TRADE UNIONS AND POLITICS IN CEYLON

This volume is sponsored by the
Center for South and Southeast Asia Studies,
University of California, Berkeley

The Center for South and Southeast Asia Studies of the University of California is the unifying organization for faculty members and students interested in South and Southeast Asia Studies, bringing together scholars from numerous disciplines. The Center's major aims are the development and support of research and language study. As part of this program the Center sponsors a publication series of books concerned with South and Southeast Asia. Manuscripts are considered from all campuses of the University of California as well as from any other individuals and institutions doing research in these areas.

PUBLICATIONS OF THE CENTER FOR SOUTH AND SOUTHEAST ASIA STUDIES :

Angela S. Burger
Opposition in a Dominant-Party System : A Study of the Jan Sangh, the Praja Socialist Party, and the Socialist Party in Uttar Pradesh, India (1969)

Robert L. Hardgrave, Jr.
Nadars of Tamilnad : The Political Culture of a Community in Change (1969)

Eugene F. Irschick
Politics and Social Conflict in South India : The Non-Brahman Movement and Tamil Separatism, 1916–1929 (1969)

Briton Martin, Jr.
New India, 1885 : British Official Policy and the Emergence of the Indian National Congress (1969)

James T. Siegel
The Rope of God (1969)

Jyotirindra Das Gupta
Language Conflict and National Development : Group Politics and National Language Policy in India (1970)

Gerald D. Berreman
Hindus of the Himalayas (Second Revised Edition, 1971)

Richard G. Fox
Kin, Clan, Raja and Rule : State-Hinterland Relations in Preindustrial India (1971)

David N. Lorenzen
The Kāpālikas and Kālāmukhas : Two Lost Śaivite Sects (1971)

David G. Marr
Vietnamese Anticolonialism, 1885–1925 (1971)

Leo E. Rose
Nepal—Strategy for Survival (1971)

Richard Sisson
The Congress System in Rajasthan (1971)

Prakash Tandon
Beyond Punjab : A Sequel to Punjabi Century (1971)

Elizabeth Whitcombe
Agrarian Conditions in Northern India. Volume One : The United Provinces under British Rule, 1860–1900 (1971)

TRADE UNIONS AND POLITICS IN CEYLON

Robert N. Kearney

UNIVERSITY OF CALIFORNIA PRESS
BERKELEY, LOS ANGELES, LONDON 1971

University of California Press
Berkeley and Los Angeles, California

University of California Press, Ltd.
London, England

ISBN: 0-520-01713-7
Library of Congress Catalog Card Number: 76-115495

PREFACE

This study is primarily a product of a great many personal interviews and discussions with trade unionists, politicians, public servants, and others in Ceylon during two three-month periods of field research in 1965 and 1967 and a brief visit in 1969. The importance of these contacts in assembling the data on which the study is based is even greater than is suggested by the frequent references to the interviews in the footnotes, since interviews and conversations very frequently led to access to trade union or party documents and other materials which have a narrowly restricted circulation and are extremely difficult to locate. While I have made considerable use of government publications, general-circulation newspapers, journals, and similar sources, research for this study essentially was conducted in trade union offices, political party headquarters, and the homes of party and union officials in Colombo.

A few events or relationships depicted here I observed personally. For the most part, however, it was necessary to rely on the perceptions and accounts of others for the "facts" on which this study rests. I was greatly impressed not only by the willingness of many persons to answer my numerous questions and to aid me in obtaining information, but also by the remarkable degree to which informants with markedly different partisan sympathies or trade union loyalties gave consistent and mutually substantiating reports of the actions and events of concern to the study. While different motives were ascribed to various participants, I found the most bitter political or trade union opponents almost invariably agreed on what had, in fact, happened in every major episode. Of course, in the reconstruction of events and description of relationships, no claim to absolute certainty can be made. I have treated as factually accurate such characterizations as were essentially agreed upon by leading participants on all sides and by informed neutral observers. Where disagreements exist between rivals or opponents, I have attempted to summarize the explanations given by spokesmen for each side. Certain matters could not be substantiated from independent sources. These I have presented as reported or claimed, with an indication of the source of the report.

The system of transliteration of Sinhalese words employed in this work generally follows the system for the transliteration of Indian languages contained in A. L. Basham, *The Wonder That Was India* (New York: Grove Press, 1954), Appendix X, with the following modifications: Because aspirates appear very infrequently in Sinhalese, I have used *th* to represent the dental *t,* as is a common practice in Ceylon, and have represented the retroflex *t* simply by *t.* Also, the sibilant rendered as *s* by Professor Basham is here represented by *sh,* consistent with its pronunciation and the more general transliteration employed in Ceylon.

The name under which a Ceylonese labor organization is registered with the Department of Labour is the organization's legal name, whether the registered name is in Sinhalese, Tamil, or English. Until about 1950, most labor organizations were registered under English names, but over the last two decades newly formed organizations increasingly have adopted Sinhalese or Tamil names. I have not used English translations of the Sinhalese or Tamil names, both because in Ceylon such organizations are regularly cited in English writing or speech by their Sinhalese or Tamil names and because in many cases confusion might occur between unions with English names and the almost identical translations of the Sinhalese or Tamil names of other unions. For the proper names of the organizations using English names, I have retained the spelling used in Ceylon, which is of course British spelling. For organizations with Sinhalese or Tamil names, I have used the form in which the organizations refer to themselves in English, which is generally identical with the transliteration of their names except for the deletion of diacritical marks distinguishing between long and short vowels and in some instances between dental and retroflex consonants. In a few cases where considerable inconsistency exists in the spelling of a name in English, I have resorted to the system of transliteration employed in this work, except that diacritical marks have not been retained.

Much the same practice has been followed regarding the names of political parties. Each party conventionally presents its name in a certain form in English, and is referred to in English by the public and press by this name, whether consisting of Sinhalese, Tamil, or English words. For example, although the United National Party is called the Eksath Jathika Pakshaya (a literal translation) in Sinhalese, it is invariably cited by its English name in English speech or writing. The Mahajana Eksath Peramuna, on the other hand, employs its Sinhalese name in both Sinhalese and English. The only party which refers to itself in more than one form in English is the Federal Party, which sometimes calls itself by its Tamil name, Ilankai Tamil Arasu Kadchi. I have cited parties by the name which they themselves employ (or in the case of the Federal Party employ most frequently) in English. Parties and unions are frequently referred to by their initials. Since both parties and unions exist in profusion in Ceylon, a large array of names and initials appear in this study, admittedly taxing the patience and memory of the reader but unavoidably resulting from the character of the Ceylonese political system and labor movement.

I am indebted to a large number of individuals and organizations for invaluable assistance of many kinds. Field research in 1965 and 1967 was made possible by grants from the Joint Committee on Asia of the American Council of Learned Societies and the Social Science Research Council. In 1965, the Program in Comparative Studies on Southern Asia of Duke University, and in 1967 the Committee on Research of the University of California, Santa Barbara, and the Center for South Asia Studies of the University of California, Berkeley, supplied supplemental financial assistance. The South Asia Program of Syracuse University provided support for a visit to Ceylon in 1969, arranged for typing of the manuscript, and rendered other aid in the later stages of this work.

The completion of this study marks the conclusion of a decade which I have devoted almost exclusively to the examination of Ceylonese politics, and the number of persons in Ceylon to whom I owe deep debts of gratitude is truly formidable. I am profoundly grateful to each of the many politicians, public servants, trade unionists, educators, and others who have extended to me the most cordial and generous assistance in connection with this and earlier studies. I wish to express special appreciation to A. Aziz, Pieter Keuneman, P. K. Liyanage, Eric Ranawake, Prins Rajasooriya, Bala Tampoe, and D. G. William, whose assistance was particularly valuable in the preparation of this study. My good friends Hector Abhayavardhana, Leslie Goonewardene, Kumari Jayawardena, Anil Moonesinghe, S. E. R. Perinpanayagam, M. J. Tissainayagam, and Sydney Wanasinghe have lent me invaluable assistance in innumerable ways over many years, and to them I extend my most sincere thanks. Among those attached to the American Embassy in Ceylon who aided me, I would like especially to mention John de Ornellas, Oscar Morrison, and the late J. J. Hediger. Finally, I wish to thank my wife for her patient and unfailing help and encouragement throughout my work on this study.

R. N. K.

Syracuse, New York
September, 1969

CONTENTS

LIST OF TABLES, CHARTS AND FIGURE

Tables

Charts

Figure

LIST OF ABBREVIATIONS USED FOR
LABOR ORGANIZATIONS AND POLITICAL PARTIES

CBEU, Ceylon Bank Employees' Union
CCCTU, Central Council of Ceylon Trade Unions
CESU, Ceylon Estates Staffs' Union
CFL, Ceylon Federation of Labour
CFTU, Ceylon Federation of Trade Unions
CMU, Ceylon Mercantile Union
CPWU, Ceylon Plantation Workers' Union
CTUF, Ceylon Trade Union Federation
CWC, Ceylon Workers' Congress
DWC, Democratic Workers' Congress
GCSU, Government Clerical Service Union
GWTUF, Government Workers' Trade Union Federation
JCTUO, Joint Committee of Trade Union Organisations
LEWU, 'Lanka Estate Workers' Union
LSSP, Lanka Sama Samaja Party
LSSP(R), Lanka Sama Samaja Party (Revolutionary)
MEP, Mahajana Eksath Peramuna
PSWTUF, Public Service Workers' Trade Union Federation
SLFP, Sri Lanka Freedom Party
SLJGS, Sri Lanka Jathika Guru Sangamaya
SLNVSS, Sri Lanka Nidahas Vurthiya Samithi Sammelanaya
SLRLS, Samastha Lanka Rajaye Lipikaru Sangamaya
UCCTU, United Committee of Ceylon Trade Unions
UNP, United National Party
UPTO, Union of Post and Telecommunication Officers
UPWU, United Port Workers' Union
VLSSP, Viplavakari Lanka Sama Samaja Party

INTRODUCTION

Trade unionism has emerged in Ceylon as a large and vigorous movement which has undergone a dramatic growth in size, self-confidence, and aggressiveness over the last fifteen or twenty years. Like labor movements in many other ex-colonial nations of Asia and Africa, Ceylonese trade unionism is characterized by pervasive political influences and the existence of intimate links between labor organizations and political parties.[1] Ceylon is one of many contemporary societies, often described as transitional or modernizing, which are experiencing a process of rapid social and political development, involving the emergence of numerous functionally specific and differentiated social structures, secularization of social values and attitudes, a widening of the horizons of social and political awareness, and a broadening of participation in the political process.[2] The pace of political and social change is reflected in the swift growth and development of the Ceylonese labor movement, and has strongly influenced the character and actions of trade unions. Trade unionism in Ceylon exhibits serious problems of fragmentation, rivalry, organizational weakness, and heavy dependence on and subordination to political parties. Unions are, nonetheless, among the few relatively

[1] On the political involvement of labor movements in the developing nations, see particularly Bruce H. Millen, *The Political Role of Labor in Developing Countries* (Washington, D.C. : Brookings Institution, 1963). Also, Subratesh Ghosh, *Trade Unionism in the Underdeveloped Countries* (Calcutta : Bookland Private, Ltd., 1960); Sidney C. Sufrin, *Unions in Emerging Societies* (Syracuse, N.Y. : Syracuse University Press, 1964); and Ioan Davies, *African Trade Unions* (Harmondsworth, England : Penguin Books, Ltd., 1966).

[2] While unresolved problems and disagreements remain, social and political development is generally considered to include, and is used in this work to refer to, a cluster of mutually inter-related social (including political) changes involving increasing structural differentiation, specificity, and autonomy, accompanied by attitudinal changes from the sacred, ascriptive, and particularistic toward the secular, achievement-oriented, and universalistic. Political development is often also considered to include a broadening of participation in the political process to encompass new and wider social groups. Among the growing volume of literature on political development and modernization, see Gabriel A. Almond and G. Bingham Powell, Jr., *Comparative Politics : A Development Approach* (Boston : Little, Brown and Co., 1966), pp. 299–332 and *passim;* Fred W. Riggs, *Administration in Developing Countries : The Theory of Prismatic Society* (Boston : Houghton Mifflin Company, 1964), pp. 3–49; Samuel P. Huntington, *Political Order in Changing Societies* (New Haven and London : Yale University Press, 1968), p. 32–39, 93–139; S. N. Eisenstadt, *Modernization : Protest and Change* (Englewood Cliffs, N.J. : Prentice-Hall, Inc., 1966), pp. 1–15 and *passim;* and Lucian W. Pye, *Aspects of Political Development* (Boston : Little, Brown and Co., 1966), pp. 31–48.

coherent, organized voluntary associations with mass memberships based on modern occupational interests to emerge in the society. They have contributed to further political development by playing a highly important role in the political socialization and recruitment of workers, particularly urban workers. Through the political activities of trade unions, the workers, who previously had few opportunities for meaningful involvement in politics, are introduced to the political process and provided with a sense of purposeful participation.

All Ceylonese labor organizations are concerned with performing the basic functions attributed to trade unions—representing and championing the common interests of the members as employees in interaction with employers and attempting to gain improvements in wages, working conditions, and other occupational matters for their memberships. Indeed, relative to the trade unions in other developing countries, many Ceylonese trade unions seem to perform the functions of "economic" trade unionism with considerable ability and success. The activities of unions in pursuit of occupational objectives are of great importance to the unions and to the economic system. Most trade unions are also involved in performing political functions, which frequently are accorded scarcely less importance by the leaders of the organizations, at least in the attainment of ultimate union goals.

Trade union involvement in politics usually is as an auxiliary or ally of a political party, and the trade union's principal political function is to contribute to the strength and position of the party. Although there are notable exceptions, as will be indicated later, a considerable portion of the labor movement is composed of unions more or less firmly committed to a particular political party, and the political interests of the trade union are identified with the interests of that party. Trade union leaders and activists commonly seem to believe that the more important objectives of the union will be won in the political arena, through the political triumph of the party with which the union is associated, rather than through collective bargaining with employers. There is, thus, a tendency among trade unionists to hold an all-or-nothing view of the political process. With the triumph of their party, virtually all objectives will be realized, and short of this triumph very little of importance can be obtained.[3] Even those unions which are not firmly committed to a party tend to act in politics in conjunction with a particular party or group of parties at any given time.

There is relatively little indication of the kind of pluralistic bargaining

[3]It has been noted that party control of interest groups inhibits the groups' formation of specific demands and gives to group activity a rigid political or ideological complexion. Gabriel A. Almond, "A Comparative Study of Interest Groups and the Political Process," in Harry Eckstein and David E. Apter (eds.), *Comparative Politics : A Reader* (New York : Free Press of Glencoe, 1963), p. 403.

and compromising on specific immediate issues in contention with other organized interest groups which is generally described as characterizing interest group behavior in the modern industrial societies of the West and particularly in the United States.[4] Excluding activities related to wages boards and industrial courts, which operate outside the conventional machinery of government, trade unions are seldom involved in piecemeal attempts to gain access to particular bureaucratic or political decision makers or to influence specific legislative proposals or administrative actions. The political activities of trade unions more commonly are partisan activities, and unions are primarily concerned not with specific individual decisions but with the winning of political power by a particular party or group of parties with which they are aligned. The major, almost the only, exceptions are provided by organizations of public servants, which often seek to influence specific political and administrative decisions on questions affecting their members' conditions of employment. Yet even public servants' unions, in promoting the demands of their members, often collide with policies of the political Government,[5] such as wage freezes or positions on strikes, and conclude that the party composition of the Government must be changed in order for their objectives to be realized.

The prevalence and intimacy of links between trade unions and parties is to a major extent a product of the presence of party activists as "outsiders" in the leadership positions of unions and the role which parties have played in establishing and assisting unions. However, a similar tendency toward partisan alignments and expectations of attaining union objectives through partisan politics characterizes many labor organizations not organized by or dependent on parties. The strong propensity of public servants' unions to develop partisan attachments, despite legal prohibitions against political activities or affiliations and against obtaining officers from outside the public service, suggests a deliberate and voluntaristic choice of partisan alignment.

The marked political involvement and strong partisan orientation of trade unions in Ceylon appear related to the same basic social and political circumstances which have impelled the labor movements of many develop-

[4]For comparative perspectives on interest groups in the West, see Samuel H. Beer, "Group Representation in Britain and the United States," *Annals of the American Academy of Political and Social Science*, CCCXIX (September, 1958), 130–140; and Joseph LaPalombara, "The Utility and Limitations of Interest Group Theory in Non-American Field Situations," in Eckstein and Apter (eds.), *Comparative Politics: A Reader*, pp. 421–430.

[5]Following a practice common in Ceylon and other states with parliamentary governmental systems, where the word "Government" appears capitalized it refers to the political executive or Ministry (much as "Administration" is used in the United States in connection with the tenure in the executive branch of a particular president or party), as distinguished from the use of "government," uncapitalized, to refer to the entire administrative and policy-formulating apparatus of the state.

ing countries toward political action. Workers in countries undergoing rapid social transformation commonly face the dislocations, stresses, and uncertainties of a changing social environment and unfamiliar patterns of life and work. A weak bargaining position, glaring social inequities, and a general dearth of social and economic amenities and opportunities have tended to produce a sense of alienation and futility. Solutions to acute and seemingly hopeless social and economic problems are often sought in political action.[6] For the worker, the trade union can become not only an association for bargaining with an employer on specific occupational grievances, but also a vehicle for the expression of more general protest against the political and social conditions which generate frustration and alienation. The trade union strength of the Marxist parties, in part attributable to early and sustained organizational efforts, is almost certainly also related to the Marxists' unrelenting hostility toward the existing social order and militant championing of radical social-protest and egalitarian doctrines.[7] Furthermore, workers' needs and wants are generally beyond the ability of individual employers to satisfy. The labor force wants and requires more plentiful and rewarding employment opportunities, improved schools and housing, a higher scale of living, and a generally more favorable and satisfying social and economic environment. Fulfillment of these needs requires action on a scale which can be undertaken only by the government.[8]

In Ceylon, the grant of universal suffrage in 1931 was explicitly intended to enhance the responsiveness of government to working-class needs. The Donoughmore Commission which recommended the franchise reform cited "the backward character of social and industrial legislation in Ceylon" as an indication of the need for a drastic widening of the franchise.[9] The commission's report was a virtual invitation to labor leaders to utilize the franchise and seek their goals in the political arena. Universal suffrage came in the early stages of the growth of trade unionism, with

[6]Wilbert E. Moore, *The Impact of Industry* (Englewood Cliffs, N.J.: Prentice-Hall, Inc., 1965), p. 105. Similarly, see William H. Knowles, "Industrial Conflict and Unions," in Wilbert E. Moore and Arnold S. Feldman (eds.), *Labor Commitment and Social Change in Developing Areas* (New York: Social Science Research Council, 1960), p. 36; and Millen, *The Political Role of Labor*, pp. 59–62.

[7]Rejection of the existing society is an attitude characteristic of most unions in the developing areas. Millen, *The Political Role of Labor*, pp. 70–71. On the Ceylonese urban working class, see S. J. Tambiah, "Ceylon," in Richard D. Lambert and Bert F. Hoselitz (eds.), *The Role of Savings and Wealth in Southern Asia and the West* (Paris: UNESCO, 1963), p. 62.

[8]This point, made regarding India, seems to be generally applicable to Ceylon and other developing countries as well. Oscar A. Ornati, "Problems of Indian Trade Unionism," *Annals of the American Academy of Political and Social Science*, CCCX (March, 1957), 156.

[9]Great Britain, Colonial Office, *Ceylon: Report of the Special Commission on the Constitution*, Cmd. 3131 (London: His Majesty's Stationery Office, 1928), p. 83. Drummond Shiels, a British Labour Party leader, was a member of the Donoughmore Commission and the Secretary of State for the Colonies approving the commission's proposals was Lord Passfield, formerly Sidney Webb, the prominent Fabian socialist.

the result that before solidarity on occupational lines had hardened or great spontaneous demand for organization had developed among workers, the potential for considerable political power was presented to workers, providing an incentive for aspiring politicians to enter the trade union field.

The thrust of trade unionism toward politics has been further encouraged by the extensive intervention of the state in industrial relations and the large and expanding role of government as an employer. The major growth and development of trade unions came after the notion of an active service state had been firmly established and the habits and styles of trade union activities have developed within a context of extensive governmental intervention, regulation, and initiative not only in labor-management relations, but in many areas of economic and social activity. Governmental intervention in industrial relations is very old in Ceylon, originating in the unique problems of immigrant labor brought from South India to work on the large British-owned coffee and later tea estates in the mid-nineteenth century. The hardships and deplorable conditions to which the Indian estate laborers were often subjected led to the intercession of the Indian government and agreement between the governments of India and Ceylon regulating conditions of recruitment and employment for estate labor. In 1927, minimum wage legislation was enacted for Indian estate labor. There followed over the next few decades a series of legislative enactments dealing with wages and hours, working conditions, and industrial disputes. Wages boards were authorized by a 1941 statute with powers to fix minimum wages, hours, and other conditions of employment for specific trades. The determination of wages for certain categories of employees was provided for in the Shop and Offices Employees Act of 1954. An Industrial Disputes Act in 1950, replacing legislation adopted in 1931, provided for extensive public intervention in industrial relations, including provisions for establishing industrial courts and compulsory arbitration. Labor tribunals, established since 1957, allow individual workers to bring minor disputes, including challenges to dismissals and other disciplinary action, before the tribunal.[10] The result of state intervention, coupled with a generally relatively weak union bargaining position, is to encourage the view among trade unions that it is through political and governmental action that they may hope for the alleviation of their grievances.

[10]The growth of state intervention in labor matters is traced in the *Report of the National Wage Policy Commission*, Sessional Paper VIII — 1961 (Colombo : Government Press, 1961), esp. pp. 5–27; and C. T. Rasaratnam, "Trade Unionism in Ceylon," *Ceylon Labour Gazette*, XVIII (August, 1967), 589–598. Also, see W. P. N. de Silva, *Industrial Law and Relations in Ceylon* (Colombo : K. V. G. de Silva & Sons, 1964); and Ceylon, Ministry of Commerce and Industries, *Handbook on Labour Law and Legislation for Industrialists* (Colombo : Government Press, [1963]).

Certain characteristics of government in Ceylon probably tend to discourage trade unions or other interest groups from attempting to influence policy and implementation on specific individual questions. The Cabinet system of government, with strong Cabinet leadership in Parliament and rigorous party discipline within the legislative chamber, tends to discourage attempts at influencing individual M.P.'s and to require concentration on the Cabinet level, which leads to concern with the party composition of the Cabinet. In addition, the character of the bureaucracy reduces the utility of direct contacts with administrators. The bureaucracy tends toward a meticulous and often ritualistic adherence to details of rules, regulations, and firmly established procedures, with little evident ability or inclination to exercise discretion or initiative. The futility of seeking objectives through access to the bureaucracy probably reinforces the proclivity of trade unionists to focus attention on political party activity as the only plausible way of realizing their goals.

As the labor movement has gained strength over the past decade, trade unions have in fact succeeded in winning many specific immediate objectives in both the industrial and the political spheres. There are some indications that at least a few of the more powerful and successful organizations in practice are gradually shifting the emphasis of their efforts from millennial political goals to incremental occupational gains for the membership through collective bargaining with employers, whether public or private. The shift in practical emphasis, however, is seldom accompanied by a professed change in political attitudes. It is possible to speculate that the character of trade unionism and the nature of the political involvement of trade unions may change considerably over the next few decades. The fact remains, however, that trade unionism is and will for some time continue to be deeply committed to politics and closely linked with political parties.

Virtually every important Ceylonese labor organization is involved in partisan politics. Although trade unionism has experienced a dramatic growth in numbers and influence in recent years, there is slight indication of diminishing partisan involvement. Rather, additional parties have entered the trade union field in order to compete for the political allegiance of organized labor. Almost the only trade unions which remain detached from partisan conflicts are very small and weak organizations with a localized membership, often representing employees of a single firm. While partisan involvement is pervasive, the nature of interaction between parties and unions varies in highly significant ways. Three general categories of politically active trade unions, based on the type of interaction with political parties, can be distinguished: (1) *party-sponsored* trade unions—those dependent on direct leadership and support from a political party; (2) *party-oriented* trade unions—those maintaining a relatively stable association or alignment with a political party without formal commitment to or heavy dependence on the party; and (3) *uncommitted* trade unions—those which participate in partisan politics but lack strong or stable ties with a particular political party.[11] Individual labor organizations may shift from one category to another, although they apparently do so infrequently, and a sharp line between categories is often difficult to draw. Nonetheless, this classification reflects important and observable differences in the relationships which major labor organizations maintain with political parties and represent significantly differing political roles and patterns of behavior of trade unions.

This study seeks to identify and describe the types and varieties of political action and association which are exhibited by trade unions in Ceylon. In particular, it is concerned with the interaction of labor organizations and political parties. Although relevant circumstances or events in the development of the labor movement or particular labor organizations are considered at certain points, no attempt is made to present a history of the labor movement.[12] Both the trade union movement and the political system had undergone fundamental alterations by the end of the first decade of independence. While some note is made of the earlier position and behavior of trade unions, this study is basically concerned with trade unions as they have functioned in politics during roughly the past decade and as they function at the present time.

While the primary concern of this work is with trade unions and politics, the characteristics of trade unionism and the functioning of trade unions in the industrial sphere are of obvious importance to explication of their political roles. The first three chapters are devoted to examination of the characteristics of trade unions and the labor movement, labor leadership, and collective bargaining and industrial conflict in Ceylon. Chapter IV explores the motives of parties in devoting time and energy to the organizing and promoting of trade unions. The following chapter seeks to present a detailed analysis of the nature of the interaction between parties and the party-sponsored unions. The sixth and seventh chapters are intended to illustrate the regularities and varieties of political behavior of party-oriented and uncommitted trade unions by presenting a series of sketches of specific labor organizations in these categories. Chapter VIII seeks to provide a more systematic examination of the political consequences of strikes and disorders resulting from union actions, which are mentioned in passing at many other points in the study. In Chapter IX, the influence of political factors in encouraging unity and disunity in the labor movemen*

[11] This typology was first used by the author in a paper presented at a seminar on comparative labor movements organized by Everett M. Kassalow in Washington, D.C., March 23, 1967.

[12] An excellent study of the origins and early growth of the Ceylonese labor movement is contained in Kumari Jayawardena, *Labour, Politics and Religion in Ceylon : The Rise of the Labour Movement, 1893–1933* (Durham, N.C. : Duke University Press, in press).

are examined. The concluding chapter attempts to evaluate the social and political consequences of the particular style and character of trade unionism as it has developed in Ceylon, and to outline and summarize the major features and significance for the labor movement and the political system of trade union involvement in politics. The study must, regretably, leave many questions of trade unionism and politics in Ceylon unanswered. It is, however, intended to provide some previously unavailable materials and interpretations concerning Ceylonese trade unionism and politics, and may suggest possible patterns and trends, as well as fruitful areas for investigation, in the political involvement of trade unions in other developing societies.

I

CHARACTERISTICS OF TRADE UNIONISM IN CEYLON

Trade unionism became established in Ceylon before the advent of industrialization and has grown rapidly, although manufacturing and factory labor have scarcely begun to appear as significant elements of the economy, despite the common assumption, based on Western experience, that the growth of organized labor follows and results from the process of industrialization. Ceylon displays the concentration of gainfully employed persons in primary production which is characteristic of the non-industrialized, economically underdeveloped countries. However, the proportion of the gainfully employed engaged in primary production in Ceylon, while much higher than in the industrialized countries, is noticeably lower than that found in neighboring countries. The 53 percent of the gainfully employed engaged in primary production in Ceylon in 1953 compares with 71 percent in India, 66 percent in the Philippines, and 65 percent in Malaya at roughly the same time.[1]

1. The Environment of Trade Unionism

The people of Ceylon are primarily rural villagers dependent on agriculture for their livelihood. In 1963, 81 percent of the population lived in rural areas,[2] and 53 percent of the gainfully employed population was engaged in agriculture and related pursuits.[3] Unlike the pattern found in many other Asian countries, however, a large proportion of the gainfully

---

[1] *Report of the National Wage Policy Commission*, Sessional Paper VIII—1961 (Colombo: Government Press, 1961), p. 33.

[2] The definition of rural and urban populations for census purposes is determined by the legal status of the locality of residence. Persons living in municipal and urban council areas, which are designated administratively, are classified as urban and all others (residents of town and village council areas) are classified as rural. The 1963 figure is based on preliminary results of the 1963 census, which has not yet been released in final form. Ceylon, Department of Census and Statistics, *Statistical Pocket Book of Ceylon, 1966* (Colombo: Government Press, 1966), p. 26.

[3] Ceylon, Department of Census and Statistics, *Census of Population, Ceylon, 1963*, Vol. I, Part II: "The Gainfully Employed Population, Tables Based on a 10% Sample" (Colombo: Government Press, 1967), Table 1, p. 1.

employed, 65 percent, are paid workers. The high proportion of paid
workers, despite the predominance of agricultural production, is largely
a result of the important position occupied by tea, rubber, and, to a
lesser extent, coconut estates, which employ relatively large numbers
of wage laborers.[4] Of 3.2 million gainfully employed persons, more than
2 million were paid workers at the time of the 1963 census. The distribution
of paid workers by industry is presented in Table 1.

Table 1

PAID WORKERS CLASSIFIED BY INDUSTRY, 1963

Industry	Number	Percent
Agriculture, forestry, hunting, and fishing	929,940	44.7
Services	426,450	20.5
Manufacturing	219,840	10.6
Commerce, banking, and finance	149,630	7.2
Transport, storage, and communication	118,190	5.7
Construction	77,260	3.7
Electricity, gas, water, and sanitary services	9,200	0.4
Mining and quarrying	8,870	0.4
Activities not adequately described	141,680	6.8
TOTAL	2,081,060	100.0

SOURCE : Ceylon, Department of Census and Statistics, *Census of Population, Ceylon, 1963,*
Vol. I, Part II : "The Gainfully Employed Population, Tables Based on a 10% Sample"
(Colombo : Government Press, 1967), Table 2, p. 4.

The Ceylonese economy has been geared for many years to the production and export of tea, rubber, and coconuts, and the import of manufactured goods and the food in excess of local production necessary to
feed the island's population.[5] For slightly more than a decade, concerted
efforts have been made by the government to stimulate manufacturing
industries, primarily through public corporations.[6] In addition, since

[4] *Report of the National Wage Policy Commission*, p. 34; "A Survey of Employment, Unemployment and Underemployment in Ceylon," *International Labour Review*, LXXXVII (March,
1963), 251. The enterprises engaged in the commercial production of tea, rubber, and coconuts on a fairly large scale by the use of wage labor are referred to interchangeably as "estates"
and "plantations" in Ceylon. The terms "estates" and "estate workers" have been used in
this study.

[5] For descriptions of the economy and problems of economic development, see Gamini
Corea, "Ceylon," in Cranley Onslow (ed.), *Asian Economic Development* (New York : Frederick
A. Praeger, 1965), pp. 29–65; Henry M. Oliver, Jr., "The Economy of Ceylon," in Calvin
B. Hoover (ed.), *Economic Systems of the Commonwealth* (Durham, N.C. : Duke University
Press, 1962), pp. 202–237; Donald R. Snodgrass, *Ceylon : An Export Economy in Transition*
(Homewood, Ill. : Richard D. Irwin, Inc., 1966); and *Ceylon Investment Guide : The General
Economic Environment* (Colombo : Industrial Development Board, Ministry of Industries and
Fisheries, 1968).

[6] The term "public corporation" is used in this study to include all industrial, transportation, distribution, and financial corporations wholly owned and controlled by the government,

about 1960 stringent restrictions on imports, produced by perennial balance-of-payments crises, have led to the growth of a number of light industries producing substitutes for previously imported manufactured goods. An index of industrial production, using the 1952–1956 annual average as a base, reached 135.0 in 1960 and rose to 170.5 in 1964.[7] As a result of the public and private import-substitution ventures, fundamental structural changes in the economy and a significant shift in the composition of the labor force which has not yet been reflected in the employment statistics may have commenced.[8]

Public employment, long of major importance outside the agricultural sector, has expanded considerably with the establishment of state industrial ventures and with the nationalization of bus services, port facilities, petroleum distribution facilities, and a major portion of commercial banking and insurance activities since 1958. In 1964, 203,481 persons were employed in the central government bureaucracy, in addition to which there were 94,853 teachers in the government schools and almost 15,000 municipal and urban council employees.[9] Excluding the conventional public service, the Ceylon Transport Board, a public corporation which operates the island's bus services, is Ceylon's largest single employer with about 35,000 employees. The labor force of thirty-four public corporations totalled more than 110,000 in 1967/1968.[10]

The island's population is divided into ethnic communities which remain of great social and political significance. About 70 percent of the people of Ceylon are Sinhalese, who speak the Sinhalese language and are predominately Buddhist. The Ceylon Tamils form about 11 percent of the population. They speak the Tamil language, are largely Hindu, and are concentrated at the northern tip of the island and along the east coast. Unlike the Ceylon Tamils, who have inhabited the island for many centuries, the Indian Tamils, about 12 percent of the population, are migrants or the descendants of migrants from South India during the past century, attracted to Ceylon by employment prospects, primarily on the tea and rubber estates. The Indian Tamils are generally looked upon as aliens and after independence almost 90 percent of the community was excluded from Ceylonese citizenship and the franchise. An agreement

---

embracing both what are commonly referred to in Ceylon as "nationalized industries" and "state corporations."

[7]Ceylon, Department of Census and Statistics, *Statistical Abstract of Ceylon, 1965* (Colombo : Government Press, 1966). Table 94, p. 103.

[8]On recent industrial growth resulting from import substitution, see Corea, "Ceylon," p. 62; and Central Bank of Ceylon, *Annual Report of the Monetary Board to the Minister of Finance for the Year 1967* (Colombo : Central Bank of Ceylon, 1968), p. 13.

[9]*Report of the Commission on Profit Sharing*, Sessional Paper XXVII—1967 (Colombo : Government Press, 1967), p. 14.

[10]Central Bank of Ceylon, *Annual Report of the Monetary Board to the Minister of Finance for the Year 1968* (Colombo : Central Bank of Ceylon, 1969), pp. 74–123.

between the governments of Ceylon and India in 1964 provided for the gradual repatriation to India of more than half a million Indian Tamils and the granting of Ceylonese citizenship to most of the remainder. The Indian Tamils, who are Tamil-speaking Hindus, are concentrated on the estates in the central highlands. Among the smaller ethnic communities are the Ceylon Moors (a name given Ceylonese Muslims by the Portuguese who ruled the coastal areas of Ceylon in the sixteenth and seventeenth centuries), who constitute less than 6 percent of the population and live on the east coast and, in smaller numbers, in the city of Colombo and north of Colombo on the west coast. The Burghers, of European or European and Ceylonese extraction, form a very small community which is almost entirely urban and Christian and generally uses English as the language of the home.[11]

Ceylon has experienced a very rapid population growth in recent decades. The 1963 census provisionally reported a population of 10,624,507, an increase of 31 percent over the slightly more than 8 million enumerated ten years earlier and double the population of 1931.[12] While gross national product has been edging slowly upward, it has scarcely been able to match the pace of population growth. Per capita gross national product in 1965 was 625 rupees (then approximately $130), which although considerably higher than in neighboring countries, was slightly below that of the preceding year.[13] An unusually high rate of growth in gross national product during 1967, nearly 5 percent, produced only a 2 percent rise in per capita gross national product and no advance in per capita national income due primarily to population growth.[14] Ceylonese labor has suffered from a relatively high incidence of unemployment and underemployment, resulting largely from the rapid population increase coupled with sluggish economic expansion. Involuntary unemployment was estimated in 1963 at 457,730, 13.8 percent of the workforce. An estimated 17.8 percent of the urban workforce was unemployed.[15]

Despite the stresses of a rapidly expanding population and slow and uncertain economic growth, great progress has been recorded in education and literacy, and Ceylon possesses a remarkably literate and informed

[11]The ethnic composition of the Ceylonese population is as follows : Sinhalese, 69.4; Ceylon Tamils, 10.9; Indian Tamils, 12.0; Ceylon Moors, 5.7; Indian Moors, 0.6; Burghers and Eurasians, 0.6; Malays, 0.3; and others, 0.5 percent. The religious composition is : Buddhists, 64.3; Hindus, 19.9; Christians, 8.9; Muslims, 6.7; and others, 0.1 percent. *Statistical Abstract of Ceylon, 1965*, Table 17, p. 27, and Table 19, p. 29.

[12]Ceylon, Department of Census and Statistics, *Ceylon Year Book, 1967* (Colombo : Government Press, 1967), p. 33.

[13]*Ceylon Today*, XV (August, 1966), 2. In November, 1967, the Ceylon rupee was devalued from about $ 0.210 to $ 0.175.

[14]Central Bank of Ceylon, *Annual Report . . . for the Year 1967*, p. 2.

[15]Central Bank of Ceylon, Department of Economic Research, *Survey of Ceylon's Consumer Finances, 1963* (Colombo : Central Bank of Ceylon, 1964), pp. 54–56. See also "A Survey of Employment, Unemployment and Underemployment in Ceylon," pp. 247–257.

mass public. In 1953, 65.4 percent of the population five years of age and over was literate.[16] Release of the 1963 census results is expected to reveal a significant further advance in literacy. Mass education has been pursued vigorously for many decades, and since 1945 education has been free from the primary through the university level. Ceylon's proportion of gross national product spent on education, 5 percent, is claimed to be the highest in Asia.[17] In 1964, 2,630,000 youths were enrolled in schools from a population of about 3,750,000 between the ages of five and nineteen.[18] The small size of the island has facilitated the development of reasonably good transportation and communications networks, which leave few villages beyond the easy reach of newspapers, radio, and inexpensive public bus service. In 1964, Ceylon possessed four daily newspapers with an average daily circulation in excess of 50,000 and three weekly newspapers with a circulation of more than 100,000, as well as at least six other widely circulated daily and four other major weekly newspapers.[19]

A survey of newspaper readership, radio listening, and cinema attendance in 1964 discovered a very high level of exposure to mass communications media. For the entire island, the survey found that 53 percent of the men and 23 percent of the women read a newspaper, 58 percent of the men and 33 percent of the women listened to the radio, and 57 percent of the men and 36 percent of the women visited the cinema. Although exposure to communications media was higher in the urban areas, remarkably high exposure was discovered in the rural villages. Among the largely Sinhalese villagers of the "wet zone" of the southern and western coastal areas, 54 percent of the men and 17 percent of the women read newspapers and similar proportions of the men and somewhat larger proportions of the women listened to the radio and attended the cinema. Media involvement was considerably lower in the "dry zone" and on the Jaffna Peninsula.

From the standpoint of the labor movement, one of the most significant findings of the survey was that among males in the urban working class, 67 percent read some publication (51 percent read a daily newspaper), 60 percent listened to the radio, and 72 percent visited the cinema. Even among women in the urban working class, who are assumed to be much less likely to have contact with the communications media, 47 percent

[16]As with most aggregate data for Ceylon, considerable variations exist between ethnic communities. Of the larger communities, the literacy rate for those five years of age and over varies from 73.4 percent for both the Low-Country Sinhalese and Ceylon Tamils to 41.2 percent for the Indian Tamils. Ceylon, Department of Census and Statistics, *Census of Ceylon, 1953*, Vol. III, Part I (Colombo : Government Press, 1960), Table 6, pp. 242–256.
[17]*Ceylon Investment Guide : The General Economic Environment*, p. 43.
[18]*Statistical Abstract of Ceylon, 1965*, Table 12, p. 24; Table 242, p. 254.
[19]*Ceylon Year Book, 1967*, pp. 297–298.

read newspapers, 45 percent listened to the radio, and 61 percent attended
the cinema. The very high incidence of exposure to communications
media suggests a high level of social mobilization and political awareness
among urban workers. In marked contrast to the urban working class,
however, is the Indian Tamil estate population, the other large and easily
identifiable group of wage earners, which had the lowest incidence of
exposure to the media of any of the strata into which the population
was divided for purposes of the survey.[20] Only 18 and 3 percent of the
men and women, respectively, read any newspaper, and 37 and 15 percent,
respectively, listened to the radio. Cinema attendance was the only form
of communications in which the male estate Tamils reached the island
average of 57 percent. Of women, however, only 13 percent attended the
cinema, compared to 36 percent of women throughout the island.[21]

2. *The Labor Movement*

The first attempts at collective action by employees in Ceylon appeared
at the end of the nineteenth century with sporadic outbreaks of restiveness
among urban workers, which led to eruptions of strikes and a few attempts
to establish committees to draft and present workers' demands. The first
labor organizations, as in India, were little more than ad hoc committees
created to protest specific and immediate grievances, and they seldom
survived the flareup which produced them.[22] The early attempts at
organizing and acting collectively were limited to the urban workers of
Colombo, with employees in the printing trade, railway workshops,
and port displaying particularly marked militancy and aggressiveness.
Attempts at concerted action by workers have been traced to a strike in
1893. The first major industrial dispute was a strike by railway workers
in 1912, followed by a general strike in 1923, a port strike in 1927, and a
tramway strike in 1929.

[20]The sample was stratified into urban upper and middle classes, lower-middle class, and
working class, and rural wet zone, dry zone, Jaffna, and estate Tamil populations, reflecting
the relevance of social class in the cities (defined for survey purposes by income) and region
and ethnic group in the rural areas.

[21]"Readership Survey, Ceylon, April–June 1964, Conducted for the Audit Bureau of
Circulations Limited by the Market Research Department of Lever Brothers (Ceylon)
Limited" (mimeographed; Colombo, September, 1964), Table 5.

[22]The discussion of early trade unionism in Ceylon is based primarily on Kumari Jayawardena, *Labour, Politics and Religion in Ceylon: The Rise of the Labour Movement, 1893–1933*
(Durham, N.C.: Duke University Press, in press). Brief histories of Ceylonese trade unionism
appear in V. Sarvaloganayagam, "Trade Unionism in Ceylon," *Ceylon Today*, VII (May,
1958), 28–31, and VII (June, 1958), 13–21; and N. S. G. Kuruppu, "A History of the Working
Class Movement in Ceylon," *Young Socialist* (Colombo), No. 1 (July–September, 1961),
pp. 12–16; No. 3 (October–December, 1961), pp. 152–156; and No. 4 (January–March,
1962), pp. 201–205. On the origins of trade unionism in India, see V. B. Karnik, *Indian
Trade Unions: A Survey* (2nd ed., rev.; Bombay: Manaktalas, 1966), pp. 1–39.

The Ceylon Workers' Welfare League was formed in 1919 to seek improvement of the circumstances of workers, but the organization was composed of middle-class social reformers and nationalists and contained no workers. In the same year, the inaugural meeting of the Ceylon National Congress, formed to work for constitutional reform and Ceylonese self-government, adopted a resolution asking for a number of improvements in the conditions of labor and "Recognition of the right of association of all workers."[23] A. E. Goonesinha, the first Ceylonese to devote himself primarily to labor organizing and leadership, entered the trade union field by way of the nationalist movement.[24] In 1922, Goonesinha founded the first major and relatively durable trade union, the Ceylon Labour Union, as an affiliate of the Ceylon National Congress. However, in 1928 Goonesinha broke with the moderate and cautious leaders of the Congress and formed a Labour Party and an All-Ceylon Trades Union Congress. The following year a collective agreement was signed between the Trades Union Congress and the newly formed Ceylon Employers' Federation, which represented the first formal recognition by employers of the right of workers to organize and bargain collectively. Following the bitter and violent tramway strike in 1929, which led to a reaction against organized labor by the government and employers, and the impact of the Great Depression a year or two later, however, Ceylonese trade unionism suffered a setback from which it did not fully recover until the conclusion of the Second World War, and Goonesinha's influence in the labor movement was permanently undermined. The early 1930's saw the beginnings of Marxist activities in Ceylon when a number of young men returned from British and American universities and plunged immediately into political and labor struggles, bringing new vigor and militancy to the labor movement.[25] Commencing with a textile mill strike in 1933, the Marxists challenged Goonesinha's leadership of organized labor and by the conclusion of the Second World War largely dominated the labor movement.

The Growth of Trade Unionism

Growing labor activity and Colonial Office pressure for labor legislation were reflected in the enactment of the Trade Unions Ordinance of 1935, which for the first time gave legal sanction to workers' right of association and right to bargain collectively. The act required trade unions to register

[23]S. W. R. D. Bandaranaike (ed.), *The Handbook of the Ceylon National Congress, 1919–1928* (Colombo : H. W. Cave & Co., 1928), pp. 212–213.

[24]Goonesinha's autobiography, "My Life and Labour," published serially in the Sunday *Ceylon Observer* commencing on July 4, 1965, indicates his early preoccupation with anti-colonialism and self-government, rather than explicitly labor issues.

[25]For an account of the early years of the Marxist movement in Ceylon, see George J. Lerski, *Origins of Trotskyism in Ceylon : A Documentary History of the Lanka Sama Samaja Party, 1935-1942* (Stanford, Calif. : Hoover Institution on War, Revolution and Peace, 1968).

Table 2
GROWTH IN MEMBERSHIP OF EMPLOYEES'
TRADE UNIONS, 1937–1967[a]

Year	Total membership of reporting trade unions	Year	Total membership of reporting trade unions
1937	6,717	1952	297,370
1938	6,066	1953	307,369
1939	5,931	1954	311,449
1940	7,703	1955	359,431
1941	147,076	1956	261,681
1942	90,552	1957	521,654
1943	104,690	1958	730,178
1944	93,479	1959	821,996
1945	144,240	1960	738,569
1946	181,774	1961	787,574
1947	169,031	1962	863,316
1948	158,178	1963	1,166,650
1949	129,327	1964	1,419,704
1950	127,809	1965	1,215,654
1951	233,653	1966	1,256,490
		1967	1,453,941

[a] Includes only trade unions submitting compulsory annual reports to the Commissioner of Labour. It is likely that misunderstanding of the requirements of the reports in the early years caused frequent failures to report and inaccurate reporting. However, from about 1941 the figures should reflect with reasonable accuracy the relative growth of trade union membership.

SOURCE : For 1937–1947, Ceylon, Department of Census and Statistics, *Ceylon Year Book, 1950* (Colombo: Government Press, 1951), p. 222; for 1948–1967, *Administration Report of the Commissioner of Labour* for the years 1948–1966/1967 (Colombo: Government Press, 1949–1969).

with and submit annual reports to the Commissioner of Labour. The growth in trade union membership from 1937 to 1967 is shown in Table 2.

After the founding of the Ceylon Indian Congress Labour Union in 1940, organization of the numerous Indian Tamil estate laborers made rapid progress, contributing to the growth of trade union membership in the 1940's. Following two general strikes in 1946 and 1947, public servants in 1948 were allowed to form trade unions with some restrictions. Much of the rapid growth in trade union membership in the early 1950's reflects the extensive organization of public servants. By 1952, public servants constituted 40 percent of all non-agricultural employees belonging to trade unions. From the conclusion of the Second World War to 1952, trade union membership doubled.

An even more dramatic growth in trade unionism followed the 1956 election (see Figure 1). This election produced the defeat of the United National Party, which had held power since independence, and the victory of a coalition led by the Sri Lanka Freedom Party. The UNP had been generally conservative and had displayed little sympathy for the Marxist-dominated labor movement. Governmental tolerance and permissiveness and a generally more egalitarian and radical political environment contributed to an astonishing growth in trade unionism in the decade after 1956. The government facilitated the organization and condoned the militancy of public servants and employees of public corporations, sought to secure recognition of unions as bargaining agents by private employers, established labor tribunals to hear workers' complaints, and provided legal aid to unions involved in disputes with employers.[26] The organizational and psychological gains scored by the labor movement survived subsequent political shifts and became an established part of the Ceylonese political and economic scene.

FIGURE 1

Growth in Membership of Employees' Trade Unions

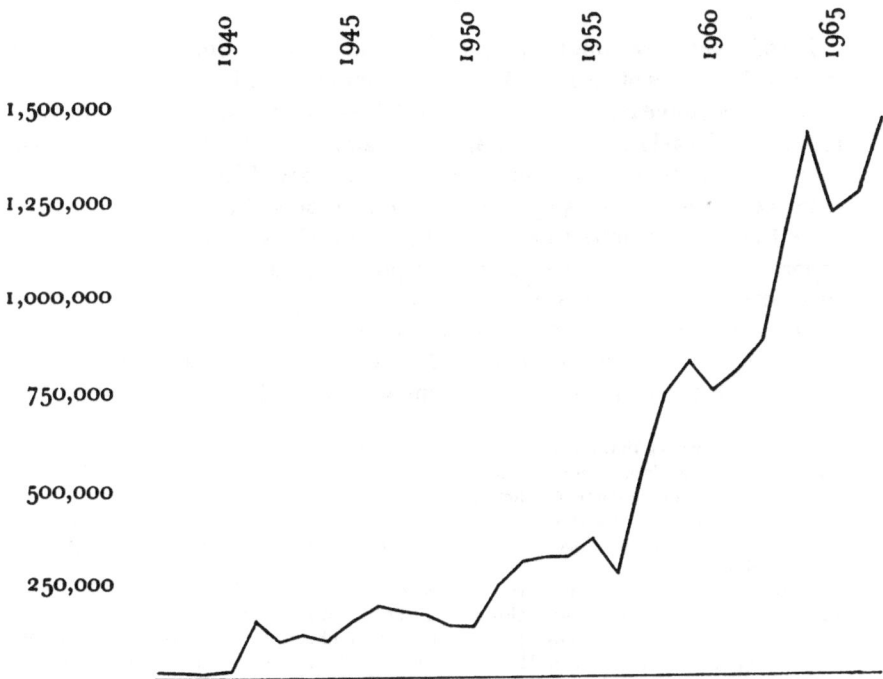

---

[26]See *Administration Report of the Commissioner of Labour for 1958* (Colombo: Government Press, 1959), p. 181.

Union Membership and Finances

While some individual trade unions have developed relatively great organizational strength and considerable membership solidarity, especially in the past decade, unions generally have been characterized by unstable and fluctuating memberships and extremely weak financial circumstances. Membership figures submitted to the Commissioner of Labour are not subject to verification, as is done in India, and considerable skepticism concerning their accuracy exists. Many workers considered within the membership are probably at most nominal members and pay dues to a union irregularly and infrequently, if at all, although they may identify themselves with the union and obey calls to strike or return to work issued by the union.[27] The reported membership figures are supposed to exclude members who are more than three months behind in the payment of dues, but it has been noted that the size of memberships reported by many unions far exceeds the membership for which dues receipts are recorded.[28]

Despite very low union dues, usually half a rupee ($0.085) a month,[29] the small incomes of most workers, often combined with weak commitment to the union, have made the collection of dues a source of constant difficulty for unions. Nearly two decades ago, the Commissioner of Labour asserted that for most unions : "If rules in regard to arrears of fees had been rigidly enforced, perhaps over 50 percent of the members of these Unions would have lost their membership."[30] In 1965, the Ceylon Workers' Congress reported that collections of dues had not kept pace with the growth in membership and complained that "a large section of our members are slack in paying their dues to the Union, and we have to report that the percentage of subscriptions collected is not at all satisfactory."[31]

The deduction of union dues from wages has been practiced in the

[27] It has been argued that the dues-paying membership of unions in the developing countries may not be of great significance since a union's influence often extends well beyond the ranks of the members who regularly pay their dues and the union may speak for and command the support of a body of workers considerably larger than its formal membership. Bruce H. Millen, *The Political Role of Labor in Developing Countries* (Washington, D.C. : Brookings Institution, 1963), p. 90.

[28] *Report of the Committee of Inquiry into the Law and Practice of the Trade Unions Ordinance*, Sessional Paper XXVIII — 1967 (Colombo : Government Press, 1967), p. 32.

[29] Clerical employees' unions usually have somewhat higher dues. GCSU dues, for example, are two rupees ($ 0.34) a month. However, the dues of some unions are as low as a quarter of a rupee a month. CWC dues were one rupee (then $ 0.21) a year until 1957, when they were increased to half a rupee a month. Ceylon Workers' Congress, "Report of the Seventeenth Annual Sessions of the Ceylon Workers' Congress Held at 'Sarvodhaya Sadukkam,' Nuwara Eliya, on 28th September, 1958" (mimeographed; Colombo, 1958), p. 8.

[30] *Administration Report of the Commissioner of Labour for 1950* (Colombo : Government Press, 1951), p. 8.

[31] *Ceylon Workers' Congress Report, 1964–1965* (Colombo : Ceylon Workers' Congress, 1965), p. 7.

public service and public corporations for about a decade and has recently begun to spread to the private sector. During 1967, the Ceylon Mercantile Union won inclusion of the checkoff of dues in a collective agreement signed with the Employers' Federation of Ceylon, and an agreement between the Ceylon Workers' Congress and the Ceylon Estates Employers' Federation provided for the checkoff on the estates. The checkoff has become a regular demand of unions and appears likely to spread to cover most workers in the larger enterprises over the next few years. The checkoff is expected to have a major impact on the financial strength of unions and, as parlous financial circumstances are among the most conspicuous handicaps of unions, may have wide ramifications for the labor movement. It is also expected by some trade unionists to help bind members more closely to the union by preventing lapses in dues payment and impeding frequent shifts of members to rival unions.

The uncertain commitment of union members is also reflected in workers' simultaneous membership in more than one union. Multiple membership, which appears to be fairly common in certain public corporations, particularly the Port (Cargo) Corporation, has been explained as possibly resulting from the workers' wish "to please the various union leaders who are persons of influence in the workplace."[32] It also seems to be viewed by workers as a way of insuring protection against discrimination and benefiting from favoritism, particularly on political grounds. Following the return to power of the UNP in 1965, employees of the Ceylon Transport Board were reported to be joining a UNP-sponsored union while retaining their membership in unions aligned with opposition parties.[33]

Fragmentation and Proliferation of Unions

The Ceylonese labor movement is marked by extreme fragmentation and the existence of a large number of very small and weak trade unions. While the total membership of unions multiplied nearly ten-fold in the two decades following independence, the number of unions in existence climbed from 141 in 1947 to 526 in 1957, and by 1967 reached 1,239.[34] In 1967, one of every three unions contained less than fifty members, and nearly three-quarters of all unions contained less than 250 members. Only about one union in eight had more than 1,000 members.[35] The

---

[32]*Report of the Committee of Inquiry into the Law and Practice of the Trade Unions Ordinance*, p. 27.
[33]Reported in interviews with several trade unionists in 1965.
[34]Ceylon, Department of Census and Statistics, *Ceylon Year Book* for the years 1954–1963 (Colombo : Government Press, 1954–1964) ; *Administration Report of the Commissioner of Labour* for the years 1947 and 1966/1967 (Colombo : Government Press, 1948 and 1969).
[35]In Ceylon, not only labor organizations but professional associations and, incongruously, employers' groups are registered as trade unions (the Employers' Federation of Ceylon possesses trade union registration number one), and many of the data of the Department of

Table 3

MEMBERSHIP STRENGTH OF TRADE UNIONS :
PERCENT OF UNIONS CLASSIFIED BY SIZE OF MEMBERSHIP

Year	Percent with membership of					Average Membership per union
	less than 50	50–249	250–999	1,000– 4,999	5,000 and over	
1945	13	33	25	25	4	3,005
1948	3	40	33	22	2	2,727
1951	17	31	39	10	3	1,899
1954	22	36	26	12	4	1,494
1957	25	39	18	13	4	2,048
1960	32	40	18	6	3	1,259
1963	30	41	17	9	3	1,516
1967	34	38	17	9	3	1,554

SOURCE : *Administration Report of the Commissioner of Labour* for the years 1960, 1963/1964, and 1966/1967 (Colombo : Government Press, 1961–1969).

ninety-five largest unions reporting to the Commissioner of Labour in 1965 included approximately 1,130,000 workers, while the other 774 reporting unions contained a total of only about 86,000 workers.[36] The proportion of unions with extremely small memberships, below 250, has tended upwards over the years, while the proportion with 1,000 or more members has gradually declined (Table 3). Although far outdistanced by the proliferation of small organizations, the number of larger unions has also increased significantly. Between 1935 and 1940, only one union had a membership above 1,000.[37] The number of unions with 1,000 or more members climbed from fourteen in 1945 and thirty-three in 1954 to 108 in 1967 (Table 4).

The proliferation of small trade unions is particularly marked in the public service, where special circumstances add to the general causes of fragmentation shared with the private sector. Of 1,239 registered trade unions in 1967, 741 were organizations of public servants. Thus, public servants' unions accounted for about 60 percent of the total number of registered trade unions, but the public servants' unions submitting reports to the Commissioner of Labour that year included less than one-fifth of all union members. Central government employees' unions averaged

Labour, including that on the membership size of trade unions, do not distinguish between workers' organizations and other organizations. The unions with very small memberships include some non-workers' organizations, but these groups constitute only a minor proportion of the small unions. In 1967, only eight employers' organizations were included, but 668 unions had less than 250 members. *Administration Report of the Commissioner of Labour for 1966–67*, pp. 55–56.

[36]Ceylon, Ministry of Labour, Employment, and Housing, *May Day, 1967* (Colombo : Government Press, 1967), pp. 33–34.

[37]Ceylon, Department of Census and Statistics, *Ceylon Year Book, 1950* (Colombo : Government Press, 1951), p. 222.

Table 4

MEMBERSHIP STRENGTH OF TRADE UNIONS :
NUMBER OF UNIONS CLASSIFIED BY SIZE OF MEMBERSHIP

Year	Number with membership of					Total number of trade unions reporting
	less than 50	50–249	250–999	1,000–4,999	5,000 and over	
1945	6	16	12	12	2	48
1948	2	23	19	13	1	58
1951	21	38	48	13	4	124
1954	46	76	54	25	8	209
1957	64	100	46	34	11	255
1960	189	236	107	38	17	587
1963	235	317	130	66	23	771
1967	314	354	160	80	28	936

SOURCE : *Administration Report of the Commissioner of Labour* for the years 1960, 1963/1964, and 1966/1967 (Colombo: Government Press, 1961–1969).

only 333 members.[38] The multiplicity of public servants' unions is encouraged by a statutory requirement that an organization be restricted to a single department or service or a single category of public servants. The Ceylonese bureaucracy contains a large number of services below the clerical grades which are limited to one of the more than one hundred departments in the administrative system and several departmental services of clerks and other intermediate-level public servants, in addition to a few interdepartmental services such as the General Clerical Service.[39] Consequently, many organizations draw members from sharply restricted categories of public servants.

The large number of public servants' unions also stems from the tendency for many splinter unions to be formed to represent the same body of public servants. Until 1958, a public servants' union had been required to include within its membership at least 40 per cent of the public servants belonging to the service, grade, or department the union sought to organize in order to obtain Treasury recognition, which was necessary for the union's spokesmen to represent its members before official bodies. In 1958, the requirement of Treasury recognition was abolished and any organization which was registered as a trade union regardless of size became eligible to represent its members.[40] With the change in recognition policy and

[38]*Administration Report of the Commissioner of Labour for 1966–67*, pp. 55, 177.

[39]Departments in Ceylon are the second-tier organizational units, equivalent to bureaus in many administrative systems. On the characteristics of bureaucracy and administration in Ceylon, see Robert N. Kearney, "Ceylon: The Contemporary Bureaucracy," in Ralph Braibanti and associates, *Asian Bureaucratic Systems Emergent from the British Imperial Tradition* (Durham, N.C.: Duke University Press, 1966), pp. 485–549.

[40]*Administration Report of the Commissioner of Labour for 1958*, p. 181.

the growth of trade unionism following the 1956 election, the number of public servants' unions jumped from 182 in 1955 to 474 in 1959.[41] The 40 percent rule is thought to have been abolished by the SLFP-dominated Government to encourage small and weak pro-SLFP unions which were being formed in the public service at the time.

The proliferation of trade unions in the private as well as the public sector is frequently attributed to the statutory provision that any seven persons may form and register a union and the absence of any legal provision for the recognition of unions by employers. The Commissioner of Labour must register any union consisting of at least seven persons if the application for registration is made in the legally prescribed form. The absence of provision for the recognition of unions as bargaining agents has relieved unions of the necessity to represent any fixed number or proportion of employees in the workplace in order to negotiate with the employer. The decision whether to deal with a union or not is left with employers, who commonly deal with all unions, irrespective of size, on matters involving the grievances of individual workers (which constitute a large proportion of trade union activity). Hence, there is little impediment to the multiplication of weak splinter unions.

The multiplicity of small unions is to some degree a carryover from the firm-oriented trade unionism which was common in the formative years of the labor movement, when organization was closely connected with immediate grievances and workers in a single workplace joined together to present their grievances and demands. Although many unions by the 1940's had begun to organize various categories of workers on an industry-wide or island-wide basis,[42] some tendency toward localism and an individual-firm orientation has persisted. The names of a host of unions—such as the Gintota Plywood Factory Workers' Union, Kankesan Cement Works Employees' Sangam, Panwila Estates Workers' Union, Paranthan Chemical Employees' Sangam, Times Sevaka Sangamaya, and Velona Carpentry Workship Workers' Union—indicate their limitation to employees of a single enterprise.

Political rivalry, which leads to the organization of duplicating unions associated with the competing political parties, is a commonly cited cause of the proliferation of unions within a single industry. In a number of industries, particularly the more extensively organized ones, rivalry

[41]Ceylon, Department of Census and Statistics, *Ceylon Year Book, 1963* (Colombo : Government Press, 1964), p. 201.

[42]Soon after the formation of the Ceylon Trade Union Federation in 1940, for example, the unions affiliated to the federation were reorganized from a firm to an industry basis. A CTUF publication explained, "Just as the workers organised in separate factory unions soon realised the need for a federation, so now workers engaged in separate factories but in the same trade realised the need for greater unity and a common organisation to fight for their common demands." Ceylon Trade Union Federation, *Ten Years of the Ceylon Trade Union Federation, 1940–1950* (Colombo : Ceylon Trade Union Federation, [1950]), p. 3.

between unions sponsored by the Lanka Sama Samaja Party, Mahajana Eksath Peramuna, and Communist Party has long been a prominent feature of labor relations. Party splits and the entry into trade unionism of other parties have frequently led to the formation of additional duplicating unions. A conspicuous example is provided by the port of Colombo, which for years has been the scene of conflict among at least four rival unions associated with opposing political parties.[43] However, while partisan competition for influence in the labor movement has contributed to the multiplicity of unions, it does not entirely explain the extent of fragmentation which exists.

The social cleavages and status consciousness which are marked characteristics of the society also contribute to the proliferation of unions. Strong consciousness of rank and status has impeded the development of a sense of solidarity and common purpose among workers of differing grade, position, or status.[44] Within a single enterprise, one union commonly exists for manual workers, while skilled workers such as truck drivers and machine operators are organized in a second, and clerical employees are represented in a third. In recent years, the Ceylon Estate Staffs' Union, Ceylon Bank Employees' Union, and Ceylon Mercantile Union, each originally limited to clerical employees, have broadened their membership to include subordinate office employees, and in the case of the CMU even non-office workers. This development may indicate the beginnings of a trend from trade unions restricted to a narrow stratum of each industry toward vertically integrated industry-wide trade unionism, but it is significant that each of these three unions was originally a white-collar organization, to which employees of lower status were subsequently admitted. It would be more unlikely that white-collar workers would join a union consisting primarily of laborers. Despite the example of these unions, it is still uncommon for a single union to incorporate successfully employees of markedly differing status.

[43]E.g., *Report of the Commission of Inquiry on the Working of the Commercial Sector of the Port of Colombo*, Sessional Paper II—1957 (Colombo: Government Press, 1957), p. 8; *Report of the National Wage Policy Commission*, p. 169.

[44]See *Reports on the Visit of a Joint Team of Experts on Labour-Management Relations to Pakistan and Ceylon, September–November 1959*, ILO Labour-Management Series No. 10 (Geneva: International Labour Office, 1961), pp. 53, 58; S. J. Tambiah, "Ceylon" in Richard D. Lambert and Bert F. Hoselitz (eds.), *The Role of Savings and Wealth in Southern Asia and the West* (Paris: UNESCO, 1963), pp. 61–62. The strong consciousness of status and marked hierarchical stratification of society are undoubtedly related to the existence of a caste system. Among the Buddhist Sinhalese, the caste system is considerably less rigid or steeply hierarchical than among the Hindus of India or Ceylon and, in contrast with India, the differences of occupational grade and rank among workers are seldom related to caste. Nonetheless, the presence of a caste system and caste ideology has tended to compartmentalize society and perpetuate, reinforce, and emphasize concern with relative status and hierarchical position. On the Sinhalese caste system, see Bryce Ryan, *Caste in Modern Ceylon* (New Brunswick, N.J.: Rutgers University Press, 1953).

In addition to the horizontal divisions produced by consciousness of rank and status, within any one level or grade workers tend to divide on communal lines, and duplicating organizations often appear which, although ostensibly seeking universal membership among a body of workers, in practice obtain their members from a particular ethnic community. It is extremely difficult for workers to develop a sense of identity and solidarity on class or occupational lines which bridges the emotional barriers between communities.[45] The ethnic community which shares a common language, social customs, and (with exceptions) religion has remained the principal focus of identification for the vast masses of the Ceylonese population, including many workers. Among government school teachers, clerks in the public service, and many other occupations, parallel organizations exist for Sinhalese and Tamils. The two largest unions on the island, the Ceylon Workers' Congress and the Democratic Workers' Congress, are composed virtually exclusively of Indian Tamils.

A considerable number of unions include members of several communities, and a predominant part of the labor movement professes hostility toward communal distinctions and loyalties. Some trade unions are probably among the most successful and determined integrative institutions on the island. Nonetheless, Ceylonese trade unionism has always been profoundly affected by the communal divisions and persisting communal rivalries of the island. The nascent labor movement was deeply shaken during the 1930's when A. E. Goonesinha, then the paramount trade union leader, began campaigning against the employment of Indians in the Colombo port and other industries, deepening and emphasizing communal suspicions and cleavages within the labor movement.[46] For decades, the Marxist unions consistently and fervently denounced communalism as dividing and weakening the working class, and the Marxist unions have commonly included both Sinhalese and Tamils within the same organization. However, after the 1965 election, when a coalition including the two largest Marxist parties attacked Government concessions to the Tamil-speaking minority, the Marxist unions faced a crisis of communal relations and lost many of their non-Sinhalese members.[47]

Communal clevages are further complicated by the emergence of occupational interests resulting from the language divisions of Ceylon and

[45]This is a problem faced by trade union movements in many of the multi-communal developing countries. See Subratesh Ghosh, *Trade Unionism in the Underdeveloped Countries* (Calcutta: Bookland Private, Ltd., 1960), p. 61.

[46]See Leslie Goonewardene, *A Short History of the Lanka Sama Samaja Party* (Colombo: Lanka Sama Samaja Party, 1960), p. 11; and Jayawardena, *Labour, Politics and Religion in Ceylon.*

[47]The problems of the Marxist unions after 1965 are discussed below, Chapter V. See also the discussions of the Government Clerical Service Union and Ceylon Mercantile Union, Chapter VI.

the eruption of the official language controversy. The Samastha Lanka Rajaye Lipikaru Sangamaya provides an example of the interaction of traditional group solidarity and modern interests based on education and occupation. The union is composed almost entirely of Sinhalese public servants and was founded specifically to agitate for a swift transition to Sinhalese as the sole language of administration, a position which is communally divisive and effectively excludes virtually all non-Sinhalese from membership. Nonetheless, the SLRLS does not profess communal exclusiveness, but claims to be open universally to all members of the General Clerical Service who accept its objectives. It is, in fact, said to contain a few Tamil members who have accepted Sinhalese as the only official language.[48] The union is largely composed of and represents the interests of the clerks with secondary educations in the Sinhalese language, who began entering the public service after 1956 and whose career prospects are closely bound up with the fortunes of Sinhalese as the language of administration. The union thus simultaneously reflects particularistic communal sentiments and a modern occupational interest based on education and bureaucratic employment.[49]

[48]Author's interview with SLRLS officers, July 17, 1967.

[49]The SLRLS is discussed further in Chapter VII. The blending of traditional, ascriptive with modern, associational and universalistic characteristics suggests the type of group frequently encountered in developing countries for which Professor Riggs has constructed the term "clect." Fred W. Riggs, *Administration in Developing Countries : The Theory of Prismatic Society* (Boston : Houghton Mifflin Company, 1964), pp. 164–173.

II

TRENDS IN INDUSTRIAL RELATIONS

Ceylonese workers, like workers in other countries undergoing fundamental social and economic change, experience many dislocations and tensions which generate unrest and contribute to a high incidence of industrial conflict. Workers' grievances are a reflection less of protest against the disappearance of traditional society and the onset of industrialization than of protest against the incomplete and unfulfilled character of the new social and economic circumstances—insufficient employment opportunities outside subsistence agriculture, insecurity of employment, inadequate housing and amenities, harsh and demeaning discipline, and a host of other conditions which indicate the partial and incomplete development of a modern society and economy.[1]

Trade unionism in Ceylon is plagued by many maladies. The multiplicity, rivalry, organizational instability, and lack of self-confidence of trade unions, along with the incomplete acceptance of organized labor and collective bargaining, all to some degree influence industrial relations. Nonetheless, trends toward greater strength, solidarity, and self-reliance are discernible within the labor movement. Relative to the recent Ceylonese past or to other developing societies of Asia and Africa, industrial relations in Ceylon exhibit signs of growing maturity, and trade unions are finding expanding opportunities for effective bargaining and articulation of workers' demands. A rising incidence of industrial conflict may indicate not only the accumulated tensions and frustrations of employment, but also the increasing capacity, self-confidence, and determination of organized labor.

1. *Problems of Collective Bargaining*

Trade unionism in Ceylon has generally suffered from the weakness of bargaining power which typifies labor in the developing countries and which contributes to the politicization of trade unions by creating despair with any avenue for the realization of labor's goals other than

[1] See William H. Knowles, "Industrial Conflict and Unions," in Wilbert E. Moore and Arnold S. Feldman (eds.), *Labor Commitment and Social Change in Developing Areas* (New York: Social Science Research Council, 1960), pp. 291-312.

political action. While a number of individual unions have developed impressive strength and the bargaining power of the entire labor movement has improved markedly in the past ten or twenty years, organized labor in Ceylon is still in a basically weak bargaining position. Relatively few workers possess scarce skills, and the number of workers seeking jobs exceeds the amount of employment available. Therefore, the threat or act of withholding labor to force concessions from employers often is ineffective and may simply result in workers being replaced by others who are unemployed and eager to take the jobs. The plight of striking workers was starkly captured in the Commissioner of Labour's report for 1949, which remarked that "where a Union or workers rushed head-long into strikes... the employers were able to replace the striking workers without much difficulty, which they proceeded to do without much ado. In such cases subsequent retreat by the workers or even obeisance in the traditional eastern fashion did not enable them to get back their jobs."[2] Furthermore, with the exception of clerical and certain other employees, workers generally lack the resources to go for extended periods without wages. Strikes often commence with great militancy and determination, but if a quick settlement is not obtained workers begin to drift back to work and the strike disintegrates before it is officially terminated by the union.

Barganing Styles and Arenas

Workers' organizations in Ceylon have customarily tended to avoid direct bargaining with employers and have sought to rely on government intervention, suggesting a marked lack of confidence in their own bargaining strength or negotiating skills.[3] As a Commissioner of Labour once lamented, the method of obtaining demands adopted by most unions was "to lodge a complaint with this Department which is thereafter expected to obtain for them all that they have asked."[4] Government officials repeatedly urge unions to deal directly with employers, rather than turning immediately to public agencies for assistance. For example, a procedure for the resolution of industrial disputes outlined by the Minister of Labour in 1957 insisted that the union "must, in the first instance, submit its demands to the employer," and provided for governmental intervention only after the union and the employer have failed to reach

[2]*Administration Report of the Commissioner of Labour for 1949* (Colombo : Government Press, 1950), p. 9.

[3]See *Reports on the Visit of a Joint Team of Experts on Labour-Management Relations to Pakistan and Ceylon, September–November 1959*, ILO Labour-Management Series No. 10 (Geneva : International Labour Office, 1961), pp. 53–54; Ceylon, Department of Labour, "Collective Bargaining in Ceylon" (mimeographed; Colombo, January, 1960), p. 68.

[4]*Administration Report of the Commissioner of Labour for 1953* (Colombo : Government Press, 1954), p. 12.

agreement.[5] Over the past ten or twenty years, however, the environment of collective bargaining has undergone gradual but significant modifications. Although many small and weak organizations continue to rely on governmental intervention, the bargaining power of the labor movement as a whole appears to have improved considerably, and several major unions such as the Ceylon Mercantile Union and the Ceylon Bank Employees' Union have displayed a marked tendency toward reliance on their own bargaining strength in direct clashes with employers. With increasing governmental permissiveness and receptivity to labor demands and with the growth in size and cohesiveness of many trade unions, many private employers appear to have accepted the necessity of dealing with trade unions.

Indicative of the mounting self-confidence of at least some trade unions and the growing maturity of industrial relations is the recent signing of a series of collective agreements. The first major collective agreement was concluded in 1957 between the Ceylon Estate Staffs' Union and the Ceylon Estates Employers' Federation. The Ceylon Mercantile Union and the Employers' Federation of Ceylon signed a collective agreement in 1961, which was revised and renewed in 1967. The Ceylon Bank Employees' Union reached an accord with the Commercial Banks' Association, the Bank of Ceylon, and the People's Bank in 1967, and in the same year a collective agreement was signed by the Ceylon Workers' Congress and the Ceylon Estates Employers' Federation. These collective agreements provide for the handling of incidental disputes and prohibit the presentation of new demands on wages, hours, working conditions, and other stipulated terms of employment during the period of the agreement. Consequently, the rapid extension of collective agreements should reduce the incidence of industrial conflict and tend to ease labor-management relations. Although as yet encompassing only a small part of organized labor, the agreements have been accepted by the most powerful and influential unions and employers' groups.

Many of labor's demands are not sought in the collision between union and employer in direct two-party conflict, but are pursued in other arenas such as those provided in the private sector by wages boards. Wages boards are created to fix minimum wages, determine holidays, and establish hours and conditions of work for specific trades. Twenty-six trades covered by wages boards were recently estimated to include approximately 800,000 workers, about 40 percent of all paid employees in Ceylon.[6] The board established for a given trade includes representatives of trade

[5] *Administration Report of the Commissioner of Labour for 1957* (Colombo : Government Press, 1958), p. 19.
[6] *Report of the Commission on Profit Sharing*, Sessional Paper XXVII—1967 (Colombo : Government Press, 1967), p. 59.

unions and employers involved in that trade and, in addition, a third group of members nominated to represent the public.[7] Wages boards were originally intended to cover trades in which workers were poorly organized and lacked bargaining power, but in practice they have generally been created in trades where trade unionism is most strongly established.[8] The wages board, as noted by the National Wage Policy Commission in 1961, has become "a bargaining forum between organized labour on the one hand and organized employers on the other...."[9] Labor organizations attach great importance to their representation on wages boards. The major organizations frequently boast of the number of boards on which they are represented and include benefits approved by the boards among the victories they claim to have won.[10]

Organizations of public servants commonly seek their demands in a somewhat different manner than unions in the private sector. Public servants' grievances and demands usually are first presented in the form of petitions and memoranda to the department head or the Secretary to the Treasury as head of the public service. If satisfaction is not obtained at lower levels and if the issue is important, a deputation will seek a meeting with the responsible minister or with the Prime Minister. On major demands, if the ministers are not responsive, the union may resort to announcements to the press and open letters to the minister or to the Cabinet in the hope of generating public support for and political pressure behind the demands.[11] Representatives of the Government Clerical Service Union, for example, climaxed a long period of agitation with a three-hour session with the Prime Minister in September, 1967.[12]

Union Proliferation and Rivalry

The proliferation of duplicating unions combined with sharp rivalry between unions in many workplaces has had a marked impact on industrial relations and has led to frequent criticism by employers. The chairman of the Employers' Federation of Ceylon recently asserted that collective

[7]The role and operation of the wages boards are described in Department of Labour, "Collective Bargaining in Ceylon," pp. 72–83.

[8]*Report of the National Wage Policy Commission*, Sessional Paper VIII—1961 (Colombo: Government Press, 1961), p. 40.

[9]*Ibid.*, p. 100.

[10]E.g., M. G. Mendis, *Ceylon Federation of Trade Unions: Report of the General Secretary to the 17th Sessions* (Colombo: Ceylon Federation of Trade Unions, 1966), p. 14; *Ceylon Workers' Congress Report, 1964–1965* (Colombo: Ceylon Workers' Congress, 1965), p. 36; *Democratic Workers' Congress Administrative Report, 1963/64* (Colombo: Democratic Workers' Congress, 1964), p. 9; and A. Aziz, "Presidential Address of Mr. A. Aziz at the Annual Sessions of the Democratic Workers' Congress Held at Yatiyantota on 27th and 28th August 1967" (mimeographed; Colombo, 1967), p. 4.

[11]Based on interviews with a large number of officers of public servants' unions in 1965 and 1967.

[12]*Ceylon Daily News*, September 13, 1967, p. 1.

bargaining "is difficult, if not impossible, because of the existence in Ceylon of numerous trade unions to represent the workers in one particular trade. It is a pity that, due to these divisive tendencies among the workers themselves, the trade union movement in Ceylon . . . still cannot claim to speak with one voice on behalf of the workers in any given trade."[13] The Ceylon Estates Employers' Federation has complained that planters on tea, rubber, and coconut estates have to deal with fifty or sixty separate unions.[14] In the private sector, where one union of substantial size and a number of splinter unions often exist in the same workplace, the customary practice is for the employer to deal with all unions, irrespective of size, concerning individual grievances of workers, but to bargain only with the largest union on wage issues and other matters of general applicability.[15] Where the workforce is splintered among a number of small unions, it is common for the unions to form a "front" or joint committee to bargain with the employer on the issues of general concern.

An important consequence of the multiplicity of unions, a number of which often battle for members from the same group of workers, is the extensive rivalry which has been blamed for much of the turbulence and volatility of industrial relations in Ceylon. The commitment of members to a particular organization or leadership is frequently tenuous, and workers shift from union to union with relative ease. An accumulation of grievances and discontents among workers is common and, with a number of rival unions competing for support within a single industry or enterprise, leaders frequently feel compelled to demonstrate the greater militancy of their leadership in order to attract and hold members. The Employers' Federation of Ceylon recently charged : "The existence of so many trade unions has made it necessary for unions to maintain their strength, membership and prestige by espousing or creating frivolous disputes, so as to avoid the danger of their members being won over by a rival trade union." The multiplicity of unions, the federation contended, "has a tendency to promote a large number and variety of disputes since the creation of disputes is necessary for the survival of a union in the face of such competition from rival unions."[16]

[13]Employers' Federation of Ceylon, "Thirty Eighth Annual General Meeting, Chairman's Address" (mimeographed; Colombo, 1967), p. 2.
[14]Ceylon Estates Employers' Federation, *Annual General Meeting, 24th August, 1963* (Colombo: Ceylon Estates Employers' Federation, n.d.), p. 5.
[15]Author's interview with Lincoln Abeywira, Commissioner of Labour, July 18, 1967. Also, see *Report of the Committee of Inquiry into the Law and Practice of the Trade Unions Ordinance,* Sessional Paper XXVIII—1967 (Colombo: Government Press, 1967), pp. 19–20.
[16]Employers' Federation of Ceylon, "Reply to Questionnaire Issued by the Industrial Disputes Commission (Ceylon)" (mimeographed; Colombo, January 7, 1967), "Annexure 'B,'" pp. ii–iii. Union rivalry and the competitive pursuit of demands are cited as conducive to a high level of industrial conflict by Arthur M. Ross and Paul T. Hartman, *Changing Patterns of Industrial Conflict* (New York: John Wiley & Sons, Inc., 1960), pp. 65–66.

Absenteeism and Indiscipline

Absenteeism, indiscipline, and similar manifestations of incomplete acceptance of the regimentation of an industrial society are prevalent among the Ceylonese wage-labor force and have affected the climate of collective bargaining. An average rate of absenteeism of 15 percent has been estimated for organized labor in Ceylon,[17] and in some industries the rate is considerably higher. Absenteeism has averaged about 30 percent in the state industrial corporations and the engineering industry.[18]

The incidence of absenteeism is generally attributed to the rural, village background of workers and their failure to understand or appreciate the demands of industrial discipline. Workers from the villages often return to help their families with harvests and also absent themselves from work to attend festivals, weddings, and other events of great importance in village life.[19] A prominent Ceylonese trade union leader has explained :

> Most workers in a country like ours have a village background, even where they do not actually live in a village, and most of them are governed in their social behaviour by their village traditions and customs. The importance of weddings, funerals, and such occasions, of religious observances and pilgrimages and the like in their minds often conflicts with the necessities of modern business....
>
> Many workers are co-owners in plots of land in their villages, and ... there are ploughing, sowing, harvesting and reaping times, and proprietary duties connected therewith, which cannot be delegated and require absence from work. ... Here we see really a conflict between two modes of production, which is essentially a social question.[20]

Furthermore, social conventions in Ceylon, at least outside the middle class, require the male head of a household to perform innumerable domestic chores such as taking a sick child to the government dispensary, dealing with the landlord or creditors, or overseeing repairs to his residence or furnishings, which in industrialized Western societies often would be handled by his wife. When a worker lives far from his place of employment,

[17]B. R. Fernando and P. U. Ratnatunga, "Discipline, Absenteeism, and Lateness," in D. S. Bandarage (ed.), *Hand Book of Personnel Management (Ceylon)* (Colombo : Institute of Personnel Management, [1964?]), p. 125.

[18]*Report of Reconnaissance Mission to Ceylon in Connection with State Industrial Corporations, February 16–March 16, 1966,* by G. W. Naylor (Colombo : Ministry of Planning and Economic Affairs, October, 1966), p. 23; *Ceylon Investment Guide : The Light Engineering Industry* (Colombo : Industrial Development Board, Ministry of Industries and Fisheries, 1968), p. 18.

[19]Fernando and Ratnatunga, "Discipline, Absenteeism and Lateness," p. 127.

[20]P. B. Tampoe, "Absenteeism," *Young Socialist* (Colombo), No. 10 (September, 1963), p. 258.

as most workers in Colombo do, such domestic responsibilities can result in frequent absence from work for a half-day or an entire day. Also, although the evidence is contradictory, reference is frequently made to the preference of workers, particularly agricultural workers or those psychologically close to the village, for leisure rather than a marginally higher living standard, once a minimum standard has been attained.[21]

Workers' indiscipline is a constant source of complaint by employers. The Employers' Federation of Ceylon, for example, denounced "the frequent walk-outs resorted to by the work force, particularly over trivial issues such as attendance at a funeral or political meeting, or in consequence of the refusal to grant a holiday to which they were not entitled."[22] An extreme form of indiscipline appears in the occasional eruptions of violence by workers, particularly on the estates. The annual reports of the Ceylon Estates Employers' Federation regularly carry a section devoted to violence against the supervisory staff.[23] The federation claimed in 1964 that incidents of violence against estate staff were reported on member estates in forty-three of the fifty-two preceding weeks. An additional twenty-six cases were reported of violent clashes between groups of workers growing out of rivalries between unions.[24] A spokesman for the estate employers' group has claimed that in legal proceedings resulting from violence on the estates, "unions invariably strongly support their members, however bad the case."[25] Although sporadic, small-scale violence is most prevalent on the estates, various forms of violence, particularly attacks against "blackleg" or "scab" workers during strikes, are not an infrequent accompaniment of industrial disputes outside the estates as well. The Employers' Federation of Ceylon expressed astonishment at the extent of violence and indiscipline which accompanied one strike by employees of the federation's member firms, since the strikers were white-collar, lower-middle-class clerical employees and the strike was

---

[21]E.g., Fernando and Ratnatunga, "Discipline, Absenteeism and Lateness," p. 127. There are, however, indications that even villagers seek material gains and are willing to substitute additional labor for leisure if reasonable opportunities are available. E.g., see B. H. Farmer, *Pioneer Peasant Colonization in Ceylon* (London : Oxford University Press, 1957), p. 286. Also, see Bryce Ryan, L. D. Jayasena, and D. C. R. Wickremesinghe, "Secularization Processes in a Ceylon Village," *Eastern Anthropologist*, XI (March–August, 1958), 155–161; and Bryce Ryan, *Sinhalese Village* (Coral Gables, Fla. : University of Miami Press, 1958), pp. 29–34.

[22]Employers' Federation of Ceylon, *Annual Report and Accounts, 1964–1965* (Colombo : Employers' Federation of Ceylon, n.d.), p. 10.

[23]See particularly Ceylon Estates Employers' Federation, *Annual General Meeting, 17th August, 1960* (Colombo : Ceylon Estates Employers' Federation, n.d.), p. 4.

[24]Ceylon Estates Employers' Federation, *XXth Annual Report and Accounts, 1963–1964* (Colombo : Ceylon Estates Employers' Federation, n.d.), p. 33.

[25]Ceylon Estates Employers' Federation, "Annual General Meeting, 19th August, 1964" (typescript), p. 8. Similarly, see *Ceylon Daily News*, August 26, 1967, p. 13.

Table 5

AVERAGE ANNUAL INCIDENCE OF STRIKES, 1946–1965 [a]

Years	Estates			Other than estates			Total		
	Average number of strikes annually	Average number of workers involved annually	Average number of man-days lost annually	Average number of strikes annually	Average number of workers involved annually	Average number of man-days lost annually	Average number of strikes annually	Average number of workers involved annually	Average number of man-days lost annually
1946–1950	64	110,085	209,720	39	18,426	166,946	104	128,512	376,666
1951–1955	51	154,587	284,431	46	10,810	43,611	97	165,397	328,042
1956–1960	140	96,637	354,333	89	38,513	244,191	229	135,151	598,512 [b]
1961–1965 [c]	151	53,443	361,831	59	25,044	370,257	211	78,487	732,088

[a] Strikes included in a particular year are those ending in that year. From 1952 on, strikes involving less than five workers or lasting less than one day are not included unless more than fifty man-days were lost. Slight discrepancies in totals are due to averaging.

[b] The discrepancy between this figure and the sum of man-days lost for estates and other than estates presented in the table (598,524) is a result of a discrepancy in the data for the year 1958, which records sixty less total man-days lost than the sum of the man-days lost in the two sub-categories.

[c] Includes the period January 1, 1961, to September 30, 1965. In 1961 the period for which data were reported was changed from a calendar year to a fiscal year ending September 30. The annual average for this period was calculated on the basis of four and three-fourths years.

SOURCE : Administration Report of the Commissioner of Labour for 1964–65 (Colombo : Government Press, 1967), Table III, pp. 58–59.

called not in support of their own demands but in sympathy with a port workers' strike.[26]

2. *Industrial Conflict*

Industrial conflict in Ceylon contains significant elements of volitility, alienation, and instability, but in comparison with other transitional societies, it is characterized by fairly general and regular adherence to the formal and informal rules of industrial relations behavior and ordinarily is relatively focused and purposive. Abrupt explosions of undirected frustration are not unknown but constitute only a minor element of industrial conflict. Industrial conflict often merges into political conflict, and, even if unintended, strikes and other forms of "direct action" often have immense political ramifications, particularly when the government is the employer. The discussion here is concerned with conflict between workers and their employers, whether the employer is a governmental agency or a private firm, which is essentially employment-related rather than political.[27]

Strikes

The strike is undoubtedly the chief and most visible instrument of industrial conflict. Strikes have been endemic in Ceylon since the Second World War, and the growth of trade unionism, particularly since 1956, has been accompanied by a rising incidence of strikes (see Table 5).[28]

Both the average number of strikes and the number of man-days lost annually have risen spectacularly. The number of workers involved,

Table 6

AVERAGE DURATION OF STRIKES : MAN-DAYS
LOST PER WORKER INVOLVED

Years	Estates	Other than estates	Total
1946–1950	1.9	9.1	2.9
1951–1955	1.8	4.0	2.0
1956–1960	3.7	6.3	4.4
1961–1965	6.8	14.8	9.3

SOURCE : From Table 5.

[26]Employers' Federation of Ceylon, *Annual Report and Accounts, 1963–1964* (Colombo : Employers' Federation of Ceylon, n.d.), p. 20.

[27]The political significance of strikes is discussed in Chapter VIII.

[28]Due to wide annual fluctuations, a five-year average has been used as more clearly indicative of the trend.

Table 7

AVERAGE NUMBER OF WORKERS INVOLVED PER STRIKE

Years	Estates	Other than estates	Total
1946–1950	1,720	472	1,236
1951–1955	3,031	235	1,705
1956–1960	690	433	590
1961–1965	354	424	372

SOURCE : From Table 5.

however, does not follow the upward trend, and, in fact, declines after 1960. This is explained by the trend on the estates, where the characteristics of strikes diverge in some respects from those of strikes elsewhere. The number of non-estate workers involved in strikes was much higher in the second than the first of the two decades included in the table. On the estates, the period 1946–1955 was marked by many brief strikes which often lasted only a day or two but involved a very large number of workers, as is demonstrated by Tables 6 and 7. Until 1955, estate strikes lasted an average of less than two days, but the average number of workers involved was well over a thousand. Estate strikes in this period frequently were brief, often abrupt, eruptions which represented demonstrations of protest and discontent, but because of the lack of bargaining strength and the relatively weak organization of estate labor they generally were not serious contests of strength with employers intended to win specific demands. In the decade after 1955, the number of workers involved in estate strikes has declined, but the strikes have tended to last considerably longer.[29]

In other industries, the duration of strikes has also risen, particularly in the period 1961–1965. The relatively long duration of non-estate strikes in the period 1946–1950, as well as the large number of workers involved, reflects the labor turbulence of the immediate post-war years. With the conclusion of· the Second World War and the approach of political independence, a restiveness and accumulation of demands both for improvements in wages and working conditions and for trade union rights, which had been suppressed during the war, erupted in major public service, transport, and general strikes in 1946 and 1947.[30] After the ebbing

[29]Lightning strikes, however, continue to be common on the estates. In 1963/1964, the Ceylon Estates Employers' Federation claimed that 169 of 185 strikes on estates of federation members were lightning strikes called without warning, most of which "were called off unconditionally within a day or two." Ceylon Estates Employers' Federation, *XXth Annual Report and Accounts, 1963–1964,* p. 14.

[30]The release of tensions suppressed during the war and the agitation for independence also produced a record level of industrial conflict in India during 1946–1947. See V. B. Karnik, *Strikes in India* (Bombay : Manaktalas, 1967), p. 401.

of the post-war strikes, virtually all indicators of the incidence of industrial conflict outside the estates have risen steadily.

These strike trends not only reveal mounting industrial conflict but suggest that the strike may be undergoing a transformation from a demonstration of protest to a test of strength between workers and employers. A number of specific strikes within recent years which have pitted strong and determined unions against employers in lengthy contests can be cited in support of this interpretation. Among the major strikes in which unions challenged employers in prolonged tests of strength are bank employees' strikes lasting three months in 1961–1962 and two months in 1967, a strike of Port (Cargo) Corporation employees of fifty-two days in 1961–1962, a seventeen-day strike by employees of the Ceylon Transport Board in 1963, port strikes called by the CMU of seventy days in 1963–1964 and forty-two days in 1968, a twenty-three day CMU strike against firms belonging to the Employers' Federation of Ceylon in 1966, and a DWC-led estate strike of forty-five days' duration in 1966. As a result of the growing strength and self-confidence of the labor movement, industrial conflict may increasingly assume the form of serious tests of strength between workers and employers over specific labor demands.[31]

Strikes on wage and other service questions have been called with considerable frequency by public servants' unions. Although the resources available to the government dim a union's prospects of winning a contest of strength, some public servants' strikes have been prolonged and bitter. Among the major strikes by public servants which seemed seriously intended to test the strength and resolve of the government were strikes in 1946 and 1947, which involved demands for trade union rights and wage increases; a 1958 strike of thirteen days organized by the Public Service Workers' Trade Union Federation, principally on wage and salary issues; and a strike by government clerks and other public servants lasting twenty-five days in 1968 for higher wages and removal of punishments against participants in the January, 1966, political strike. All of these strikes had political motives as well as wage and other job-related objectives, and in all except the 1958 strike the unions involved and the political parties to which they were allied were strongly opposed to the Government in power at the time.

There are few legal impediments to strikes in Ceylon. The most significant

---

[31]It has been noted that in industrialized Western countries during the present century strikes have tended to become shorter and less frequently represent a test of strength between workers and employers. Ross and Hartman, *Changing Patterns of Industrial Conflict*, pp. 24–25, 38–39. It can be argued, however, that in the developing countries where industrialization has only commenced and labor movements are yet weak, if trade unions are not suppressed or smothered by state paternalism, the consolidation and strengthening of trade unionism will be followed by mounting industrial conflict and lengthening duration of strikes as the unions are increasingly able to challenge employers.

limitations on strikes outside the public service are prohibitions against any strike without twenty-one days' notice in any industry which has been declared "essential" to the life of the community and any strike after a dispute has been referred to an industrial court or to arbitration and before an award has been made. Also prohibited are strikes to obtain modification of an order by a labor tribunal or of a settlement or award by an arbitrator or industrial court, or to alter the terms of a collective agreement binding on the union and employer involved.[32] Public servants' unions are prohibited from organizing or aiding strikes intended "wholly or partly for the purpose of influencing or overawing the Government on any political issue not affecting public servants in their capacity as such, or wholly or mainly for the purpose of supporting workmen, other than public servants, in any strike or trade dispute."[33] These limitations have, in fact, placed slight practical constraint on strikes. Strikes have occurred in industries designated "essential" and have continued despite compulsory referral to arbitration without action being taken against the strikers or their unions. Furthermore, public servants have been frequent and conspicuous participants in political and sympathy strikes.[34] Following the political strike of January 8, 1966, disciplinary action was taken against striking public servants for the first time in more than a decade.[35]

Strikes, largely limited to the Colombo vicinity and the estate areas until recent years, have begun to spread throughout the island. Until ten or twelve years ago, there were few trade union members outside the shops and offices of Colombo and the self-contained and socially isolated estates. Following the nationalization of the island's bus services in 1958 and petroleum distribution facilities in 1961, the employees of the Ceylon Transport Board and Ceylon Petroleum Corporation were rapidly unionized. These public corporations and the People's Bank, established in 1961, have depots, outlets, branches, or offices spread widely through the rural areas, and strikes by corporation employees have involved workers in the towns and countryside throughout much of the island. The CBEU journal remarked of a 1966 bank employees' strike : "For the first time in the history of this country the strike was taken to the villages when the numerous branches of the People's Bank closed down completely."[36] The result is that trade unionism and strikes, once familiar only to the cities and estates, have been introduced to the much larger population of rural, village Ceylon.

[32]For a summary, see Eric Ranawake, "The Right to Strike," *Enterprise* (Journal of the Ceylon Chamber of Commerce), II (March, 1968), 29–33. "Stay-in" strikes were outlawed in 1955, but the prohibition was repealed in 1958.

[33]Trade Unions (Amendment) Act, No. 15 of 1948.

[34]Strikes by public servants have been discussed in Robert N. Kearney, "Militant Public Service Trade Unionism in a New State : The Case of Ceylon," *Journal of Asian Studies*, XXV (May, 1966), esp. pp. 402–404.

[35]The January, 1966, political strike and its consequences are examined in Chapter VIII.

[36]*Bank Worker*, October, 1966, p. 7.

Causes of Strikes

A large proportion of labor disputes are produced by non-wage issues such as security of employment, disciplinary action, working conditions, and protest against abusive and degrading treatment. As a number of grievances commonly are involved in a single strike and a wide assortment of accumulated discontents may suddenly crystalize into a strike, it is often difficult to attribute disputes to single cause.[37] Nonetheless, the causes of strikes as classified by the Department of Labour for selected years reveal the importance attached to dismissals, disciplinary questions, and other non-wage matters (Table 8). With the paucity of alternative employment opportunities, the typical Ceylonese worker is deeply con-

Table 8

CAUSES OF STRIKES

| Causes | Percent attributed to each cause | | | | | | | | | | | |
| | 1956 | | | 1960 | | | 1962/1963[a] | | | 1965/1966[a] | | |
	Estates	Other	Total	Estates	Other	Total	Estates	Other	Total	Estates	Other	Total
Dismissals, loss of employment	20	18	19	20	16	19	17	33	21	29	32	30
Demands for wage increases	1	12	7	1	5	2	1	11	4	5	12	6
Other wage disputes	11	29	21	8	19	11	7	11	8	9	18	11
Rules and discipline	29	15	21	33	35	34	37	17	32	33	21	31
Right of association and meeting	4	—	2	2	8	4	5	—	4	3	—	2
Assaults by employer or agent	5	2	3	11	3	9	5	4	4	5	3	4
"General" demands	9	20	15	13	5	11	13	19	14	12	12	12
Other causes[b]	20	4	12	12	8	11	15	6	13	5	3	5
TOTAL NUMBER OF STRIKES	99	115	214	123	37	160	169	54	223	155	34	189

[a] Year commencing October 1 and ending September 30.

[b] Includes food and welfare, "factional disputes and domestic matters," "external matters" (described as "e.g., arrest by Police"), and sympathy strikes.

SOURCE : *Administration Report of the Commissioner of Labour* for the years 1960–1965/1966 (Colombo: Government Press, 1961–1968).

[37] Thus, for example, the Employers' Federation reported a fifty-three day strike which resulted from disciplinary action taken against a group of workers but which was complicated by the subsequent addition of a number of other issues unrelated to the original grievance. Employers' Federation of Ceylon, *Annual Report and Accounts, 1964–1965*, p. 10.

cerned with retaining his job at all costs, and trade unions are repeatedly called upon to intercede on behalf of dismissed workers.[38] The Employers' Federation of Ceylon complained to the recent Industrial Disputes Commission that it was not uncommon for unions to demand reinstatement even of workers "whose services have been terminated for theft and who have been convicted in a criminal court."[39] Discipline is another constant source of grievances and disputes. Usually disputes originating in disciplinary issues are small and inconspicuous, but in late 1961 an abrupt strike of Ceylon Transport Board employees which was precipitated by the issuance of a circular revising disciplinary rules paralysed bus services throughout the island for six days and was ended only when the Cabinet ordered withdrawal of the new rules.

That "assaults on workers" is retained in the Labour Department's classification of strike causes suggests another type of problem in Ceylonese industrial relations. Ceylon has only quite recently entered a period in which the worker is assumed to be entitled to rights and dignity. The development of humane and egalitarian relationships in industry has been handicapped by the tremendous cultural gap and social distance which has typically separated employers and managers from their workers, originating in traditional social attitudes and practices emphasizing status, deference, and hierarchy, sometimes complicated by ethnic and language differences.[40] Although in general employers' attitudes and behavior toward workers have changed considerably in the past several decades, particularly among the larger commercial firms represented in the Employers' Federation and the public corporations and public service, some pockets remain where ill treatment, abuse, and contempt are not uncommon.[41]

---

[38]See *Report of the National Wage Policy Commission*, p. 174. Preoccupation with dismissals has been an important feature of the labor movement for many years. In 1940, the Controller of Labour remarked that during the year trade unions had "largely confined their attention to interference in cases where members of the unions have been discharged from employment. Very little other form of trade union activity has been observed." *Administration Report of the Controller of Labour for 1940* (Colombo: Government Press, 1941), p. 5.

[39]Employers' Federation of Ceylon, "Reply to Questionnaire Issued by the Industrial Disputes Commission (Ceylon)," "Annexure 'B,'" p. ii. The importance accorded dismissals and layoffs by Ceylonese trade unions is reflected in the CMU's lengthy treatment of the subject in answering the same questionnaire: Ceylon Mercantile Union, "Answer to the Questionnaire of Industrial Disputes Commission" (mimeographed; Colombo, n.d.), section XI.

[40]On the stratification and status distinctions and ceremonial symbols of rank of traditional society, see Ralph Pieris, *Sinhalese Social Organization: The Kandyan Period* (Colombo: Ceylon University Press Board, 1956), esp. pp. 169–177; Ralph Pieris, "Speech and Society: A Sociological Approach to Language," *American Sociological Review*, XVI (August, 1951), 499–505; and Gananath Obeyesekere, *Land Tenure in Village Ceylon* (Cambridge: Cambridge University Press, 1967), pp. 215–226.

[41]E.g., *Report of the National Wage Policy Commission*, p. 171.

Other Forms of Industrial Conflict

To the conventional weapon of the strike, the Ceylon Mercantile Union in recent years has added an unconventional and controversial technique for bringing pressure to bear on employers. The union has called on its branches in the port of Colombo to refuse to handle shipments of firms with which other branches of the union have a dispute. As most private-sector firms are dependent on either imports or exports, most of which must pass through the port of Colombo, the port boycott has proved to be a highly effective device where strike action is impractical or ineffective. The boycott has been used particularly where the CMU was attempting to organize a group of employees for the first time but was faced with "victimization" of new members and other obstacles to formation of a branch by management. The technique has also been used where the union was very weak, as with many small shops and family-owned distribution firms, or where striking workers were in a particularly weak bargaining position due to the ease with which they could be replaced by new employees. The CMU, in justifying use of the boycott to the recent Industrial Disputes Commission, explained :

> The new manufacturing companies ... utilise their present unrestricted legal rights of suspension and dismissal of workers at the very inception of the formation of a union amongst them. The workers in these establishments consequently have to choose between having no union to safeguard their rights, as workers, and trying to form a union, in the full knowledge that they will face an immediate attack by the employer, on all sorts of pretexts.
>
> A large Union like ours can only use the "weapon" of boycott against such employers, since the "weapon" of strike cannot be exercised in such cases.[42]

In late 1966, after employees in the port of Trincomalee were dismissed from their jobs—and hence could scarcely threaten to strike—the CMU boycotted tea shipments of the offending firms through the port of Colombo. The dispute was settled following government intervention. At the same time, after negotiations for renewal of a collective agreement with the Employers' Federation stalled, the CMU declared a boycott against imports or exports of sixty-seven federation firms in support of a strike against the firms. After a week, the boycott and strike were called off and negotiations resumed on the basis of proposals by the Minister of Labour which the Employers' Federation had earlier rejected.[43]

[42]CMU, "Answer to the Questionnaire of Industrial Disputes Commission," section XI, p. 3.
[43]Ceylon Mercantile Union, "The Struggle for a Collective Agreement with the Employers' Federation of Ceylon—1966" (mimeographed; Colombo, n.d.), pp. 18–23; Ceylon Mercantile Union, "Ninth Annual Delegates Conference, 16th and 17th April 1967 : General Secretary's Report" (mimeographed; Colombo, April 14, 1967), p. 3.

Another device of labor to bring pressure to bear against employers is the "slowdown" or "go-slow" campaign, which has the advantage of not resulting in a loss of wages since workers appear for work and ostensibly carry out their duties. A varient of the slowdown often employed by public servants is the "work to rule," by which government employees have resorted to such meticulous and elaborate attention to the detail of procedures and regulations that the work of the unit is backed up and thrown into confusion or brought to a standstill. Announcements are often made that slowdowns and "work-to-rule" campaigns will commence at a particular time unless certain demands are met, just as strike deadlines are set. Although frequently utilized, the slowdown is not an accepted technique of collective bargaining and can result in disciplinary action against workers using it.[44]

[44]In 1967, a labor tribunal refused to order reinstatement of employees dismissed for conducting a slowdown called by their trade union on grounds that it was not a legitimate bargaining weapon. *Ceylon Daily News*, November 14, 1967, p. 1.

III

LABOR LEADERSHIP

For most of its history, trade unionism in Ceylon has been heavily dependent on the leadership of persons who are not themselves workers or members of unions. In the first years of the labor movement, before the development of permanent and coherently organized unions, immediate workers' grievances occasionally produced spontaneous protests and strikes led by militant workers, who became the spokesmen and leaders of their fellow employees.[1] The first workers' organizations were formed and directed by nationalists and social reformers, who were wealthy professionals and landowners. With the 1923 general strike, the Ceylonese labor movement gained its first professional labor leader, A. E. Goonesinha, a middle-class nationalist and radical who devoted his efforts for many subsequent years to labor organizing and working-class politics. Typical of the pattern of early labor disputes, Goonesinha related that at the commencement of the 1923 strike he was approached by a group of workers who told him they had gone on strike and asked him to become their spokesman and leader.[2]

1. *The Role of Outsiders*

Although in recent years labor leaders have increasingly emerged from the ranks of workers' organizations, the "outsider" has continued to provide much of the leadership of the trade union movement. Union leaders are frequently persons who are not and have never been associated with the work performed by union members. Often they are middle-class, university-educated professionals and intellectuals.[3] The president

---

[1] For an examination of the workers who became strike leaders in the early years of the labor movement, see Kumari Jayawardena, "Pioneer Rebels among the Colombo Working Class," *Young Socialist* (Colombo), No. 18 (November, 1968), pp. 80–87.

[2] A. E. Goonesinha, "My Life and Labour" (part 5), *Ceylon Observer*, August 1, 1965, p. 5.

[3] The prevalence in Ceylonese trade union delegations of "lawyers, school-masters, journalists, ex-Government employees, and similar persons of education" was noted many years ago by G. St. J. Orde Browne, *Labour Conditions in Ceylon, Mauritius, and Malaya*, Cmd. 6423 (London: His Majesty's Stationery Office, 1943), p. 34. The phenomenon of the "outsider" as a trade union leader is frequently encountered in the developing countries. For example, see Bruce H. Millen, *The Political Role of Labor in Developing Countries* (Washington, D. C.: Brookings Institution, 1963), pp. 27–32; Charles A. Myers, *Labor Problems in the Industrialization of India* (Cambridge, Mass.: Harvard University Press, 1958), pp. 76–80; Everett

of the Ceylon Federation of Labour, N. M. Perera, holds two doctoral degrees from the University of London and was once an academic economist. Colvin R. de Silva, a CFL official long involved in trade unionism, enjoys a lucrative legal practice and holds a University of London doctorate in history. Pieter Keuneman, president of the Ceylon Federation of Trade Unions, is a graduate of Cambridge University and a son of a prominent Supreme Court judge. The founder of the SLFP trade unions, W. D. de Silva, was a medical doctor. S. Thondaman, president of the Ceylon Workers' Congress, is a wealthy estate owner. The general secretary of the Ceylon Mercantile Union, Bala Tampoe, is a lawyer and was a lecturer at the Agricultural School until his dismissal for participation in the public servants' strike of 1947. Prins Rajasooriya, one-time general secretary of the CFL and now secretary of the United Committee of Ceylon Trade Unions, and P. K. Liyanage, long active in the CFL, are both lawyers.

The necessity for trade union leadership by middle-class "outsiders" stems from fundamental social and cultural circumstances. Despite a very high literacy rate in Ceylon relative to neighboring countries, workers frequently are illiterate or barely literate and are separated by a wide social and cultural gulf from the executives, lawyers, and public service officers with whom union leaders must deal. The worker with little education is unlikely to be able to understand the statutes, administrative orders, and court decisions regulating collective bargaining or defining workers' rights. As with many aspects of Ceylonese life, language has been of great significance to trade union leadership. All public and business documents, records, and correspondence until very recently were in English. Education in English, nearly universal in the middle class but rare among workers, has been almost indispensable to the effective promotion of a labor organization. During a debate on trade union rights for government employees a few months after independence, N. M. Perera asserted in defense of the outsider:

> I do not know whether hon. Members are aware of the difficulties of running these trade unions. Large numbers of Government workers, particularly in a [formerly] colonial country like this where everything is done in English, have to fill in umpteen forms—various forms issued by the Labour Department. They have not the knowledge nor the capacity to understand all these forms. It is only the outsiders who can help them and their unions.[4]

M. Kassalow, "Unions in the New and Developing Countries," in Everett M. Kassalow (ed.), *National Labor Movements in the Postwar World* (Evenston, Ill.: Northwestern University Press, 1963), pp. 236–237; and Van Dusen Kennedy, *Unions, Employers and Government: Essays on Indian Labour Questions* (Bombay: Manaktalas, 1966), pp. 85–90.

[4]Ceylon, House of Representatives, *Parliamentary Debates (Hansard)*, vol. 3, col. 608 (June 3, 1948).

The state plays a major role in labor-management relations in Ceylon either as the employer of a considerable segment of the wage-labor force or through regulation of and intervention in labor relations. The growth of public corporations in the past decade has considerably expanded the role of the state as an employer. Even when the government is not involved as the employer, labor-management issues often are decided by industrial courts and labor tribunals rather than by bargaining between the parties. Consequently, trade unions have considerable need for legal advice and for advocates to present their cases before tribunals. A union which has one or more lawyers among its officers may profit substantially from the availability of free legal talent, and a trade union leader with legal training has an advantage in securing gains for his followers.

The towering social barrier separating workers from middle-class employers and bureaucrats and the deferential behavior normal to the lower classes in contacts with those of superior social status make the vigorous assertion of workers' demands by the workers themselves extremely difficult. The report of the National Wage Policy Commission in 1961 commented that trade unions "find it necessary to have 'outsiders' to conduct negotiations with employers since workers, however congenial the general atmosphere may be, find it difficult to bargain on equal terms round the table with employers who exercise direct supervision and authority over them in their daily work."[5] The outsider has the further advantage of being beyond the disciplinary control of the employer and thus free from the threat of penalty or discharge, which in the state of labor relations prevalent in Ceylon is widely feared and at least until recent years seems to have been common. Mutual distrust, suspicion, and jealousy among workers may also encourage reliance on leadership from outside the workers' ranks. A member of the group, in the absence of unusual capability or talent, might have great difficulty in establishing a claim to leadership and holding the loyalty of the group, whereas an outsider, particularly one considered to be of superior status, may readily be accepted as leader.

Even if unions contain individual members competent to perform many of the essential organizational tasks, few have been financially able to pay a capable full-time staff, including any able insiders, and hence have been dependent on a volunteer or semi-volunteer staff and leadership composed of individuals who are willing to conduct union activities and provide their skills through idealistic or ideological motives or for the possibility of political rewards. Although union members frequently volunteer clerical or menial service, they often possess neither the needed skills nor the leisure to provide the services required by the organization.

[5]*Report of the National Wage Policy Commission*, Sessional Paper VIII—1961 (Colombo: Government Press, 1961), p. 170.

Consequently, financial weakness and shortage of available talent from within the union have made many labor organizations dependent on assistance volunteered by outsiders.

The affluent outsider leading a trade union not only provides needed skills and services to the union he leads, generally with little or no monetary compensation, but may even assist in providing funds to keep the organization functioning, particularly during an exhausting strike or other time of crisis. One outsider who has spent many years as a labor leader, S. Thondaman, the president of the Ceylon Workers' Congress, is frequently said to have contributed to the financial support of the estate workers' union from his personal wealth, notably during the early and lean years of the organization. Often attacked for being both a leader of an estate workers' union and an employer of estate labor, Thondaman recently exclaimed, "The so-called great leaders of the labour movement go there [to the estates] and say: 'Oh! Thondaman is a capitalist.' I have never said I am a pauper. . . . Everybody knows that Thondaman owns estates and is employer. . . ." He recalled that when he had ordered estate workers out on an extended strike, "I did not ask them to buy their rations. When the moneys in the union's funds were exhausted, I drew my own money out of the bank every week and paid them."[6]

Excluding public servants' unions, all the officers of which must be members of the public service, at least half the officers of trade unions are required by statute to be persons actually employed in an industry or trade represented by the union.[7] "Officers," however, are defined as including all members of the union's executive committee and, consequently, it is possible and not uncommon for outsiders to hold all the leading posts, while a sufficient number of workers are included in a generally passive capacity as members of the executive committee to comply with the statute.[8] The post of effective top leadership is the president in some labor organizations and the general secretary in others. In the accompanying chart (Chart I), the two principal officers of each of the major federations and the larger and more powerful unaffiliated unions are classified as either "outsiders," or as "insiders" who at some time in their lives have been employees in the trades which their unions represent. Except for public servants' organizations, which are prohibited from drawing leaders from outside the public service, the top posts are with very few exceptions held by outsiders. Of the insiders, CTUF president Watson Fernando is a former mercantile clerk and a regional Communist Party functionary who became president of the federation after a Com-

---

[6]House, *Debates,* vol. 67, cols. 661–662 (July 20, 1966).

[7]Trade Unions Ordinance, Sec. 32 (1).

[8]See *Report of the Committee of Inquiry into the Law and Practice of the Trade Unions Ordinance,* Sessional Paper XXVIII—1967 (Colombo: Government Press, 1967), p. 25.

Chart 1
"OUTSIDERS" AND "INSIDERS" IN LEADERSHIP POSITIONS OF MAJOR LABOR ORGANIZATIONS

	"Outsiders"	"Insiders"
Federations		
Ceylon Federation of Labour		
President	N. M. Perera	
General Secretary		D. G. William
Ceylon Federation of Trade Unions		
President	Pieter Keuneman	
General Secretary	M. G. Mendis	
Ceylon Trade Union Federation		
President		Watson Fernando
General Secretary	N. Sanmugathasan	
Central Council of Ceylon Trade Unions		
President	Tilak Kulasekera	
General Secretary	Philip Gunawardena	
Sri Lanka Nidahas Vurthiya Samithi Sammelanaya		
President	Harold Jayawardena	
General Secretaty	Lakshman Jayakody	
Public Service Workers' Trade Union Federation		
President		Piyadasa Adipola
General Secretary		A. W. Singho
Government Workers' Trade Union Federation		
President		G. E. H. Perera
General Secretary		James Kariyawasam
Unaffiliated Unions		
Ceylon Workers' Congress		
President	S. Thondaman	
General Secretary		M. S. Sellasamy
Democratic Workers' Congress		
President	A. Aziz	
General Secretary	V. P. Ganeshan	
Ceylon Mercantile Union		
President		Ivor Mendis
General Secretary	Bala Tampoe	
Government Clerical Service Union		
President		I. J. Wickrema
General Secretary		P. A. Wanasinghe
Ceylon Bank Employees' Union		
President		W. E. V. de Mel
General Secretary		Chandra Jayawardena
Sri Lanka Jathika Guru Sangamaya		
President		D. Peter Silva
General Secretary		L. Ariyawanse

munist Party split in 1963 and the capture of the CTUF by the pro-Peking Communists. M. S. Sellasamy, general secretary of the Ceylon Workers' Congress, formerly held a minor supervisory post on an estate. Ivor Mendis has continued his employment as a mercantile clerk while serving as president of the Ceylon Mercantile Union. W. E. V. de Mel and Chandra P. Jayawardena of the Ceylon Bank Employees' Union are employed as bank clerks. The most striking of the insiders is D. G. William, a onetime waiter in a hotel dining room who became a labor leader by organizing his fellow workers and leading strikes. A singularly forceful and dynamic individual, William rose to be general secretary of one of the largest labor organizations on the island when an outsider who long held the post, Prins Rajasooriya, broke with the LSSP in a 1964 party split. Although the veteran politician Dr. N. M. Perera has been president of the CFL for many years and is recognized as its principal leader, William appears to be responsible for the day-to-day management of federation affairs. In each of the other three instances in which one of the leading posts is held by an insider and the other by an outsider, effective control of the organization rests with the outsider. Insiders are considerably more numerous in the second- and third-level positions and at the head of smaller unions.

It is possible to distinguish two types of leaders of the major federations and unions. One is the prominent top political party leader, invariably an outsider, who formally heads the federation or unions linked with his party but who is also immersed in party duties, is usually a member of Parliament, and may be involved in municipal politics. Although these leaders may have been active trade unionists in the past, today they are seldom able to devote much time and attention to the daily affairs of the labor organizations they head. Dr. Perera, for example, in earlier years was deeply involved in day-to-day trade union affairs and still takes a part in directing major strikes and negotiations. However, in addition to heading the CFL, he has been the principal public spokesman and parliamentary leader of the LSSP, has served in Parliament and the pre-independence State Council for more than thirty years, was a member of the Colombo Municipal Council from 1950 to 1956 including a period as Mayor of Colombo from 1954 to 1956, and in 1964–1965 was Minister of Finance. Other examples of leaders of this type are Pieter Keuneman, Philip Gunawardena, and J.R. Jayewardene, each of whom while heading the federation or unions sponsored by his political party is primarily identified as a party leader and legislator rather than as a trade unionist.

The second type of trade union leader may also be an outsider and a party activist and may be motivated toward trade unionism by partisan or ideological considerations. In contrast to the prominent politician heading the party's labor organization, however, he is primarily a trade

unionist and is directly involved in the day-to-day duties of union leadership. Unlike the prominent party leaders, the leaders of the second type
are often not well known outside the labour movement, and, even though
they may be party activists and may occasionally seek public office, their
principal identification is with trade unionism. Among the trade unionists
of the latter type are N. Sanmugathasan,[9] D. G. William, Bala Tampoe,
L. W. Panditha, and leaders of several public servants' organizations.
A listing of the dozen most prominent and influential individuals in the
labor movement today would probably include only two members of the
working class, D. G. William and Piyadasa Adipola, and perhaps one or
two other insiders belonging to the lower-middle class of clerical employees.

2. Leadership from the Union Ranks

Despite the continued role played by outsiders, particularly in the large
federations and unions, trade union leaders have increasingly emerged
from the ranks of the union membership in recent years. Several developments appear to have contributed to this trend. Knowledge of the English
language, although unquestionably still of considerable value for a trade
union leader, is no longer an essential requisite for successful labor leadership, at least in the public service. Since the adoption of Sinhalese as the
official language in 1956, progress has been made in publishing government
documents in Sinhalese and substituting Sinhalese for English for official
correspondence, forms, and notices.[10] A number of important unions in
the public service are headed by officers with little or no command of
English, the most important example of which is the huge Public Service
Workers' Trade Union Federation. The federation's president, Piyadasa
Adipola, a minor employee in the public service, knows scarcely any
English but effectively controls the day-to-day functioning of the organization and is probably among the most powerful and able trade union
leaders on the island.

The recently instituted practice of the government and public corporations of releasing an officer of every trade union of any substantial size
for full-time union work probably has also contributed significantly to

---

[9]A biographical note on the back cover of a pamphlet containing a collection of articles
by Sanmugathasan, published at the time of the Communist Party split in 1963, observed
that Sanmugathasan was completing his twentieth year as a full-time functionary of the
Ceylon Trade Union Federation and described him as "one of the few leftist leaders who
have devoted their entire adult life [sic] in the service of the working class." N. Sanmugathasan,
How Can the Working Class Achieve Power? (Colombo: Worker Publication [1963]).

[10]For example, by 1960, the Colombo Port Commission claimed to be conducting all its
correspondence with trade unions in Sinhalese. *Administration Report of the Commissioner and
Chairman, Colombo Port Commission, for 1960* (Colombo: Government Press, 1961), p. 38.
Since 1958, the Commissioner of Labour's annual reports, previously published only in
English, have been published in Sinhalese, Tamil, and English.

the capacity of insiders to lead their organizations effectively. Previously, workers seldom enjoyed the leisure to manage union affairs while continuing their regular employment or the financial security to give up their customary employment and sacrifice pension and other benefits for full-time trade union work, even if they possessed the required competence and the union the ability to pay their salaries. The salary of a union officer released for trade union work is generally paid by the union, but his allowances are paid by the government and on relinquishing or losing his trade union office he is able to resume his employment in the public service or corporation without loss of pension, seniority, or similar benefits. A few public corporations, including the large Ceylon Transport Board and Port (Cargo) Corporation, pay the entire salary and allowances of union officers released for full-time trade union duties.[11] The release of union officers undoubtedly facilitates the development of effective insider leadership and may contribute to the professionalization of trade union leadership and the strengthening of labor organizations. It may also tend to entrench incumbent leaders in office by giving them, or allowing them to claim, experience and knowledge gained from full-time involvement in union affairs not shared by a potential rival or successor, and may make union leadership unduly attractive for personal reasons by allowing the officer to retain the benefits of public service employment but escape the discipline and routine of the bureaucratic office.[12] Unions have also been strengthened financially by the checkoff of union dues, now established in the public service and public corporations and rapidly spreading to the private sector, which enables them more frequently to meet the cost of full-time paid functionaries.

Since 1963, the Labour Department has conducted workers' education courses in trade unionism, largely intended to facilitate the leadership of unions by the workers themselves. By 1965, more than 350 union representatives had enrolled in the courses.[13] In addition, the intangible influences of the increasing strength and self-confidence of the labor movement, the wider acceptance of trade unionism by the employers and the public, and perhaps growing sophistication among workers also have probably contributed to the emergence of labor leaders from the ranks of the unions.

[11]*Report of the Committee of Inquiry into the Law and Practice of the Trade Unions Ordinance*, p. 34. The Port (Cargo) Corporation releases an officer of each union with a membership of more than 1,000 for trade union work on full pay and also provides office accommodations for all unions with more than 500 members. Ceylon, Ministry of Labour, Employment, and Housing, *May Day, 1967* (Colombo : Government Press, 1967), p. 71.

[12]These possibilities, particularly the considerable attractiveness of full-time trade union work, have been brought to the author's attention in a number of interviews with trade unionists both within and outside the public service.

[13]*Administration Report of the Commissioner of Labour for 1964–65* (Colombo : Government Press, 1967), p. 196.

Able and effective officers drawn from the union membership are still relatively rare among unions of laborers and unskilled workers. The organizations which first produced capable leaders from the ranks of their own members were unions of white-collar employees, and these unions continue to provide the most conspicuous examples of successful leadership by insiders. Clerical and other white-collar office workers enjoyed the obvious advantage of being able to maintain the financial records and prepare the reports required of the union. In the government service until the last decade and in the private sector to the present, the clerks have been English-educated and consequently even when English was virtually essential to directing a union, they did not suffer from the language handicap faced by many other workers, who spoke and, if literate, read and wrote only Sinhalese or Tamil. But even the clerks' unions often had to await the growth of sophistication and self-confidence of the clerical employees and increased acceptance of trade unionism by employers before they were able to provide their own leaders.

A case of a union begun under outside leadership which eventually developed leaders from its own ranks is provided by the Ceylon Bank Employees' Union, called the Ceylon Bank Clerks' Union until 1956, when membership in the union was broadened to include subordinate bank staff in addition to the clerks. During the Second World War, clerks employed by the foreign-owned commercial banks of Colombo became restive and in 1943 organized the Ceylon Bank Clerks' Union. A. E. Goonesinha, the ubiquitous labor organizer, was asked to become president of the newly established union, although he had had no connection with the banking industry. This followed the common pattern of the Ceylonese labor movement, in which mounting grievances would lead employees to organize and invite a prominent or militant outsider to assume leadership of the union. By the time the bank clerks' union was formed, Goonesinha had passed the militant and radical phase of his career, however. Although the restiveness which led to the formation of the union was evident in bank strikes called in 1944, 1945, and 1946, rank-and-file dissatisfaction with Goonsinha's lack of aggressiveness began to mount, and when efforts to oust him as president failed the union became divided and inactive. After Goonesinha went abroad in 1952, restiveness again rose, producing several major strikes and pressure on the associate of Goonesinha, also an outsider, to whom leadership of the union had been passed. Finally in 1957, the union rank-and-file deposed the outside leadership and elected officers who were union members and bank clerks.

As the leadership struggle was described in a CBEU publication, between 1952 and 1956, "the young [rank] and file, and the comparatively junior leaders gained sufficient experience and confidence, and agitated for the throwing-out of the outside leaders...." In 1957, although the union members "were diffident at that time of the capabilities of it's [the union's] own members where leadership was concerned, the militant sections spearheaded the ousting of outsiders from the Union, and one of it's [sic] members was elected as the President, for the first time. This dawned a new era for Bank employees, and after some time, the entire membership was enthusiastic and rallied round the new leaders."[14] W. E. V. de Mel, a clerk at the Hongkong and Shanghai Bank in Colombo, became president and has remained at the head of the union to the present. In the following decade, the CBEU gained a reputation as an ably led, aggressive, and successful trade union. Without doubt, the CBEU example of successful leadership by insiders has suggested the dispensability of outsiders to members of other unions and has reduced the lack of confidence of many workers in the leadership capacites of their co-workers.

Leadership by outsiders has become a subject of considerable recent controversy. The usual criticism of outsiders is that they are politicians who, it is assumed, use their union offices not for the benefit of the members but for partisan purposes. There is wide agreement that the labor movement in the past obviously needed more, and more skillful, leaders than the workers could provide. The statutory requirement that outsiders hold less than half the offices in a union was intended to restrict the role of outsiders, but it also represented a recognition of the essential function performed by outsiders in the labor movement. However, it has been contended that the need for outsiders has declined or disappeared with rising educational levels among workers. A government-appointed committee which investigated trade unionism during 1967, while acknowledging the useful role of outsiders in earlier periods of the trade union movement, alleged that "the 'outsider' has, through the years, tended to use the trade union more and more for his own ends, which are mainly political." The committee concluded that the circumstances which necessitated outsiders as union officers in earlier years no longer existed, since "workers today are sufficiently educated to manage by themselves the affairs of their own trade unions." The committee recommended amendment of the Trade Unions Ordinance to limit union officers to persons employed in the industry or trade in which the union is involved, but added that unions should remain free to be represented by whomever they chose in negotiating with employers.[15]

Many trade unionists and politicians and some neutral observers, however, have contended that the removal of outsiders would seriously weaken the labor movement. The National Wage Policy Commission

[14]"The Short History of the Ceylon Bank Employees Union," *Bank Worker*, February–March, 1961, pp. 4–5.
[15]*Report of the Committee of Inquiry into the Law and Practice of the Trade Unions Ordinance*, pp. 25–26.

in 1961 expressed fear that a prohibition on outsiders holding union offices would provide employers with an undue advantage in collective bargaining, and observed that in the past "the political 'outsiders' acting on behalf of employees have redressed the balance of bargaining strength between such employers and their employees."[16] The political parties which are deeply involved in trade unionism have viewed proposals for removing outsiders from union leadership as a covert attempt to cripple the labor movement, not only by depriving trade unions of officers with knowledge and training which union members lack but also by removing from the labor movement many of the most energetic, combative, and fearless of the labor leaders. In a statement issued in 1965, the Communist Party charged that an attempt to drive outsiders from the labor movement by the UNP-dominated Government was intended "on the one hand, to decapitate the trade union movement by removing militant leaders and, on the other hand, to encourage docile trade unions that will lick the boots of the UNP and the bosses."[17]

3. Leaders and Internal Democracy

The leadership of Ceylonese trade unions in the formative years of the labor movement can best be described as autocratic and paternalistic. The leader was the benevolent patron and guardian, to whom the member extended deferential loyalty, a type of relationship rooted in traditional Ceylonese culture and social structure.[18] While several decades of aggressive trade unionism and rising sophistication and political awareness among workers have weakened deference and modified leader-follower relations in the labor movement, oligarchic leadership, long tenure of office, and minimal restraints on leaders' control of union activities remain typical of much of the labor movement.[19] A considerable number of trade unions are identified with an individual leader, who often is the union's founder and has been its chief official throughout all or most of its existence. Many unions appear to be regarded by the officeholders as their personal property, and even the unions with a relatively high degree of rank-and-

---

[16]Report of the National Wage Policy Commission, p. 182.

[17]Forward (Colombo), July 23, 1965, p. 3.

[18]E.g., Gananath Obeyesekere, Land Tenure in Village Ceylon (Cambridge: Cambridge University Press, 1967), pp. 243–244.

[19]The absence of internal democracy within trade unions is, of course, not limited to Ceylon, but has been regularly noted since the classic critique of Robert Michels, Political Parties (New York: Dover Publications, Inc., 1959). For a suggestive analysis of impediments to democracy within trade unions, based largely on American labor organizations, see Seymour M. Lipset, "The Political Process in Trade Unions: A Theoretical Statement," in Walter Galenson and Seymour M. Lipset (eds.), Labor and Trade Unionism: An Interdisciplinary Reader (New York: John Wiley & Sons, Inc., 1960), pp. 216–242. On trade unions in the developing countries, see Walter Galenson's introduction, Labor and Economic Development (New York: John Wiley & Sons, Inc., 1959), p. 12.

file participation are often headed by a hero-leader who possesses tremendous personal influence and prestige.

The leadership of a trade union typically consists of a president, two or three vice-presidents, a general secretary, an assistant secretary, a treasurer, and an executive committee or general council. In some unions, the officers are directly chosen by a general membership meeting or a conference of delegates chosen by the union's branches. In other unions, the membership or delegates' conference selects the executive committee, which chooses the officers. For example, the officers of the Government Clerical Service Union are elected at an annual conference composed of about 700 delegates from the union's branches. The Ceylon Bank Employees' Union holds a general membership meeting which choses a general council, and the union's officers are selected by the general council, meeting about a month after the general membership meeting. Similarly, officers of the Samastha Lanka Rajaye Lipikaru Sangamaya are elected by a central committee, which in turn is chosen at an annual membership meeting.[20] The president of the Ceylon Workers' Congress is elected at a biennial delegates' conference, and other officers are chosen by a national council composed of representatives of regional units of the CWC and the union's officers.[21] Among the officers of the Ceylon Mercantile Union are a president, two vice-presidents, two assistant secretaries, a treasurer, and an assistant treasurer, all elected by the annual delegates' conference. In addition, a general secretary, who is entrusted with responsibility for conducting union negotiations, corresponding and speaking on behalf of the union, and the day-to-day management of union affairs, is appointed by an executive committee consisting of the officers (excluding the general secretary) and eight others selected by the annually elected general council.[22]

Although formally officers are invariably held responsible to the general membership through periodic elections, if the officers are well entrenched, elections in practice represent little more than ritual affirmations of support for the leadership. Furthermore, in some cases when rank-and-file discontent exists, irregularities and manipulation of voting procedures have been claimed. The 1967 committee inquiring into the operation of the Trade Unions Ordinance reported receiving complaints that officers of some unions failed to hold membership meetings required by the unions' constitutions, chiefly because of "the likelihood of the office bearers in power being thrown out of office."[23]

[20]Based on information provided by officers of these unions during 1967.

[21]"Constitution of the Ceylon Workers' Congress" (mimeographed; Colombo, September 1, 1965), pp. 4–7.

[22]Ceylon Mercantile Union, *The Constitution* (Colombo: Ceylon Mercantile Union, n.d.), pp. 5–12.

[23]*Report of the Committee of Inquiry into the Law and Practice of the Trade Unions Ordinance*, p. 23.

Despite strong oligarchic and autocratic tendencies in the labor movement, some individual unions exhibit characteristics which could reasonably be described as democratic. In these unions there is relatively wide membership participation in union affairs including branch activities, involvement in the process of selecting officers or at least delegates to annual meetings, and some opportunity for the expression of opinion on major union matters such as strike calls and agreements negotiated with employers. Between November, 1965, and January, 1967, the CMU held three general membership meetings, with a claimed average attendance of about 10,000, on major issues confronting the union.[24] A few organizations have experienced serious competition for union offices, with rival candidates attempting to mobilize wide rank-and-file support. As an indication of the competition for office which occurs in some unions, in the 1967 election of officers of the Government Clerical Service Union, there were two candidates for president, three for the two vice-presidential posts, two for general secretary, two for deputy general secretary, five for the two positions of assistant secretary, and twenty-seven for the twelve-member central executive committee.[25]

The extent to which the leadership is effectively held responsible to the general membership and is subject to competition for office is closely related to the educational level and sophistication of the members and to the phenomenon of the outsider as union leader. Effective restraints on officers, competition for office, and the articulation of rank-and-file sentiments on union issues are exhibited much more frequently by unions of white-collar, urban, office employees than those of the less educated or sophisticated industrial laborers or estate workers. The educated, articulate, and influential outsider heading an organization of scarcely literate laborers is unlikely to face a serious challenge to his position or to be held responsible to the membership for his conduct of union affairs in any meaningful way, since few members are in a position to challenge or question his stewardship.

[24]Ceylon Mercantile Union, "Ninth Annual Delegates Conference, 16th and 17th April 1967 : General Secretary's Report" (mimeographed, Colombo, April 14, 1967), p. 28.
[25]Government Clerical Service Union, *47th Annual Conference of Delegates* (leaflet; Colombo, May 5, 1967), pp. 14–16.

IV

THE TRADE UNION'S PARTISAN ROLE

Trade unionism has come to be accepted as a normal and essential facet of political party life in Ceylon. For about two decades, from the 1930's to the 1950's, the Marxist parties were almost alone among Ceylonese parties in their involvement in the labor movement. During the past fifteen years, the attempt to compete for the political allegiance of workers through trade union activity has spread until every major party is now engaged in sponsoring labor organizations. The political process which has emerged in Ceylon is highly competitive and pluralistic, and although some politicians look with annoyance on the arduous duties involved in trade union sponsorship, no significant party is willing to forfeit an advantage to a rival party by failure to exploit trade unionism as a possible source of strength and support.

1. Party Competition and the Party System

Ceylonese politics since shortly after independence has been characterized by intense party competition, a multiplicity of rival parties, and the frequent transfer of control of the government between rival parties. Within few of the Asian and African nations which became independent since the Second World War have electoral struggles between competing parties played as significant and effective a role in politics as in Ceylon. Control of the government passed between opposing parties or groups of parties as a result of elections no less than four times in the two decades following independence. Party competition through parliamentary elections has not only determined the personnel comprising the Government but strongly influenced the content and direction of governmental policies and actions. A strickingly high level of popular participation in elections has appeared, undoubtedly related to the high literacy and exposure to mass communication media of the Ceylonese public and experience with universal suffrage since 1931, but also probably encouraged by the vigorous competition among parties and the uncertainty of the outcome of election contests. After 1947, participation in parliamentary elections has never been below 69.0 percent of the electorate, and in 1965 ballots were cast by 82.1 percent of all eligible voters.[1]

[1] *Report on the Sixth Parliamentary General Election of Ceylon*, Sessional Paper XX-1966

The political party system which has developed over the past two decades is marked by the multiplicity of parties which display considerable resiliency and durability.[2] The election performance of parties (Table 9) reveals a wide scattering of popular votes and parliamentary representation. Although a large number of separate parties contest elections and win parliamentary seats, independents and ephemeral parties have declined to negligible proportions, and, except among the small Muslim minority which has supplied most of the independents elected in recent contests, party voting seems to be firmly established. No party enjoys a perpetual dominance, nor is one party so situated that its participation is virtually essential for the formation of a governing coalition. The principal contenders for power have been the United National Party and the Sri Lanka Freedom Party. The lines of competition, however, are complicated by the existence of a number of other parties which while able to mobilize only limited electoral support nonethless remain as active participants in the system.

Since the founding of the first Marxist party, the Lanka Sama Samaja Party,[3] fissures and schisms have led to the creation of several additional Marxist parties. A Trotskyist-Communist clash in 1940 was followed by the expulsion from the LSSP of the Communists, who formed the Ceylon Communist Party in 1943. A second permanent split in 1950 produced the Viplavakari (Revolutionary) Lanka Sama Samaja Party, which since 1959 has called itself the Mahajana Eksath Peramuna (People's United Front). Further splintering of the Left occurred in 1963, when a Communist Party split, reflecting the Moscow-Peking cleavage in international Communism, produced two separate parties, each claiming to be the true Ceylon Communist Party.[4] The following year a group of dissidents

---

(Colombo: Government Press, 1966), p. 37. In 1959, the voting age was reduced from twenty-one to eighteen. The only significant element of the population excluded from the franchise are approximately one million Indian Tamils, who are not citizens of Ceylon and consequently are ineligible to vote.

[2]The political party system in Ceylon approximates in many respects what is termed "extreme pluralism" by Giovanni Sartori, "European Political Parties: The Case of Polarized Pluralism," in Joseph LaPalombara and Myron Weiner (eds.), *Political Parties and Political Development* (Princeton, N.J.: Princeton University Press, 1966), pp. 137-176. However, whereas Sartori characterizes "extreme pluralism" as discouraging competition and alterations in power, the Ceylonese party system is marked by sharp competition and has produced alterations in power. The system is polarized, in Sartori's sense of great distance or strong opposition, essentially between the UNP on the one hand and the SLFP, LSSP, and Communist Party on the other, with the Federal Party and Tamil Congress operating in a subsystem with little electoral contact with the other participants, but interacting with them in the parliamentary arena.

[3]The term *sama samāja* (or *samasamāja*), literally meaning "equal society," was adopted by the early Ceylonese Marxists as the nearest Sinhalese equivalent for the English term "socialist." After the creation of a separate Communist Party adhering to the Third International, the designation "Samasamajist" distinguished the members of the Trotskyist LSSP from the "Communist" members of the Ceylon Communist Party.

[4]As the pro-Moscow party is considerably stronger and generally accepted as the conti-

Table 9

PARTY PERFORMANCE IN PARLIAMENTARY ELECTIONS, 1947–1965

Party	1947		1952		1956	
	Percent popular vote	Number seats won	Percent popular vote	Number seats won	Percent popular vote	Number seats won
United National Party	39.9	42	44.1	54	27.3	8
Sri Lanka Freedom Party	—	—	15.5	9	40.7[a]	51[a]
Lanka Sama Samaja Party	16.9[b]	15[b]	13.1	9	10.2	14
Federal Party	—	—	1.9	2	5.4	10
Communist Party	4.9[c]	5[c]	5.7[d]	4[d]	4.5	3
Tamil Congress	4.3	7	2.8	4	0.3	1
Mahajana Eksath Peramuna	—	—	—	—	—	—
Other parties	6.2	7	2.9	2	0.6	—
Independents	27.7	19	14.0	11	11.0	8
TOTAL	100.0	95	100.0	95	100.0	95

Party	March, 1960		July, 1960		1965	
	Percent popular vote	Number seats won	Percent popular vote	Number seats won	Percent popular vote	Number seats won
United National Party	29.6	50	37.6	30	39.3	66[e]
Sri Lanka Freedom Party	21.1	46	33.6	75	30.2	41
Lanka Sama Samaja Party	10.5	10	7.4	12	7.5	10[e]
Federal Party	5.8	15	7.2	16	5.4	14
Communist Party	4.6	3	3.0	4	2.7	4
Tamil Congress	1.2	1	1.5	1	2.4	3
Mahajana Eksath Peramuna	10.6	10	3.4	3	2.4	1
Other parties	7.7	9	1.8	4	3.7	6
Independents	8.8	7	4.6	6	6.4	6
TOTAL	100.0	151	100.0	151	100.0	151

[a]Results for the MEP coalition, the principal component of which was the SLFP.

[b]Includes two factions contesting the election separately.

[c]Includes two candidates who were elected as independents and joined the Communist Party immediately after the election.

[d]Results for the united front of the Communist Party and the VLSSP. Three Communists and one VLSSP member were elected.

[e]One candidate of the UNP and one of the LSSP were returned unopposed from the two-member Colombo South constituency.

SOURCE : For 1947 : Ceylon Daily News, *Parliament of Ceylon, 1947* (Colombo : Associated Newspapers of Ceylon, Ltd., n.d.). For 1952 : I. D. S. Weerawardana, "The General Elections in Ceylon, 1952," *Ceylon Historical Journal,* II (July–October, 1952), 111–178. For 1956 : I. D. S. Weerawardana, *Ceylon General Election, 1956* (Colombo : M. D. Gunasena & Co., Ltd., 1960); and Ceylon Daily News, *Parliament of Ceylon, 1956* (Colombo : Associated Newspapers of Ceylon, Ltd., n.d.). For March and July, 1960 : Ceylon Daily News, *Parliaments of Ceylon, 1960* (Colombo : Associated Newspapers of Ceylon, Ltd., [1962]). For 1965 : *Report on the Sixth Parliamentary General Election of Ceylon*, Sessional Paper XX—1966 (Colombo : Government Press, 1966).

left the LSSP and formed the Lanka Sama Samaja Party (Revolutionary), which in turn split in 1968 with the formation by LSSP(R) dissidents of a Revolutionary Samasamaja Party. Although both the "left" Communist Party and the LSSP(R) offered candidates at the 1965 election, neither won representation in Parliament. In 1968, however, an M.P. who had been elecfed as an SLFP candidate joined the "left" Communist Party.

Another source of the multiplicity of parties lies in the ethnic divisions of Ceylon. The competition of the UNP, SLFP, and Marxist parties is primarily among the Sinhalese ethnic majority. The eruption of the official language issue, which resulted in the declaration in 1956 that Sinhalese was to be the sole official language, deepened the political divisions between Sinhalese and Tamils, but even earlier, the Ceylon Tamils had shown a tendency to support parties exclusively dedicated to serving the interests of the Tamil community.[5] Orginally, the Tamil Congress was the leading party of the Ceylon Tamils, but since 1956 it has been largely displaced by the Federal Party. Except for scattered Federal Party support from east-coast Muslims, both parties depend exclusively on the votes of the Ceylon Tamil community.

The 1947 election, held in anticipation of independence which came early in 1948, was the first to be fought primarily on party lines, although elections for the colonial legislative chamber based on universal suffrage had been held in 1931 and 1936. The UNP emerged from the 1947 election as the largest party in Parliament and with the support of a few minor groups and independents formed the first Government of independent Ceylon. Returned to power in 1952, the UNP held control of the government until its surprising and shattering election defeat in 1956, which conclusively demonstrated to both voters and politicians that substantial changes in the composition and policies of Governments were possible through election contests.[6] The SLFP's leader, S. W. R. D. Bandaranaike, engineered the defeat of the UNP by arranging a "no contest" agreement with the LSSP and the Communist Party to avoid contesting the same constituencies and splitting the anti-UNP vote and forming a coalition

nuation of the old Ceylon Communist Party, unless otherwise indicated, references to the Communist Party after the 1963 schism will refer to the pro-Moscow party. Where necessary for clarity, this party will be referred to as the "regular" Communist Party and the pro-Peking party as the "left" Communist Party.

[5]The only candidates of parties which were not exclusively Tamil parties to win parliamentary seats in constituencies with Tamil majorities since 1952 were one Communist candidate in 1956 and one UNP candidate in 1965. The SLFP has never contested a Tamil constituency and the UNP did not do so between 1952 and 1965. The language issue and ethnic communities in Ceylonese politics are discussed in Robert N. Kearney, *Communalism and Language in the Politics of Ceylon* (Durham, N.C.: Duke University Press, 1967).

[6]On the 1956 election and its significance, see I. D. S. Weerawardana, *Ceylon General Election, 1956* (Colombo: M. D. Gunasena & Co., Ltd., 1960); and W. Howard Wriggins, *Ceylon: Dilemmas of a New Nation* (Princeton, N.J.: Princeton University Press, 1960), pp. 326–369.

called the Mahajana Eksath Peramuna with the VLSSP and a few minor groups. This coalition broke up in 1959 (with the coalition's name henceforth used by the former VLSSP), and a few months later Bandaranaike was assassinated. An election held in March, 1960, produced a parliamentary deadlock and when a minority Government formed by the UNP as the largest single party was defeated in its first test before Parliament, a second election was called for the following July. The SLFP, led by Bandaranaike's widow, Sirimavo Bandaranaike, again fought the election allied to the LSSP and Communist Party by a no-contest pact and won control of Parliament by a narrow margin.[7]

After gradual attrition of its parliamentary strength, in June, 1964, the SLFP formed a coalition with the LSSP. Entrance into the coalition Government caused the LSSP to be expelled from the Fourth International, to which it had been affiliated for nearly a quarter of a century, and led to a party split when the orthodox Trotskysts condemned the LSSP leadership for "class collaboration" and withdrew to form the LSSP(R). The following December, the more conservative wing of the SLFP broke with the party on a critical parliamentary test, which the coalition Government lost by a single vote. In the resulting 1965 election, the UNP once more emerged as the largest single party, but without a parliamentary majority. A coalition Government called the "National Government" was formed by the UNP, Federal Party, Tamil Congress, MEP, and a few minor groups, with UNP leader Dudley Senanayake as Prime Minister. In 1968, the Federal Party detached itself from the National Government, but continued to lend the Government qualified support. The Communist Party fought the 1965 election in alliance with the SLFP-LSSP coalition and soon after the election became a recognized partner in the coalition. Although it lost the bitterly contested election, the SLFP-Marxist coalition (still called "the coalition" although the National Government is also a coalition) continued in existence and tended to coalesce into a relatively cohesive and durable political grouping.[8]

[7]The arithmetic of parliamentary strength is complicated by the presence of six appointed members of the House of Representatives, along with the ninety-five members elected to the first three Parliaments and 151 elected to the last three. The appointed members are named on the advice of the Cabinet to represent ethnic or economic interests deemed inadequately represented by the electoral process, and by convention they almost invariably vote with the Government. The patronage available to the Government also allows it to attract the support of a few independents. Thus, after the July, 1960, election, the SLFP Government could expect the votes not only of the party's seventy-five successful candidates but also those of the six appointed members, along with two independents and a deserter from the UNP who joined the Government Parliamentary Group, giving the Government initially a total of eighty-four votes in the 157-member House. However, in December, 1964, when the SLFP-LSSP Government fell on losing a confidence motion by a single vote, one appointed M.P. voted against the Government and a second abstained.

[8]I have discussed the political trends and alignments since the 1965 election in "New Directions in the Politics of Ceylon," *Asian Survey*, VII (February, 1967), 111–116; and "Ceylon: Political Stresses and Cohesion," *ibid.*, VIII (February, 1968), 105–109.

Despite the changing electoral performance of individual parties, certain regularities appear in the election results. The UNP and the SLFP consistently divide approximately two-thirds of the popular vote and parliamentary seats between them, although the relative fortunes of the two parties vary widely from one election to the next. The LSSP and Communist Party together capture about one-tenth of the parliamentary seats and popular vote, while the Federal Party and Tamil Congress divide about one-tenth of the seats in Parliament and one-twelfth of the popular vote in each election.

The alterations in power between opposing parties within the fragmented party system result primarily from the existence of two relatively large opposing parties, the UNP and the SLFP, one of which has formed the core of each Government since independence. Each is sufficiently large to be within plausible reach of power, which encourages the hope of victory and hence tends to intensify the competition. Also, the two are closely enough balanced in many constituencies to allow small shifts in popular votes or the benefits of electoral alliances to tip the balance from one to the other.[9] The persistent strength of other parties, however, generally denies clear control of Parliament to either the UNP or SLFP and, hence, provides the smaller parties with opportunities for bargaining and influencing the composition or policies of the Government. Ideological rigidities, however, tend to limit the bargaining flexibility of most of the smaller parties. The LSSP and Communist Party are implacably opposed to the UNP and face the practical choice of either co-operating with the SLFP or refusing co-operation to the SLFP and thereby enhancing the prospects of a UNP victory. The conservative Tamil Congress is unlikely to find a basis for agreement with the left-oriented SLFP. Only the Federal Party has had the ideological flexibility and roughly center position to make bargaining between the SLFP and UNP feasible. On several occasions since 1960, the SLFP and UNP have vied for the Federal Party's support, but the party's parliamentary strength is not sufficiently great to assure it a pivotal role in the formation of coalitions. The small MEP, reduced to a single seat in Parliament in 1965, is the only party to serve in coalition Governments with both the SLFP and UNP.

The character of the party system has had direct consequences for the

[9]For elections to the House of Representatives, the lower house of Parliament, to which the Government is responsible, a plurality, single-ballot electoral system is employed. There are 140 single-member, four two-member, and one three-member constituencies. In the multi-member constituencies, created to facilitate the representation of ethnic minorities, each voter may cast as many ballots as there are members to be elected and the two or, in the three-member constituency, three candidates with the largest number of votes are elected. The upper house of Parliament, the Senate, possesses only limited powers to delay legislation. Half the thirty members of the Senate are elected by the House of Representatives by proportional representation, with voting in practice strictly along party lines, and the other half are appointed by the Governor-General on the advice of the Cabinet.

trade union movement. The competitiveness of the system has contributed to the impetus for additional parties to join in sponsoring labor organizations, as each party has sought to exploit all possible sources of strength or neutralize strengths of opposing parties. Hence, the circumstances of political competition apparently have increased the resources and energies invested in building trade unionism and probably have enhanced the position and influence of organized labor. Furthermore, the multiplicity of existing parties is reflected in the large number of parties involved in trade unionism. Seven parties—the LSSP, MEP, SLFP, UNP, Federal Party, and both Communist Parties—are closely associated with labor organizations. In addition, an eighth, the LSSP(R), enjoys considerable influence in certain segments of the labor movement. The parties with the largest trade union followings are not those which enjoy the greatest election and parliamentary strength, but are the smaller parties, principally the LSSP and the two Communist Parties, which play only limited supportive roles in election contests and parliamentary affairs.

2. Party Attitudes and Motivations

While trade unionism has become an established part of political party activities and the major parties all maintain associated labor organizations, seldom is one clear and specific partisan motive cited in explanation of the investment of time, attention, and energy by party leaders and activists in trade union affairs. To some party leaders, trade unions seem to be simply another activity along with branch organizations, youth leagues, and party newspapers which must be maintained in order to compete with rival parties. A fairly common attitude is that a party "just has to do it," because other parties are active in the labor movement. The extent of involvement in labor affairs and the type of role ascribed to the party's trade unions, however, vary considerably from the Marxists, who are deeply committed to trade unionism and who view labor organizations as inevitable and essential concomitants of the party, to the parties which more recently became involved in trade unionism and view their labor organizations as party auxiliaries of relatively restricted and specific utility.

Marxist Perspectives on Trade Unions

The labor movement has long been identified politically with the Marxists, and their pre-eminence was not seriously shaken by the later entry of other parties. The Marxists received their first experience in labor organization and agitation in a textile mill strike in 1933, nearly three years before the founding of the first Marxist political party. They seem to have turned to trade unionism almost automatically in an attempt to

establish links with the working class and to mobilize mass support for
their political and social objectives. As Marxists, they viewed the working
class as the revolutionary class to be led toward the eventual proletarian
revolution. Trade unions have been seen as the natural organizations of
the working class through which class consciousness and solidarity could
be built and capitalism could be attacked. Trade union leadership gave
access to a mass working-class following and provided a weapon to fight
the bourgeoisie. The Ceylonese Marxists presumably were acting in
accordance with Lenin's contention that "the development of the prole-
tariat did not, and could not, proceed anywhere in the world otherwise
than through the trade unions, through reciprocal action between them
and the party of the working class."[10]

For the Marxists, trade union and party activities and interests are
virtually inseparable. Basically, the party and the trade union are closely
related organizations working toward the same broad socio-economic
objectives, with the party providing leadership and guidance and the
trade union providing a mass following. A Communist labor leader
claimed that through trade union activities the party's labor federation
was "bringing closer the day when the working class will emerge as the
decisive force in our society destined to play the role which it has been
entrusted by history, namely smashing imperialism and capitalism and
leading the country towards socialism and ultimately communism."[11]

Trade unionism was the avenue through which the Marxists first
obtained organizational and agitational experience and developed mass
contacts. Communist Party general secretary Pieter Keuneman, for
example, while in his early twenties and soon after his graduation from
Cambridge University, was assigned to organize Colombo dock workers.[12]
For the dedicated party member, trade union work represents merely an
extension of party work. The LSSP requires of its members regular services
for the party and active participation in party affairs, and the holding
of a trade union office or other union duties is one type of activity accepted
as fulfilling this party requirement.[13] Although a division of function
between party and trade union duties is recognized in day-to-day activities,

---

[10]V. I. Lenin, *"Left-Wing" Communism, an Infantile Disorder* (Moscow : Foreign Languages
Publishing House, n.d.), pp. 41–42. Lenin's earlier call for Marxists to assume control of
the trade unions and insistence on trade union subordination to the party was contained
in his famous pamphlet, *What Is to Be Done?* (Moscow : Foreign Languages Publishing
House, n.d.), esp. pp. 185–198. On the development of Lenin's attitudes toward trade unions,
see Thomas T. Hammond, *Lenin on Trade Unions and Revolution, 1893–1917* (New York :
Columbia University Press, 1957). For Marx, see A. Lozovsky, *Marx and the Trade Unions*
(New York : International Publishers, 1942).

[11]M. G. Mendis, "The Communist Party and the Workers," *Forward* (Colombo), July 2,
1965, p. 7.

[12]Basil Perera, *Pieter Keuneman : A Profile* (Colombo : Communist Party, 1967), p. 32.

[13]Author's interviews with LSSP general secretary Leslie Goonewardene on a number
of occasions since 1961.

a major strike, even though without discernible political objectives, is likely to receive the assistance of party members, virtually as a matter of course, although they hold no trade union office and are not normally involved in labor affairs.

Over the years, the two major Marxist parties have tended to downgrade the importance of "direct action" and extra-constitutional struggle in achieving their objectives and have gradually placed increasing emphasis on parliamentary and electoral activities. The Communist Party by 1960 had accepted the possibility of establishing "full democracy and socialism in Ceylon by peaceful means."[14] The party leaders' emphasis on parliamentary affairs was a major issue in the 1963 party schism. The LSSP has long displayed ambivalence toward the possibilities of achieving party objectives through elections. For many years, the Samasamajists clung to the myth that theirs was a revolutionary party dedicated to a fundamental uprooting of the social order which could not be achieved through elections and legislation. However, since independence the party has contained a strong parliamentary wing including nearly all the top party leaders, and in practice has devoted its primary attention and efforts to election contests and the functioning of Parliament and local government bodies. In 1950, the party proclaimed that its aims "cannot be realized through bourgeois parliaments,"[15] but by 1964 the party was willing to form a coalition Government with the non-Marxist SLFP even at the cost of a party schism and the expulsion of the LSSP from the Fourth International. The schism removed the doctrinaire Trotskyist wing of the party, which had disparaged elections and representative institutions, and presumably greatly reduced the doctrinal inhibitions on acceptance of the electoral and parliamentary path to the party's goals.

Some change in attitudes toward trade unionism may be occurring within the LSSP, and possibly also within the Communist Party, reflecting a generational cleavage in the party as well as the significantly altered political circumstances within which the party functions. The veteran Marxists, who are now the aging party leaders, entered politics during the period of colonial rule, when the scope for political action was limited and the possibilities for attaining party goals through elections and legislation were uncertain. Then, it is said, trade unionism held much of the glamor and drama of the Marxist movement. However, the younger Samasama-

---

[14] *Draft Thesis for the 6th National Congress of the Ceylon Communist Party* (Colombo : Communist Party, 1960), p. 52.

[15] Lanka Sama Samaja Party, *Programme of Action, Adopted at the Unity Conference, June 4th, 1950* (leaflet; Colombo : Lanka Sama Samaja Party, 1950), p. 4. Samasamajists continue to argue for the necessity of some form of mass revolutionary action as essential to overcome the alienation and apathy of the masses produced by capitalist society, in order to make possible the new human relationships and attitudes required for the new socialist order. The revolutionary action, however, need not be violent or even be primarily political so long as it leads to the mobilization and involvement of the masses.

jists, recruited to politics after independence and in a period when electoral campaigns were being vigorously conducted from the local to the national level, reportedly find more drama, excitement, and sense of purpose in election contests and the activities of elective bodies. Whereas two or three decades ago, the young party militant commonly wished to devote himself to trade union organizing, today he is more likely to wish to contest a seat on a village or town council.[16] While no detectable decline in the party's deep commitment to trade unionism has yet appeared, the tendency for many young party activists to look to election contests rather than labor organizing contains significant implications for the party's future relationship with the labor movement.

Other Parties and Trade Unionism

The trade union activities of the non-Marxist parties represent, in part, an attempt to deprive the Marxists of their virtual monopoly of influence in the labor movement and to develop some element of support for the party from organized labor. It also sometimes represents an effort to develop a party auxiliary intended to meet particular needs of the party. Given the political complexion of labor movements throughout Asia and the examples of the British Labour Party and the Indian National Congress, it is scarcely surprising that the organization of trade unions under party auspices suggested itself to non-Marxist as well as Marxist party leaders. In the early 1950's, labor activities were debated within the generally conservative and middle-class oriented United National Party,[17] although no lasting involvement resulted at that time.

The Sri Lanka Freedom Party, founded in 1951, did not enter the labor field until after it had come to power as the largest component of a coalition Government in 1956. Unlike the Marxist parties, the SLFP was not initially or primarily concerned with the urban working class. The party's support has come primarily from the Sinhalese Buddhist rural villagers, attracted largely by the party's linguistic and religious appeals. The SLFP, nonetheless, claimed to be a democratic socialist party dedicated to establishing equality of opportunity and a classless society,[18] and styled itself the "party of the common man." Although principally dependent on rural support, the party probably hoped to expand its support to wage laborers in the urban areas and Sinhalese workers on the tea and rubber estates. The founder of the SLFP trade unions later wrote, "I was requested by the late PM [Prime Minister

[16]This interpretation is a product of many conversations with Samasamajists and ex-Samasamajists over a period of nearly a decade. It is possible to speculate that a similar development is occurring in the Communist Party.
[17]E.g., *U.N.P. Journal*, June 12, 1953, and November 19, 1954.
[18]*Srī Laṅkā Nidahas Pakshayē Vyavasthā* [Sri Lanka Freedom Party's Constitution] (Colombo : Sri Lanka Freedom Party, 1958), p. 1.

S. W. R. D. Bandaranaike] to organise the working people. I acceded
to his request even though I had to sacrifice a hard-built medical practice
because I knew he was in difficulty and needed the support of organised
labour."[19]

Following the 1956 election, a dramatic expansion of the labor movement
occurred, stimulated by governmental tolerance and encouragement of
trade unionism. A 1964 government publication claimed:

> Until the victory of the late Mr. S. W. R. D. Bandaranaike [in 1956],
> the aspirations of the working class to emancipate itself from exploi-
> tation and servitude had been thwarted, and workers and trade
> unions were regarded as a nuisance. They had no place in Society.
> The two Bandaranaike Governments have since 1956 given workers
> and their unions an honoured place in Society and have taken several
> steps to protect their interests and improve their conditions. Before
> 1956, the grievances of workers were ignored or resisted. The
> tremendous trade union activity since 1956 fully exposes the
> limitations of social policy of the period prior to 1956.[20]

The SLFP was not, however, able to attract strong urban working-class
support and while in power repeatedly clashed with organized labor.
Coupled with the growth of the labor movement after 1956 was a steep
rise in labor restiveness and industrial conflict, including demands and
strikes directed against the Government. An SLFP Cabinet minister in
1958 charged that the unprecedented trade union militancy resulted
from the fear by labor leaders "that their own leadership of the working
class may be replaced by the Government itself. In a desperate attempt
to retain their political power, they sought to create labour unrest on the
least possible pretext."[21] In 1961, the organizer of the SLFP trade unions,
Dr. W. D. de Silva, resigned from the party in protest against the Government's budget, which he charged was anti-working class. Commencing
in late 1961, the SLFP Government faced a series of strikes in the major
nationalized industries. Sirimavo Bandaranaike, who became Prime
Minister in 1960, repeatedly urged restraint and charged that labor
demands and strikes imperiled economic development and represented a
claim to an unjust share of the national wealth relative to the rural
peasants.[22] The party's trade unions, grouped into a federation in 1961,

[19]Dr. W. D. de Silva, in an open letter to S. W. R. D. Bandaranaike's widow and successor
as SLFP leader, Sirimavo Bandaranaike, in *Ceylon Daily News*, September 11, 1961, p. 4.
[20]Ceylon, Department of Broadcasting and Information, *Labour Policy Since 1956*, Information Brouchure No. 3 (Colombo: Government Press, [1964]), p. 1.
[21]Ceylon, House of Representatives, *Parliamentary Debates (Hansard)*, vol. 31, col. 1161
(July 17, 1958).
[22]E.g., *Ceylon Daily News*, May 2, 1962, p. 5; *Ceylon Today*, XIII (January, 1964), 2; *ibid.*,
XIII (February, 1964), 7.

seem increasingly to have been thought of as a means of enforcing restraint on labor demands and an instrument for resisting strikes opposed by the Government. The SLFP federation's efforts to resist strikes, coinciding with mounting labor restiveness and militant calls by other unions, eventually led to a sharp decline in the strength of the party's labor following. The SLFP had shown interest in developing trade union strength and had had some success while in power, but had largely sacrificed its labor support in the interest of upholding Government policy against strikes and wage demands.

Following formation of the SLFP-Marxist coalition, the SLFP's public attitudes toward labor issues have been identical with those of its Marxist allies. The 1967 SLFP conference resolved that "the Party should take all possible steps to remove repressive regulations imposed on trade unions and the Co-operative movement by the UNP-Federalist Government and pledges to restore the democratic rights and privilleges [sic] enjoyed by the trade unions and cooperatives under the Sri Lanka Freedom Party."[23] Despite her criticism of strikes while she was in office, Mrs. Bandaranaike pointedly declared her approval of and support for a strike called by pro-coalition unions in 1967–1968 and a public servants' strike late in 1968.[24] While remaining active in the labor movement, the SLFP appears to be only marginally concerned with trade unionism, and party officers seem prepared to concede leadership of the labor movement to their Marxist coalition partners.[25]

UNP concern with the labor movement emerged from an effort to reform and revitalize the party after its crushing defeat in 1956. The UNP, which was identified by the Marxists as the political organization of the class enemy and which was considered anti-labor by many trade unionists, formed two trade unions and simultaneously convened the first UNP-sponsored May Day rally in 1961. In a message to the rally, J. R. Jayewardene, a prominent party leader and the president of both UNP unions, proclaimed "the United National Party's radical change in its attitude to the trade union movement."[26] The UNP entry into the labor movement indicated a growing appreciation of the political significance of organized labor and a desire to contain Marxist influence in the rapidly expanding trade union movement by providing a non-Marxist alternative. In addition, party leaders believed the UNP's public image would be improved

[23]*Nation* (Colombo), July 21, 1967, p. 1.
[24]*Ceylon Daily News,* January 3, 1968, pp. 1, 14; and December 1, 1968, p. 1.
[25]Based on the author's interviews with officers of the party and its labor federation, principally in 1967.
[26]*U.N.P. Journal,* April 28, 1961, p. 1. In a May Day message six years later, LSSP leader N. M. Perera referred to Marxist observances of May Day commencing in 1933, and asserted, "We have progressed so far that we have been able to compel the political instrument of the capitalist class—the UNP—to celebrate May Day and pretend to take an interest in the working class of Ceylon." *Tribune* (Colombo), May 7, 1967, p. 9.

by identification with the labor movement. The party was thought to have suffered from identification with the wealthy and privileged classes. After its 1956 defeat, an effort commenced to revamp the party and broaden its appeal.[27] The trade union venture was looked upon less as a serious challenge to Marxist hegemony in the labor movement than as a refutation of the charge that the party was anti-labor and as a symbol of the UNP's sincerity in its expressed concern for the common people.[28] UNP spokesmen have repeatedly stressed that trade unions should not be used for partisan purposes and particularly have denounced political strikes. Although the party was adamantly opposed to the SLFP Government then in power, pro-UNP trade unions refused on principle to join in the general strike of January, 1962, on grounds that it was a political strike.[29]

The entrance of the Federal Party into the trade union field provides an illustration of a party attempting to use a labor organization explicitly to create a link with a segment of the population not readily accessible through other forms of party activity. The Federal Party is the principal party of the Ceylon Tamil ethnic minority and derives its electoral support from the Ceylon Tamils of the Northern and Eastern Provinces. In their efforts to maximize the unity and solidarity of the island's Tamil-speaking peoples, the Federalists have sought to cooperate with the Indian Tamils employed on the tea and rubber estates in the interior hill country. For some years the Federal Party maintained an informal alliance with the Ceylon Workers' Congress, the principal labor organization of the estate workers, but after relations with the CWC deteriorated by 1962, the Federalists sought to establish direct contact with the Indian Tamils. Some party branches were established in the estate areas, but the Indian Tamils, largely voteless and isolated on the estates, have been politically quiescent and have manifested concern chiefly with employment and labor questions. In December, 1962, the Federalists formed a trade union for estate workers, the Ilankai Thollilalar Kazham, the professed purpose of which was to demonstrate the Federalists' concern for and solidarity with the Tamil-speaking estate workers. The objective sought presumably is not electoral support, as a large majority of the Indian Tamils are non-citizens without the franchise and the Federal Party has not contested any

---

[27]A revised party program adopted in 1958 stressed the party's dedication to socialism and concern with the welfare and aspirations of the common man : *Progress Through Stability* . *United National Party Manifesto* (Colombo : United National Party, 1958). A further revision of the UNP program appeared in 1963 as *What We Believe* (Colombo : United National Party, 1963).

[28]Based on the author's interviews with party officers, M.P.'s, and trade union officials during 1965 and 1967. In several interviews in 1965, party leaders frankly assessed the strength and prospects of their unions as limited, but stressed the symbolic importance of the unions in combating the charge that the UNP is anti-labor. A rapid growth of the party's trade unions after the UNP came to power in 1965, however, appears to have led to a somewhat less modest evaluation of their prospects and utility by 1967.

[29]House, *Debates*, vol. 46, col. 1329 (February 14, 1962).

seats in the estate areas, but rather a general collaboration and mutual support on political issues affecting either or both of the Tamil-speaking communities. After the Federal Party entered the Government in 1965, the party expanded its labor activities to include a few other types of workers, but this appeared to alter only slightly the basic purpose of the party's involvement in trade unionism, the establishment of a link with the Indian Tamil community.[30]

3. Partisan Functions of Trade Unions

The partisan function of a labor organization of which politicians are most conscious is that of a channel to "the people" or "the masses," a link between the party and a relatively broad segment of the population which is not effectively reached by the party's own organization.[31] Trade unions and youth leagues are the two types of mass organizations employed by most Ceylonese parties in the attempt to project their influence beyond the narrow and predominately middle-class membership of the party. As an adjunct to a political party, trade unions suffer from the disadvantage of the modest size of the wage-labor force, discounted by the disfranchisement of many estate workers, and the concentration of organized workers in a relatively few parliamentary constituencies. Inaccessible through trade unionism are the numerous village cultivators who form by far the largest occupational category and who constitute the primary arbitor of political party fortunes. Nonetheless, although trade unionism can directly reach only a small part of the population, other organized interest groups with a mass base are almost unknown. Politicians turn to trade unions in the absence of any more promising channels to a mass audience. As trade unions are among the society's few coherently organized and fairly durable associational groups with a relatively accessible and politically conscious membership, the attention politicians pay to organized labour is vastly greater than its proportionate size in the total population. In addition, many politicians feel that by championing organized workers' interests, they are helping to identify the party as the friend of the common man, and thus eliciting sympathy and support beyond the rather restricted confines of the organized labor force.

Partisan Loyalties of Union Members

A major question regarding the partisan utility of trade union sponsorship arises from the uncertain political commitment of the rank-and-file

[30]Author's interviews with Federal Party leader S. J. V. Chelvanayakam, July 2, 1965, and July 26, 1967.

[31]This is a role frequently assigned to trade unions in the developing nations. See Bruce H. Millen, *The Political Role of Labor in Developing Countries* (Washington, D.C.: Brookings Institution, 1963), pp. 83–84.

union member. Where sharp rivalry exists among unions sponsored by opposing parties, as in the Colombo port and the Ceylon Transport Board, there may be a tendency for workers to express their partisan preferences by their choice of labor organizations. However, in many industries, one union is dominant, despite the existence of numerous smaller organizations, and workers are thought to gravitate toward the dominant union irrespective of partisan considerations. It is widely believed by trade union leaders that workers join a union which is aggressive in defending their interests and successful in winning their demands. Consequently, members of a party-sponsored union cannot be assumed to be political supporters of the sponsoring party. A number of examples are often cited of unions led by militant leftists but with members who tend to support such non-radical parties as the UNP and Federal Party or to be politically apathetic. Indeed, some feeling exists within the parties deeply involved in trade unionism that workers have "exploited" the party by accepting the efforts on their behalf by party activists without in turn providing reliable political support for the party.

The political support a party can expect from a trade union was explained by veteran LSSP leader Leslie Goonewardene[32] as determined by the extent to which the party has developed a strong "political base" within the union. An example was cited of one union long associated with the LSSP in which a particularly strong political base existed. The union contained about one hundred party members, who supplied the officers and activists of the organization. Workers belonging to the union in addition to the party members were believed to be predominantly LSSP sympathizers and the party could regularly count on the union for a large turnout for party activities such as rallies and demonstrations. In contrast, other unions sponsored by the same party contained few or no party members and even officers of the unions were sometimes not party members. A firm political base within a union is built by the association of the party and its leaders with the demands and aspirations of the union members and the indoctrination of the membership in the merits of the party, but also depends on the political consciousness and sophistication and the educational level of the workers.

The apparent conclusion is that workers frequently join a union without regard to its political alignment and the sponsoring party will not automatically receive their support in its political activities, but that the party has a favorable opportunity to build political loyalties among the union's members. Lectures and meetings for union members specifically designed to stimulate political awareness and sympathy for the sponsoring party are conducted by many trade unions. The Ceylon Federation of Labour, thus, recently held a day-long "study camp" at which members of CFL

[32]In an interview by the author, July 4, 1967.

.unions were lectured on the "class nature of the principal political parties in Ceylon" and the joint program of the SLFP-Marxist coalition.[33] May Day and other labor rallies which are addressed by party leaders also encourage union members' identification with the party and faith that the party will best serve their interests in the political arena.[34] Many union members may never become committed to the party, and may even vote for candidates of opposing parties in national and local elections. Nonetheless, a correspondence undeniably exists between party sponsorship and the predominant political sympathies of the membership, whether through selective joining or later conversion. There is no doubt, for example, that a much higher level of support for the LSSP exists within the CFL unions than within unions affiliated with the Ceylon Federation of Trade Unions and, conversely, much more support for the Communist Party is present within the CFTU unions than within those of the CFL.

Trade Unions and Elections

One of the principal forms of political support which a party seeks from the membership of its labor organizations is support in election contests. It is generally hoped that many members of the party's unions will vote for the party's candidates and some will actively work on their behalf. The CTUF a few years after independence asserted: "In parliamentary and local elections the CTUF has always supported the progressive candidates, and, in particular, the candidates of the Communist Party which has played such a leading part in organising the CTUF."[35] More recently, the general secretary of the successor CFTU claimed that in the 1965 election "our Federation together with other trade-union centres standing foursquare against reaction played our full part in furthering the progressive cause and ensuring the return of a large number of progressive candidates to the new Parliament." Each candidate specifically mentioned was a candidate of the Communist Party.[36]

Trade unions play little if any direct role in election campaigns as organizations, but active and politically committed union members may participate as individuals and, at least in the case of the Marxist parties, may make a significant contribution to the campaign efforts. A ready

[33]*Ceylon Federation of Labour News,* February 10, 1969, p. 1.

[34]An LSSP publication commemorating the twenty-fifth anniversary of the party's founding contained advertisements by a number of labor organizations, most of which are closely aligned with the LSSP, praising the party for its years of service to the working class. Lanka Sama Samaja Party, *Visipas Vasarak : Lanka Sama Samāja Pakshayē Rajatha Jayanthiya Nimiththen Nikuth Kerena Sangrahayayi* [Twenty-five Years: Publication Issued for the Lanka Sama Samaja Party's Silver Jubilee] (Colombo: Lanka Sama Samaja Party, 1960).

[35]Ceylon Trade Union Federation, *Ten Years of the Ceylon Trade Union Federation, 1940–1950* (Colombo: Ceylon Trade Union Federation, [1950]), p. 19.

[36]M. G. Mendis, *Ceylon Federation of Trade Unions : Report of the General Secretary to the 17th Sessions* (Colombo: Ceylon Federation of Trade Unions, 1966), p. 4.

cadre of campaign workers can be a considerable political asset in view of the limitations of party organization and scarcity of communication channels to the voters. Trade unions may also play a part in a party's campaign in other ways, such as providing a union office to serve as a meeting place and temporary headquarters in a town in which the party does not maintain an office.

Trade union leadership gives a politician a platform from which to appeal to workers in the role of their friend and benefactor and an opportunity to assert the identity of his party's goals and the workers' interests. In a message to the voters of a constituency contested by Bala Tampoe in 1960, LSSP leader N. M. Perera wrote, "Bala Tampoe has been one of the best advisers to the Party on matters affecting Labour. He is one of the men we badly need in Parliament to fight the battles of Labour in that arena."[37] The labor organization may also be used as a forum for partisan attacks against opponents. Thus, at a annual conference of the CTUF, "left" Communist leader N. Sanmugathasan utilized his general secretary's report to excoriate the UNP as "the party of our employers, the most loyal servitor of foreign imperialism, the most reactionary party in Ceylon and the sworn enemy of the working class."[38]

For the Marxists, in particular, trade unionism has been an important device by which party activists have become popularly known and have developed a political base from which to seek elective office. As an indication of the role trade union activities can play in launching a political career, in 1955 Anil Moonesinghe, a young lawyer and LSSP member recently returned from study in Britain, was dispatched by the LSSP to the Agala-watte constituency to assist in a strike of estate workers. He lived and worked in the area in association with the local trade unionists and party members for several weeks during the strike. As a result, when an impending election was announced early the following year, local party members recalled his activity during the strike and suggested that he be the party's parliamentary candidate for that constituency. He won the seat in 1956 and held it in each of the three subsequent elections.[39]

Recruitment of Party Members

Trade unions are frequently viewed by the sponsoring party as recruiting grounds for party members. For the committed and active member of the union, membership and work in the sponsoring party may readily appear to be a logical extension of trade union activities. Trade unions,

[37] N. M. Perera, *To the Voters of Colombo Central* (leaflet; Colombo, January 4, 1960), unpaged.
[38] N. Sanmugathasan, *17th Congress Session of the CTUF (Colombo, November 1965) : Report by General Secretary* (Colombo : Ceylon Trade Union Federation, 1965), p. 2.
[39] Based on many conversations with Anil Moonesinghe over a number of years. After being re-elected by a comfortable margin in 1965, Moonesinghe was unseated on a finding of campaign irregularities, but in a subsequent by-election the seat was retained by the LSSP.

however, have not been a channel through which workers in huge numbers have been recruited to party membership, in part because no Ceylonese political parties are large mass parties.[40] It has long been the hope of the Marxists to bring the most militant and able of the trade unionists into the party, and the Marxist parties are probably the only ones which have recruited any significant number of workers to party membership. The Communist Party has stressed the participation of workers in the party and claimed that a substantial proportion of the membership is from the working class. Forty percent of the delegates to the 1964 congress of the "regular" party were described as industrial or estate workers and nine percent as clerical employees.[41] However, although the party in recent years has sought to broaden its membership base, it has remained quite small, probably not exceeding 2,000 members.[42] At the time of the party schism, "regular" Communist leader Pieter Keuneman complained of the small number of CTUF members who had joined the party and charged that N. Sanmugathasan, head of the federation and leader of the "left" Communists, had deliberately kept "militant workers out of our Party." Keuneman claimed that among workers in the tea and rubber processing industry, long a stronghold of Communist trade unionism, there were less than twenty party members.[43]

The LSSP has not sought to create a mass party, setting rigorous conditions for membership and requiring members to participate regularly in party activities. The party has grown over the past decade from about 2,000 to nearly 4,000 members.[44] Both the LSSP and Communist Party contain a number of lawyers, doctors, university lecturers, and other

[40]Except for the LSSP and (with qualifications) the Communist Party, the major Ceylonese political parties all aspire to be mass parties, in the sense of Professor Duverger's mass as distinguished from cadre parties. They have formally defined memberships which require certain simple procedures of enlistment and the payment of a small subscription (one rupee a year for the SLFP). Membership is open to virtually anyone willing to declare general agreement with the party's aims and indicate an intention to support the party's candidates for public office. However, claimed memberships are not impressively large, as is discussed below, and membership lists are notoriously out of date and inaccurate. It is widely assumed that many persons leave one party in order to join another without the formality of resigning, so that the same individual may be recorded as a member simultaneously by several parties. Duverger's discussion of mass and cadre parties is contained in Maurice Duverger, *Political Parties* (London : Methuen & Co., Ltd., 1954), pp. 62–79.

[41]*Forward* (Colombo), July 5, 1967, p. 3.

[42]Author's estimate in mid-1967, based on discussions with members of both Communist Parties and other Ceylonese political activists. Official party membership claims are much higher. A U.S. Department of State estimate at the end of 1967 listed 1,100 probable members for the "regular" Communist Party. U.S. Department of State, Bureau of Intelligence and Research, *World Strength of the Communist Party Organizations, 1968* (Washington, D.C. : Government Printing Office, 1968), p. 103.

[43]Pieter Keuneman, *Under the Banner of Unity : Report of Pieter Keuneman, General Secretary, on Behalf of the Central Committee* (Colombo : Communist Party, 1964), p. 47.

[44]Based on the author's interviews with a number of Samasamajist leaders between 1961 and 1969.

upper-middle-class professionals and intellectuals, from whom most of the top leadership is drawn. The LSSP, in particular, also contains a significant number of clerks and other white-collar employees. The number of party members who have been recruited through the parties' trade unions must, therefore, be quite small and constitute a minute fraction of the total membership of the labor organizations linked with parties.

The manner in which party members are recruited through trade union activity is illustrated by the career of G. P. Perera. As a worker in a cigarette factory during the late 1930's, Perera participated in formulating workers' demands and became involved in collective bargaining and the labor movement. At about the same time his concern with trade unionism was developing, he was attracted by nationalist agitation. Through his involvement in the labor movement, Perera came into contact with N. M. Perera and other early Samasamajists. As the newly formed LSSP was deeply concerned with the problems of organized labor and also was an uninhibited critic of colonial rule, G. P. Perera found himself drawn toward the party, which he soon joined. He continued his labor activity in the LSSP-led trade unions, organizing and leading one notable three-month strike in 1942. Later, he became a vice president of the CFL and an officer of several affiliated unions, as well as a member of the LSSP central committee. Along with his colleague, D. G. William, he was one of the first workers from the ranks of labor below the white-collar clerical employees to rise to a leadership post in an important labor organization and an influential political party position.[45]

The memberships of parties other than the LSSP and Communist Party are generally poorly defined and amorphous, and are largely composed of members of the middle class in the cities and towns or of planters, landowners, traders, school teachers, and a few other local notables in the rural areas. The SLFP has possibly the largest membership, with about 30,000 dues-paying members in 1967.[46] While some SLFP members belong to clerks' or teachers' unions, it is doubtful that the trade unions played a significant role in their recruitment to the party.[47] The SLFP probably contains no more than a handful of industrial or estate workers. The UNP has not revealed its membership figures, but despite the most elaborate and well-financed organization of any Ceylonese party, it is

[45]Author's interview with G. P. Perera, June, 25, 1962. G. P. Perera, now deceased, was generally known as "Elephant" Perera from his employment in a factory producing "Elephant" brand cigarettes and to distinguish him from another worker who was an early recruit to the LSSP, W. J. Perera, known as "Hospital" Perera, a one-time hospital worker. D. G. William is still widely known as "Galle Face" William, from his early employment as a waiter in the Galle Face Hotel.

[46]Author's interview with SLFP general secretary T. B. Subasinghe, August 8, 1967.

[47]One SLFP leader and former Cabinet minister, T. B. Ilangaratne, is a former president of the Government Clerical Service Union.

likely that it contains somewhat fewer members than the SLFP.[48] Although over the past decade major efforts have been made to extend participation in the party to new social groups, particularly through the UNP's youth league, party membership probably remains largely composed of professionals, businessmen, planters, landowners, and members of local government bodies. It is doubtful that trade unions have made any discernible contribution of party members.

Trade Unions and Party Funds

Trade unions in the West have served as valuable assets to parties by providing a major share of party funds. This, however, is not the case in Ceylon. Trade unions, except organizations of public servants, are legally permitted to maintain political funds but almost none of them has done so. In recent years, only the Ceylon Workers' Congress, which is not linked with a political party, has possessed a political fund of significant size, but the fund is used primarily for propaganda, legal, and other expenses in connection with obtaining citizenship for Indian Tamil estate workers, rather than for the expenses of election campaigns.[49] Several unions which had maintained very small political funds, including the Ceylon Mercantile Union and the Ceylon Bank Employees' Union, have discontinued them. Trade union and party officers universally deny that the parties receive financial support from their associated trade unions. Occasionally, at rallies and meetings, contributions reportedly will be sought for the party from union members as individuals, but the amounts derived in this manner must be extremely modest.

Few labor organizations are sufficiently affluent to be a plausible source of party financing. Union dues are very low and frequently difficult to collect. Only a fe   unions have a large membership base. It is likely that most trade unions with partisan connections are indirectly subsidized to some degree by the party. A veteran Communist labor leader, citing the difficulty of collecting membership dues and the poverty of most trade unions, has ridiculed suggestions that trade union funds were used for political party purposes, but added, "The reverse can, sometimes, be true."[50] The recent extension of the checkoff for union dues, with its important implications for the financial strength of unions, could, however, enhance the future capacity of trade unions to collect and spend money for political purposes.

[48]The UNP membership probably grew considerably while the party was in power after 1965. Between 1965 and 1969, the number of UNP branches nearly doubled, climbing from 1,041 to 1,907. The figure for 1965 was supplied to the author by the UNP headquarters in 1965, and the 1969 figure is from *United National Party 18th Annual Sessions, 23rd & 24th February, 1969* (Colombo : United National Party, 1969), p. 30.

[49]Author's interview with CWC president S. Thondaman, July 16, 1967.

[50]N. Sanmugathasan, "Outsiders in the Trade Unions," *Red Flag* (Colombo), July 14, 1967, p. 8.

The "Direct Action" Role

The trade unions' most conspicuous and, in the short run, perhaps most significant partisan role is as an instrument of "direct action." Among the most vital functions trade unions perform for parties is to provide the personnel for mass rallies and street demonstrations called by the sponsoring party and, occasionally, to dramatize a party demand or position by staging a political strike.[51] The control of trade unions gives a party a potentially important lever for exercising political pressure outside election contests and Parliament. The influence the Marxist parties have maintained in the labor movement, while not readily capable of translation into election results, has unquestionably been a major source of Marxist strength in bargaining with other parties and has expanded considerably the Marxists' ability to influence the course of political events.

The political value of trade unions is to a major degree a product of their mass memberships and concentration in the urban areas, particularly in the politically sensitive capital of Colombo, where disruption of normal economic activities or massive street demonstrations have a maximum political impact.[52] All political parties have come to attach great importance to huge rallies and demonstrations, apparently in the belief that a large turnout creates an impression of wide popular support and hence lends legitimacy to the party's activities. Trade unions are the principal instruments utilized to mobilize political rallies and demonstrations, particularly by parties with considerable labor support. Parties which lack great trade union strength tend to rely more heavily on their youth leagues to provide the crowds which make party rallies a success.

May Day rallies, which for nearly a decade have been staged by all major parties, have become symbolic tests of strength and popular support. Demonstrations, occasionally including a general strike, are often staged by parties to protest in dramatic fashion a specific event or issue. When the SLFP-LSSP coalition Government was defeated in Parliament in December, 1964, for example, the trade unions of those parties and the Communist Party were utilized to call a half-day general strike and assemble a massive demonstration and rally protesting the fall of the Government. About 80,000 workers were claimed to have participated in the demonstration and more than 200,000 to have attended the rally.[53]

[51] Political strikes are discussed at length in Chapter VIII.

[52] Estate workers, who constitute a large proportion of the organized labor force, are not located in close proximity to Colombo, which is one reason they do not play a political role commensurate with their numbers. Estate workers in large numbers were claimed to have first participated in a major rally in Colombo with other workers' organizations in March, 1964. *Democratic Workers' Congress Administrative Report, 1963/1964* (Colombo: Democratic Workers' Congress, 1964), p. 4.

[53] *25 Years of the Ceylon Communist Party* (Colombo: People's Publishing House, 1968), pp. 101–102.

The Defensive Role of Trade Unions

Control of trade unions is an asset not only for opposition groups wishing to harass the Government, but for the party in power attempting to resist pressure exerted through strikes. In a 1961 speech to an SLFP conference, Prime Minister Sirimavo Bandaranaike emphasized the defensive role assigned to the party's unions, declaring: "Our trade unions have a vital role to play in the days ahead and I am confident that they will not only act with responsibility but will prevent their fellow workers from being misled by those opposed to us."[54] The president of the SLFP's labor federation credited the party's trade unions with protecting the SLFP Government and possibly preventing its fall when it was besieged by a series of strikes in the public corporations after 1961.[55]

The National Government formed in 1965 by the UNP and smaller parties, including the MEP, anticipated the hostility of a large segment of the labor movement led by members of the opposition, but claimed that the UNP- and MEP-sponsored unions would blunt the attack of the opposition labor organizations.[56] It is likely that MEP leader Philip Gunawardena's trade union support and identification with the labor movement was an important factor in his appointment to a Cabinet post, although he was the only member of his party elected to Parliament. When a strike of Ceylon Transport Board employees was threatened by unions associated with the opposition parties in 1967, the UNP's National Employees' Union and MEP's Lanka Motor Sevaka Samithiya pledged their members would work overtime in support of the corporation management throughout the strike.[57] A UNP report boasted that during a strike by opposition-led unions the following year members of the UNP-sponsored union "remained steadfast at their posts demonstrating truly their loyalty to the Government."[58] Trade unions, it appears, have added to their political functions the role of acting as a defensive shield against strikes and labor turbulence when their sponsoring party is in power.

[54]*Sunday Times of Ceylon*, December 3, 1961, p. 12.
[55]Harold Jayawardena, "Kamkaru Handa [Voice of Labor]," *Sri Lanka Nidahas Pakshaye Saṅvathsara Kalapaya, 1964* [Sri Lanka Freedom Party's Anniversary Volume, 1964] (Colombo: Sri Lanka Freedom Party, 1964), pp. 83, 85.
[56]Author's interview with J. R. Jayewardene, Minister of State, June 26, 1965.
[57]*Ceylon Daily News*, August 19, 1967, p. 1.
[58]*United National Party 18th Annual Sessions*, p. 34.

V

PARTY SPONSORSHIP AND CONTROL

With a few exceptions, trade unions directly sponsored by political parties are organized into large federations established through the initiative of the party and closely linked with the party. Party-sponsored labor organizations probably include between 300,000 and 400,000 workers, one-fourth to one-third of all organized employees. All the major federations in Ceylon except the Public Service Workers' Trade Union Federation[1] can be classified as party-sponsored. These federations are the only major trade union centers which combine employees from a number of different industries functioning in Ceylon. Before the growth of trade unionism and the consolidation of several strong and influential unaffiliated unions during the past ten or fifteen years, they and the Ceylon Workers' Congress were virtually the only large and prominent labor organizations in existence.

In 1940, soon after the Communists were expelled from the Lanka Sama Samaja Party, the unions under Communist leadership were grouped together in the Ceylon Trade Union Federation,[2] which continued under close party supervision until a Communist Party split in 1963, when the federation was captured by pro-Peking dissidents who formed a rival Communist Party. The "regular" Communist Party thereafter formed the Ceylon Federation of Trade Unions, which claimed to be "in fact and in substance the old Ceylon Trade Union Federation under a new name."[3] In 1963, immediately before the schism, the CTUF reported 68,130 members in thirty-one affiliated unions, and a year earlier the highest membership to that date, almost 80,000, was reported.[4]

[1] The PSWTUF is identified with the "regular" Communist Party, but is classified as a party-oriented rather than a party-sponsored organization because only in the last few years has the identification become unambiguous and the close association with the party and dependence on party support which characterizes party sponsorship does not seem to exist. The PSWTUF is discussed in Chapter VI.

[2] The federation, hence, is older than the Communist Party. After their expulsion from the LSSP, the Communists functioned for a few years in the United Socialist Party, which in 1943 was transformed into the Ceylon Communist Party.

[3] M. G. Mendis, *Ceylon Federation of Trade Unions: Report of the General Secretary to the 17th Sessions* (Colombo: Ceylon Federation of Trade Unions, 1966), p. 1. The split and subsequent rivalry between the two Communist groups is discussed later in this chapter.

[4] Membership figures for the private-sector federations are from the annual reports of the Commissioner of Labour for the years cited.

Shortly after the Second World War and the resumption of activity by the LSSP, which had been proscribed during the war, the party assumed control of the Ceylon Federation of Labour, which had recently been registered by a minor political group, and began to organize and affiliate new unions and build the federation.[5] The CFL, which reported about 15,000 members in 1951, reached a peak of 113,794 claimed members in 1963 but slumped to 84,517 members in 1966. The major affiliates of the CFL are the Lanka Estate Workers' Union, the All-Ceylon Commercial and Industrial Workers' Union, the All-Ceylon United Motor Workers' Union, and the United Port Workers' Union. Despite prohibitions against political connections by public servants or their organizations, the Government Workers' Trade Union Federation has functioned in close and scarcely disguised association with the LSSP for a quarter of a century. Unlike the party's CFL, the GWTUF is not led by professed members and officers of the LSSP, and the GWTUF's headquarters and staff are separated from those of the party in deference to the statutory restrictions on public servants' organizations. Nonetheless, there appears to be slight difference between the two federations in the extent of effective party support and influence. Since federations of public servants' unions are technically prohibited, the GWTUF is not formally recognized as existing and consequently does not submit reports to the Commissioner of Labour. The memberships of unions affiliated to the GWTUF are estimated to total about 75,000.

The Central Council of Ceylon Trade Unions was organized in 1957 by the Viplavakari Lanka Sama Samaja Party, which since 1959 has been called the Mahajana Eksath Peramuna. Philip Gunawardena, the MEP leader, was an active organizer of harbor workers several decades ago, and the All-Ceylon Harbour and Dock Workers' Union remains the principal union within the CCCTU. Other MEP unions were organized after Gunawardena became a minister in the S. W. R. D. Bandaranaike Cabinet in 1956. In most recent years, the CCCTU has reported a membership of a little more than 30,000, with a peak in 1965 of 36,841. The following year, however, the reported membership fell to 23,941.

The first serious trade union venture by a non-Marxist party since the creation of the now defunct Labour Party and All-Ceylon Trades Union Congress by A. E. Goonesinha in 1928 was launched by the Sri Lanka Freedom Party in 1956, less than a month after an SLFP-dominated coalition had come to power. The SLFP unions were collected into the Sri Lanka Nidahas Vurthiya Samithi Sammelanaya (Ceylon Independent Trade Union Federation)[6] in 1961. Membership of the SLNVSS climbed

[5]Leslie Goonewardene, *A Short History of the Lanka Sama Samaja Party* (Colombo: Lanka Sama Samaja Party, 1960), p. 28.

[6]The Sinhalese word *nidahas*, which in the name of the SLFP (in Sinhalese, Srı Lanka

to over 30,000 in 1962, but plunged to 7,072 two years later. Recently, the Sri Lanka Nidahas Rajaya Seva Vurthiya Samithi Sammelanaya (Ceylon Independent Government Service Trade Union Federation) was formed under SLFP auspices, but its significance is still uncertain.

Not organized into federations but characterized by the same direct party control and sponsorship are the unions formed by the United National Party and the Federal Party. The UNP entered the trade union field in 1961 with the formation of the Lanka Jathika Estate Workers' Union and the National Employees' Union. The following year, the Ilankai Thollilalar Kazham (Ceylon Workers' Federation)[7] was formed under Federal Party auspices, originally as a union of estate workers but after 1965 expanded to include a few other groups of Tamil-speaking workers, principally port workers in Trincomalee. Until 1965, each of the UNP and Federalist unions included 2,000–3,000 members, but since the two sponsoring parties entered the Government in 1965 they are said to have undergone rapid expansion.[8]

1. Benefits of Party Sponsorship

The partisan connections of trade unions result in part from important advantages which unions derive from association with political parties. These benefits are most vital to party sponsored organizations, but in some cases are significant for party-oriented unions as well. Party-sponsored unions and federaions generally are heavily dependent on the support of parties for their effective functioning, if not for their very existence. Most of these unions and federations were organized through the efforts and initiative of party activists. They have remained heavily dependent on party support because they commonly are not organizationally self-sufficient. Some of the requirements for the effective performance of their functions and achievement of their goals are not obtainable from their internal resources.

Among the most critical weaknesses of labor organizations has been a pronounced lack of leadership from their own ranks. Although the necessity for leaders from outside the union membership appears to be declining, many organizations are still dependent on outsiders for basic administrative, negotiating, and legal skills, and where they may no longer be indispensi-

---

Nidahas Pakshaya) is invariably translated as "freedom," is usually translated as "independent" in the federation's name. The federation is often also referred to, even in its own publications, as the Sri Lanka Freedom Party Trade Union Federation.

[7]According to Federal Party officers, the labor organization was not in fact organized as a federation. However, the Tamil word *kazham* is usually employed to denote a federation and the word *sangam* is customarily used as the Tamil equivalent of union.

[8]Based on interviews with UNP and Federal Party officers in 1965 and 1967. The National Employees' Union membership was claimed to have reached 10,000 in 1967.

ble, the outsider officers are well entrenched and supported by the habit
of reliance on their services. The party-sponsored unions are generally
composed of unskilled and semi-skilled laborers who have slight education,
relatively little sophistication, and no experience in managing an organization. The middle-class intellectuals and professionals who are willing
to assume the duties of a trade union leader are almost invariably politicians. Union leadership is arduous, time-consuming, and contentious and
seldom provides appreciable material rewards. Politicians have assumed
the leadership of labor organizations because outside leadership has been
virtually essential and politicians are usually the only persons willing to
assume the burdens involved.[9]

Many labor organizations are unable to afford not only required
professional expertise such as legal and accounting services but sometimes
even the office staff and facilities to carry on union business. These needs,
reflecting gaps in the independent capabilities of the labor organizations,
are filled by party assistance. Both the SLFP and the UNP provide headquarters accommodations for their trade unions in the party headquarters
buildings. The LSSP and its federation share a common headquarters,
which in fact is identified only by the labor organization's name. The
party and federation were reported to have once taken common office
accommodations a number of years ago in order to share the same
telephone.[10] The first trade union formed under SLFP auspices was
provided with an office, furniture, and supplies by the party leader.[11]
Most of the party-sponsored organizations, unable to provide adequate
paid staffs, are heavily dependent on volunteers to perform services
ranging from routine correspondence to maintaining financial records
and preparing briefs for court appearances. Some of the volunteer work
is performed by activists from the unions themselves, but in the party-
sponsored organizations a considerable amount, often including provision
of the most critical and scarce skills, comes from party members.

A further reason for workers' submission to political leadership stems
from an apparent belief that the worker can be better protected by a
politician than by another outsider. Party and trade union activists
argue that many workers, particularly the unskilled and unsophisticated
workers most frequently found in party-sponsored unions, obtain a sense

[9]In his report for 1940, the Controller of Labour noted a "dearth of persons who have the
time and leisure ... to organize the administration of a trade union which is nearly always
unpaid work involving much toil and many discouragements and which brings more criticism
and less thanks." *Administration Report of the Controller of Labour for 1940* (Colombo : Government
Press, 1941), p. 5. The role of outsiders as trade unions leaders was discussed in Chapter III.

[10]Author's interview with P. K. Liyanage, July 8, 1967.

[11]Lakshman Jayakody, "Śrī Laṅkā Nidahas Pakshaya saha Kamkaru Samithi Vyāpāraya
[Sri Lanka Freedom Party and the Labor Union Movement]," in *Śrī Laṅkā Nidahas Pakshaya
Dasavāni Sāṅvathsarika Kalāpaya, 1961* [Sri Lanka Freedom Party Tenth Anniversary Volume,
1961] (Colombo : Sri Lanka Freedom Party, 1961), p. 115.

of strength and security from membership in an organization headed by an influential political figure. As an official of one union sponsored by a major political party remarked, workers "want the backing of strong politicians."[12] The desire of workers to place themselves under the protection of a powerful guardian may be related to the patron-client relations of traditional society and the distrust and insecurity prevalent in the culture.[13] This may be one reason why the formal head of a party's trade union center is usually one of the most prominent top party leaders, although he is presumably seldom able to devote much time and attention to union matters.

The political party also serves as the trade union's link to the general public, the political system, and often the rest of the labor movement. During a crisis or major struggle, the union often can call upon the resources and energies of the party and may receive the backing of other unions allied with the same party, including the calling of a sympathy strike by the entire federation. An official of the LSSP-sponsored CFL has claimed that independent unions often "fail to reap much for the membership due to lack of public support and support from other unions."[14] Furthermore, the party leader may utilize the political platform, the floor of Parliament, or the party press and other mass communications media to vent union grievances and attract public attention to claimed abuses or victimization. Even if in the opposition, a prominent politician can usually command the attention of public servants and officials of public corporations. M.P.'s belonging to parties involved in trade unionism frequently use the question period, adjournment debate, or other parliamentary opportunities to demand inquiry into complaints by unions or even individual workers which would otherwise be very unlikely to obtain a high-level hearing. Membership in one of the LSSP unions opens to workers the prospect of having their individual or collective interests championed in Parliament by such articulate and skilled parliamentary spokesmen as N. M. Perera, Colvin R. de Silva, Leslie Goonewardene, or Bernard Soysa. Pieter Keuneman has performed similar functions for unions linked with the Communist Party.

Access to the administrative and political authorities is of particular

[12]Author's interview with P. Sumathiratne, July 1, 1965.

[13]See T. L. Green, "The Cultural Determination of Personality in Ceylon," *School and Society*, LV (March 15, 1952), 164-166; Murray A. Straus, "Childhood Experience and Emotional Security in the Context of Sinhalese Social Organization," *Social Forces*, XXXIII (December, 1954), 152-160; Murray A. Straus and Jacqueline H. Straus, "Personal Insecurity and Sinhalese Social Structure: Rorschach Evidence for Primary School Children," *Eastern Anthropologist*, X (December, 1956-February, 1957), 97-111; and Murray A. Straus and Solomon Cytrynbaum, "Support and Power Structure in Sinhalese, Tamil, and Burgher Student Families," *International Journal of Comparative Sociology* III (September, 1962), 138-153.

[14]Wimalasiri de Mel, "Trade Unions Cannot Escape Politics," *Nation* (Colombo), July 6, 1967, p. 6.

importance to the large numbers of workers employed by government departments and public corporations. Favoritism toward the unions and members of unions associated with the party in power is almost universally claimed and anticipated by both supporters and opponents of the Government.[15] While the extent of favoritism is difficult to estimate, it is significant that during the period of the SLFP Government the membership of SLFP unions was largely in the public corporations. When the UNP came to power in 1965, party leaders expected an almost automatic expansion of their unions' membership, particularly in the public corporations.[16] Within two years, the UNP's National Employees' Union had surpassed all other unions in membership among Ceylon Transport Board employees. The value accorded association with the governing party and the advantage of holding political power in attracting labor support were revealed in a statement appearing in a 1962 publication of the SLFP's federation. The secretary of the Paranthan Chemicals Employees' Sangam, a union of the largely Tamil employees of a public corporation located in the North, complained of victimization of workers and hostility toward the union by the corporation management. He continued :

> The Paranthan Chemicals Employees Sangam had carried on all these days without any party affiliation. They [union spokesmen] approached a few Tamil Members of Parliament and requested their intervention in the matter. The results were disappointing. Other sources were contacted with the same degree of success. There was only one solution. The ears of the Government had to be reached to place the workers' case for impartial inquiry.... The quickest way to reach the Government's ears was obviously through the Government party. With the blessing of a few Tamil Members of Parliament we went to the S.L.F.P. Headquarters. Our case was patiently given a hearing. We were assured that if we were found to be right the Party's Trade Union Federation would give us all support. We were shown by action that the party meant what it said. Action was taken swiftly and effectively. Three victimised workers have got back to work. Other cases are pending and action is being taken. We felt it our duty to ask the members for a mandate to affiliate the Paranthan Chemicals Employees Sangam with the Sri Lanka

[15]Fairly typical of the accusations of favoritism while the SLFP was in power are a charge that the president of an industrial court was dropped from the court after he criticized an SLFP union, and a charge that after two watchers were discovered sleeping on duty, disciplinary action was taken against one, who belonged to an LSSP union, but not against the other, who belonged to an SLFP union. Ceylon, House of Representatives, *Parliamentary Debates (Hansard)*, vol. 34, cols. 1769–1771 (March 12, 1959), and vol. 55, cols. 2922–2923 (February 28, 1964), respectively.

[16]Reported in interviews by the author a few months after the 1965 election.

Freedom Party Trade Union Federation. The membership gave a unanimous vote for it.[17]

2. *Party-Union Links*

Ceylonese labor organizations, even those most intimately associated with political parties, are not formally affiliated or structurally connected with political parties. There has been no apparent effort to define and commit to writing the precise relationship between unions and their sponsoring parties.[18] Trade unions are bound to parties principally through the leadership provided to the labor organizations by party activists. Party-sponsored labor organizations, except public servants' unions, are invariably headed by a party leader, usually a prominent member of Parliament. CFL president N. M. Perera is the parliamentary leader of the LSSP, has been a member of the colonial legislature or Parliament for more than three decades, and was briefly mayor of Colombo and Minister of Finance. Pieter Keuneman, the president of the CFTU, is the general secretary of the Communist Party and has been a member of Parliament for over twenty years. The secretary of the CCCTU, MEP leader Philip Gunawardena, is a veteran legislator who has served in two Cabinets. J. R. Jayewardene, a prominent UNP official and Cabinet minister, is the president of both UNP unions. The general secretary of the SLFP's SLNVSS, Lakshman Jayakody, has been a member of Parliament since 1960.

It is likely that every full-time officer and staff member of each federation and most officers of the affiliated unions are active party members. Some members of a federation's general council and a few officers of affiliated unions are reported not to be party members, but are considered "sympathizers."[19] While some union activists at the lower levels may not be firm supporters of the party, it is highly unlikely that they would be supporters of opposing parties. The only probable exception is when a party schism leaves a supporter of one faction in a union controlled by the other. Thus, for example, following the LSSP split in 1964, the rebels who founded the LSSP(R) considered forming their own trade unions as rivals to the CFL unions, but eventually decided to leave their supporters

[17] K. Vinayagmoorthy, "Paranthan Chemicals Employees Sangam," in Sri Lanka Nidahas Vurthiya Samithi Sammelanaya, *1962 Māyi Dina* [1962 May Day] (Colombo: Sri Lanka Nidahas Vurthiya Samithi Sammelanaya, 1962), p. 140.

[18] No Ceylonese party or union presumably has considered it necessary to attempt as specific a statement of the nature of the association between the labor organization and its sponsoring party as was formulated by the Indian National Congress and the Indian National Trade Union Congress in 1958. On the Congress-INTUC formula, see N. Pattabhi Raman, *Political Involvement of India's Trade Unions* (New York: Asia Publishing House, 1967), pp. 45–48.

[19] Reported in the author's interviews with officers and former officers of the CFL and CFTU.

within the CFL in the interest of labor unity and in the hope of influencing the LSSP-sponsored unions from within.[20] In contrast, the pro-Peking Communists claimed that when the CTUF-affiliated All-Ceylon Toddy Workers' Union was captured by the pro-Moscow CFTU following the Communist Party split, the union's secretary, a supporter of the pro-Peking group, was dismissed from office and expelled from the union.[21] A number of similar incidents have been charged by both contestants in the battle for the Communist-sponsored unions.

Although it is through interlocking personnel that the trade union is tied to the party, the continued influence of the party is reinforced by the multi-faceted dependence of many unions on the sponsoring party and the blow to the viability of the labor organization which the withdrawal of party support is likely to produce. A rebellious trade unionist could scarcely ignore the costs in terms of union effectiveness produced by a loss of volunteered expertise and assistance, perhaps loss or disruption of headquarters facilities and staff, and the loss of possible support by other unions associated with the party, as well as the rupturing of the union's channel to the political sphere.

With the exception of the unions sponsored by the UNP and the Federal Party, nearly all the unions which are closely associated with and dependent on political parties are grouped in federations. It is at the federation level that the linkage with the party is most pronounced and significant. The unions affiliated with the federations generally seem to possess little self-sufficiency or autonomy and to be heavily dependent on the federation in many of their operations. Policies apparently are formulated and decisions made at the federation level, not only on questions involving the entire federation but on most matters of consequence concerning individual unions. Many of the constituent unions do not maintain headquarters separate from that of the federation,[22] and federation officers often also hold office in the constituent unions. Of twenty-two unions affiliated with the CFTU, for example, ten list their headquarters at the Malay Street headquarters of the federation in Colombo and three others share headquarters locations with federation branch offices outside Colombo.[23] The CFL maintains two offices in Colombo, a headquarters on Jayantha Weerasekera Mavatha in Maradana and a branch office on Kew Road in Slave Island. Of twenty-three affiliated unions, three share the Maradana office and seven the Slave Island office with the parent

[20]Author's interview with Prins Rajasooriya, June 27, 1967.

[21]*Red Flag* (Colombo), July 14, 1967, p. 8.

[22]All trade unions are required by law to have a headquarters address, to which communications can be directed by the Department of Labour.

[23]Mendis, *Ceylon Federation of Trade Unions*, p. 19. Most of the other unions are organizations of public corporation employees and list the corporation, where they are provided with office accommodations, as their headquarters address.

federation. CFL president N. M. Perera is also president of five affiliated unions. D. G. William, CFL general secretary, is general secretary of five unions and Wimalasiri de Mel, administrative secretary of the federation, is treasurer of four unions affiliated to the CFL.[24] William and de Mel are both full-time federation officials.

The Style of Party Control

The Marxist parties follow the Leninist tenet of giving directives not to trade unions but to party members in the trade unions.[25] As explained by Pieter Keuneman, who is both general secretary of the Communist Party and president of the party's labor federation, "the party gives political guidance to the federation, but through the party members who are in the federation."[26] If party members have a firm hold on the leadership posts of the trade union, the party is in practice effectively in control of the union. When the principal officers of the federation are also leaders of the party, difficulties in securing compliance with party instructions are unlikely, in normal circumstances. A decision taken by the directing organs of the party will seldom be challenged by trade union officers who as party leaders participated in the decision. Conversely, seldom will the leadership of a trade union take action contrary to the party's interests when the union leadership is composed predominately of men who are aslo party militants.

As is often the case in regard to Ceylonese trade unionism, the practices established by the Marxists were generally followed by the other parties which became involved in trade unionism much later. However, the SLFP and UNP seem less concerned than the Marxists with preserving an appearance of independence for their labor organizations, as is evident in the location of the trade union headquarters in a corner of the prominently labeled party headquarters, and in the case of the SLFP in the regular inclusion of a section on the party's labor federation along with sections on the youth and women's activities of the party in an annual SLFP publication.[27]

An indication of the nature of party-union relations may be obtained

[24]Information supplied by CFL headquarters in 1967. The affiliated unions headed by Dr. Perera include three of the federation's most important affiliates, the Lanka Estate Workers' Union, All-Ceylon Commercial and Industrial Workers' Union, and All-Ceylon United Motor Workers' Union.

[25]Lenin's views on the exercise of party control over trade unions through party members in the unions and particularly in union leadership positions are discussed in Thomas T. Hammond, *Lenin on Trade Unions and Revolution, 1893-1917* (New York : Columbia University Press, 1957), pp. 71-73.

[26]Author's interview, August 3, 1967.

[27]E.g., *Śrī Laṅkā Nidahas Pakshayē Pasalosväni Sāhvathsarika Kalāpaya* [Sri Lanka Freedom Party's Fifteenth Anniversary Volume] (Colombo : Sri Lanka Freedom Party, 1967), pp. 65-72.

from the characterizations made by veteran leaders of the major federations and the parties with which they are associated.[28] All agree that co-ordination between party and federation is very close. The interlocking leadership is invariably cited as the tie between the political and the labor organization and the way in which party influence is transmitted to the federation. None denies that the party does exercise influence over the federation or that party and federation policy is expected to be identical on questions of concern to both. Generally, day-to-day activities and labor disputes of limited impact appear to be left to the labor organization. It is expected, however, that most decisions on strikes and other matters which have political implications or reflect larger policy considerations will be referred to the leading organs of the party for approval. Also, in nearly all cases, decisions for strikes and demonstrations by the unions, including those for immediate political objectives, are made by the union organs, although the party may "recommend" the action.

For example, a large majority of the CFL's officers and executive committee members have always been members of the LSSP. The party is said not directly to control and regulate CFL affairs, but the federation is in agreement with the party and consistently follows the party's lead, particularly on political questions. More direct party control than is customary was exercised during 1958 and 1959, when the party decided on action and the CFL acquiesced in the party decision. In one instance, the LSSP central committee decided to oppose the use of troops by the Government during a Communist-led strike in 1958. Contemplated action included a conference of labor representatives and, if necessary, a strike. The party asked the CFL to agree and the federation's executive committee accepted the party's recommendation without opposition. The strike, however, did not prove necessary. In 1959, the LSSP decided on a political strike to protest an amendment to the Public Security Act introduced in Parliament. Again, however, while the decision of political course was determined by the party, the formal strike decision was made by the executive committee of the CFL.[29]

It has been claimed that the idea for the political protest strike on the language issue staged on January 8, 1966, originated with the labor organizations rather than with the political parties involved. Strike action as a means of protesting the Government's language measures reportedly was proposed to leaders of the SLFP, LSSP, and "regular" Communist Party on January 5 by officers of the trade unions aligned with those parties, following a meeting of the union officers the preceding day.

[28]The following is based on the author's interviews with N. M. Perera, Leslie Goonewardene, D. G. William, P. K. Liyanage, Prins Rajasooriya, Pieter Keuneman, M. G. Mendis, L. W. Panditha, and N. Sanmugathasan in 1967.

[29]Information on the 1958 and 1959 episodes was supplied by Prins Rajasooriya, who was CFL general secretary when the incidents occurred.

The party leaders accepted the trade unionists' suggestion and incorporated the strike into their plans for protest action.[30]

The 1963 Transport Strike

A strike by employees of the Ceylon Transport Board in January, 1963, presented an unusual situation in the relations between the Communist Party and the CTUF, which was the first fissure in a developing party schism. While not typical of party-union relations, it is claimed, at least, to be an example of the subordination of union interests to the short-run political goals of the party. According to the general secretary of the CTUF, N. Sanmugathasan, who later in the year was expelled from the party and established the rival, pro-Peking party, strong rank-and-file grievances existed within the CTUF transport workers' union and the workers were demanding militant action. The federation officials wanted to champion the discontent and lead a strike to win the workers' demands, but the party opposed a strike at that time because of its political attitude toward the SLFP Government. The federation, however, defied the party and called the strike.

Sanmugathasan attributes great significance to the strike. He sees the conflicting attitudes toward the strike as exemplifying the differences between pro-Moscow and pro-Peking wings of the party. The veteran, pro-Moscow party leaders, according to Sanmugathasan, were deeply committed to electoral and parliamentary politics, and sought to restrain the workers in the interest of maintaining harmonious relations with the governing SLFP. In contrast, party members who were active in trade union affairs more fully appreciated the workers' plight and feared that failure to provide aggressive leadership would result in rank-and-file desertions from the union, and therefore wished to undertake militant action on the workers' grievances. Sanmugathasan charges that the pro-Moscow party leaders who dominated the leading party organs were prepared to sacrifice their trade union following for the preservation of their political relations with the SLFP and betrayed the strike by failing to back it and thus encouraging resistance to the strike demands.[31]

The strike is seen in a markedly different light by "regular" Communist leader Pieter Keuneman. In his view, Sanmugathasan, who was already determined to split the party, precipitated the transport strike in order to embarrass the veteran party leaders and to disrupt negotiations then in progress between the Communist Party and the LSSP for a United Left

---

[30]Author's interviews with Pieter Keuneman, August 3, 1967, and M. G. Mendis, August 15, 1967. Also, see House, *Debates*, vol. 64, col. 1171 (January 26, 1966).

[31]Author's interview with N. Sanmugathasan, July 1, 1967. The pro-Peking Communists' view of the strike is contained in *The History of 25 Years of Proud Service to the Working Class by the Ceylon Trade Union Federation* (Colombo: Ceylon Trade Union Federation, 1965), pp. 32–33.

Front. Sanmugathasan is said by Keuneman to have called the strike in the name of the party and the CTUF without party authorization, in the belief that the party would be forced to go along with the action. Although astonished by the move and convinced the strike was hopeless, the party leadership lent formal support to the strike but attempted to bring it to a conclusion as quickly as possible.[32] The "regular" party's CFTU later charged that while the strike was in progress Sanmugathasan "went about maliging the acknowledged leaders of the Left movement and thereby demoralising the workers."[33]

3. Threats to Party Control

With the heavy party investment of time and energy in trade unionism and the organizational dependence of many trade unions on services provided by party members, strong and secure party control might be expected. Parties can confidently expect their associated unions to adopt political resolutions supporting the party, produce participants for party rallies and demonstrations, and usually follow calls for brief general strikes on political issues or in support of the party's other unions. When a political resolution is drafted, leaders scarcely need to consider rank-and-file sentiments. Even one-day strikes and demonstrations provide diversion from the work routine for many union members and little difficulty normally seems to be encountered in securing a turnout. Nonetheless, party leaders face some significant limitations on their control over trade unions, and they are not spared considerable concern and anxiety in maintaining their labor following.

Rank and File Desertions

The ability of the leaders to subordinate the workers' interests and desires to the partisan objectives of their parties is considerably narrowed by their need to maintain the membership strength of their labor organizations. The members' weak discipline and the uncertain commitment to the union, combined with intense rivalry among unions, lead to frequent desertions and shifts to rival unions. As additional parties have commenced trade union activities during the past fifteen years, the competition for labor support has tended to multiply and the anxieties of labor leaders concerning members' loyalty has grown. Trade union leaders almost without exception stress the necessity to support demands popular with the rank and file and win occupational gains for the membership as essential to the maintenance of their organizations.

[32] Author's interview with Pieter Keuneman, August 3, 1967.
[33] *The C.F.T.U. and the Working Class Movement* (Colombo: Ceylon Federation of Trade Unions, 1966), p. 31.

The politicians leading trade unions are confronted with a dilemma. If they formulate trade union policy to serve their partisan interests they risk the decline or disintegration of their organizations, but if they emphasize promotion of the organizational interests of their unions they fail to secure the political benefits for which they engage in trade unionism.[34] Union leaders seek to influence the direction and timing of trade union action, urging restraint at one point and militancy at another, to secure their immediate political objectives, but they seldom have appeared willing to risk estrangement of their membership by ordering trade union action in direct conflict with rank-and-file moods. Leaders who guide their unions into positions unpopular with the rank and file or fail to remain attentive to the moods and wishes of the membership risk the disintegration of the organization as members shift to rival unions.

This was the fate of the SLFP trade unions when the party, then in power, attempted to resist growing labor demands in the major public corporations between 1961 and 1964. A strike in late 1961 among employees of the Ceylon Transport Board involving the SLFP's transport workers' union, one of the party's principal unions, along with other unions encountered a stern initial response from the SLFP Government. The strikers were threatened with discharge, and the strike was denounced as irresponsible and politically inspired. The awkward situation created by an SLFP union participating in a strike condemned as politically motivated by the SLFP Government was further complicated by the appearance of support for the strike among the party's M.P.'s. Within a few days the Government secured the return to work of the SLFP union and simultaneously granted the strikers' principal demand.[35]

Thereafter, it appeared that the Government's determination to resist labor demands hardened and the SLFP's control over its unions tightened. The SLFP unions were not only restrained from militant championing of workers' demands, they were used to mobilize labor to replace strikers during work stoppages in the port and transport system. Immediately after the 1961 transport strike, the leadership of the SLFP unions pledged unqualified support for the Government in opposing a prolonged and bitter strike of harbor workers.[36] Another major transport workers' strike in 1963 failed in the face of determined resistance by the Government, including the assignment of armed troops to the buses. The strike, however, shattered the SLFP's transport workers' union, which attempted

---

[34]This dilemma is of course also encountered by politically motivated trade unionists elsewhere. The problem of conflicting agitational and organizational interests is discussed in Arthur M. Ross, "The Natural History of the Strike," in Arthur Kornhauser, Robert Dubin, and Arthur M. Ross (eds.), *Industrial Conflict* (New York: McGraw-Hill, 1954), pp. 23-36.

[35]*Ceylon Observer*, December 11, 12, and 14, 1961.

[36]*Ibid.*, December 28, 1961, p. 3.

to support the Government's position, and apparently weakened the entire SLFP trade union effort. The total membership of the party's federation plummeted from 30,000 in 1962 to 7,000 the following year. The party had maintained discipline over its trade unions only at the cost of nearly destroying the federation, as members deserted it for the less inhibited leadership provided by rival organizations.

The LSSP suffered considerable discomfiture in securing compliance with party policy by its trade unions in 1964. Early in the year a list of labor demands, known as the "twenty-one demands," had been endorsed by nearly all the major labor organizations on the island with the enthusiastic backing of the LSSP trade unionists and party leaders. In June, 1964, the LSSP entered a coalition Government with the SLFP, and the Samasamajist leaders asked that agitation for the demands be halted, contending that the demands were no longer necessary since the Government now contained a workers' party which would promote workers' interests. The appeal for restraint was vigorously denounced by the orthodox Trotskyist faction of the party which broke away to form the LSSP(R) and the "left" Communists.[37] Although the pro-LSSP trade unions eventually acceded to the request, disenchantment and confusion appeared within a number of the unions. An Employers' Federation report wryly noted of the LSSP's Ceylon Federation of Labour : "There was obvious evidence of the embarrassment confronting a once militant union, in consequence of its political leadership becoming part of the Government."[38]

Further disruption of the unions aligned with the LSSP, and those led by the "regular" Communist Party, followed the 1965 election, when adherence to party positions on political issues not immediately related to trade unionism alienated many rank-and-file members. The SLFP, LSSP, and Communist opposition concentrated its attack on the newly formed National Government's proposals for the use of the Tamil language for certain governmental purposes and allegedly excessive reliance on and concessions to the ethnic and religious minorities, a strategy of opposition popularly labeled the "communal line." The appeal to language and communal sentiments marked a sharp reversal of policy by the Marxist parties and caused consternation and protest among the Marxist-controlled trade unions, leading to numerous resignations by Tamil members of the unions.[39] The LSSP's large Lanka Estate Workers' Union suffered a

[37]The fight over the "twenty-one demands" is discussed further in Chapter IX.
[38]Employers' Federation of Ceylon, *Annual Report and Accounts, 1964–65* (Colombo : Employers' Federation of Ceylon, 1965), p. 12.
[39]E.g., *Ceylon Daily News*, May 31, August 2, and December 20, 1965. However, reports in the press, which was bitterly hostile to the coalition, tended to exaggerate the coalition parties' trade union troubles. Leaders of the unions claimed in interviews by the author that by mid-1967 their Tamil members were beginning to return, except on the estates.

particularly severe loss of Indian Tamil members, who had accounted for perhaps two-thirds of the union's total members. Desertions from the union probably amounted to more than half its membership.[40] When the SLFP-Marxist coalition called a one-day strike and demonstration to protest regulations providing for the use of the Tamil language for certain governmental purposes in January, 1966, the LSSP and "regular" Communist unions responded to the strike call, but the turnout was unimpressive and the participating unions were subjected to internal dissension and further rank-and-file resignations.[41]

Defections of Leaders

While rank-and-file discontent may weaken a trade union, seldom does it endanger the hold of the leadership and the party on the organization. Disaffection of the membership is typically expressed by abandoning the union for a rival organization. Serious prospects of a party losing control of a labor organization it sponsors only appear to arise from changes in the union leadership or the defection of the party members who hold the leading trade union offices.

One of the few instances of a union breaking with a major federation and the sponsoring party was provided by the Ceylon Estates Staffs' Union, which for a number of years had been affiliated with the Communists' CTUF. The CESU, however, was not a typical party-sponsored organization. It was not founded through the intiative of the party—in fact, it was organized before the party existed—and was not organizationally dependent on the federation and the party to the same degree as are most unions affiliated with the major federations. The union reportedly became affiliated with the CTUF largely through the efforts of one enthusiastic supporter of the Communist Party who was then the CESU's principal leader. However, party members did not obtain the majority of union offices, as commonly occurs among party-sponsored unions, and the link with the party was essentially provided by one individual leader. When he relinquished office, support for the partisan association waned in the union. At the time of the CTUF split during 1963–1964, the CESU withdrew from the federation, but rather than joining the rival CFTU, it remained independent.[42] Two years later, the union joined in forming the United Committee of Ceylon Trade Unions, a grouping which was not aligned with either of the two main political camps existing after the 1965 election.

Party control of the SLFP trade unions appeared to be in jeopardy

[40]CFL officials in 1967 estimated that the union's membership fell from between 60,000 and 70,000 to about 30,000 after 1965.

[41]*Ceylon Daily News*, January 7, 8, and 9, and February 18, 1966.

[42]Based on the author's interview with Pieter Keuneman, August 3, 1967.

in 1961 when the general secretary and organizer of the SLFP unions, Dr. W. D. de Silva, broke with the party in disagreement over the SLFP Government's budget proposals, but refused to relinquish his trade union post. After a brief period of uncertainty, SLFP leader Sirimavo Bandaranaike issued a statement declaring that the party's trade unions were "inviolably tied up with the Sri Lanka Freedom Party in their basic structure" and contending that a person who was no longer a party member could not remain as an official of the SLFP unions. She challenged union members to "decide between allegiance to the party and allegiance to a non-party General Secretary."[43] The party maintained the support of the second-level officials and activists and was able to substitute new leaders and preserve its control of the unions. The dispute, however, may have contributed to the decline of the SLFP's labor organization a few years later.

The Battle for the Communist Trade Unions

The Communist Party faced a more dramatic and costly challenge to its control of the CTUF as a result of the party split in 1963, which touched off possibly the most bitter and intense battle for the control of trade unions ever witnessed by the Ceylonese labor movement. A dissident pro-Peking faction was expelled from the "regular" Communist Party in late 1963 and established a separate "left" Communist group which claimed to be the true continuation of the Ceylon Communist Party.[44] The split in the party ignited an acrimonious debate on the issues dividing international communism between Moscow and Peking, and particularly on the question of the relative emphasis to be placed on the "peaceful" and the "revolutionary" paths to socialism.[45] Although labor issues were involved only indirectly, if at all,[46] the Communist trade unions became the chief battleground of the struggle between the two contending groups.

The leader of the "left" Communists, N. Sanmugathasan, was the

---

[43]The statement is quoted in *Ceylon Observer*, August 30, 1961, p. 7.

[44]I have discussed the party schism in greater detail in "The Communist Parties of Ceylon : Rivalry and Alliance," in Robert A. Scalapino (ed.), *The Communist Revolution in Asia* (2nd ed., rev.; Englewood Cliffs, N.J. : Prentice-Hall, Inc., 1969), pp. 391–416.

[45]The "left" dissidents' position is stated in *Reply to the Central Committee of the Ceylon Communist Party* (Colombo : Worker Publication, n.d.); and N. Sanmugathasan, *The Lessons of the October Revolution* (Colombo : Worker Publication, 1964). The pro-Moscow, "regular" leadership's attitudes appear in Ceylon Communist Party, *On Questions of the International Communist Movement : Statement of the Central Committee of the Ceylon Communist Party* (Colombo : Communist Party, September 26, 1963).

[46]One of the charges brought by the "left" dissidents against the veteran party leaders was that they opposed and refused to provide leadership for the 1963 transport workers' strike and did not campaign vigorously for the "twenty-one demands." "To All Marxist-Leninists Inside the Ceylon Communist Party," a statement dated November 17, 1963, contained in *Statement of Ten Central Committee Members of the Ceylon Communist Party* (Peking : Foreign Languages Press, 1964), pp. 30–33.

general secretary of the CTUF. He had been engaged in the immediate daily tasks of trade union leadership for many years and apparently had developed a core of support among the officers and activists in the Communist unions. The "regular" party leadership charged that Sanmugathasan's initial aim was "to discredit our Party among the workers, to break the connections between the Party and the trade unions, [and] to oppose the trade unions to the Party."[47] Sanmugathasan and his supporters were able to oust the "regular" Communists and consolidate their hold on the federation at a CTUF annual conference held in December, 1963, soon after the party schism. M. G. Mendis, the president of the CTUF and a member of the "regular" party leadership, withdrew from the conference after the dissidents' control became obvious and moved to the party headquarters, where plans were formulated for a new federation. The next month, the "regular" Communists formed the rival Ceylon Federation of Trade Unions, with Communist Party general secretary Pieter Keuneman as president and Mendis as general secretary.[48]

The newly formed CFTU immediately launched a counter-attack against the "left" Communists and the CTUF. The new federation won over the Ceylon Harbour Workers' Union and a few other unions which abandoned the CTUF and affiliated with the CFTU. In other trades, rival unions were established which sought to split the CTUF-affiliated unions and detach their members.[49] The Communist unions were severely jarred by bitter rivalry between the contending and violently hostile groups for several years. The "regular" party leadership apparently expended tremendous time and energy on the campaign, during which Keuneman, Mendis, and others systematically solicited the support of workers, union by union and branch by branch, in their places of employment. The CTUF, which remained in the hands of the "left" Communists, gave this description of the "regular" Communists' campaign against it :

> The weeks and months that followed the 16th Congress of the CTUF [in December, 1963] saw feverish activity by the Keuneman-Mendis clique of revisionists who went all out in an attempt to split the CTUF unions. They used every dirty calumny, including the communal slander against the CTUF's General Secretary. It is a matter for great joy and pride that, despite the fact that almost all the national figures, including all the revisionist members of Parliament and their LSSP allies were ranged against us, the over-whelming majority of the membership of the CTUF decided to remain loyal and faithful to the revolutionary principles of the CTUF.

[47]Pieter Keuneman, *Under the Banner of Unity : Report of Pieter Keuneman, General Secretary, on Behalf of the Central Committee* (Colombo : Communist Party, 1964), p. 45.
[48]Author's interview with M. G. Mendis, August 15, 1967; and *The C.F.T.U. and the Working Class Movement*, pp. 32–33.
[49]Mendis, *Ceylon Federation of Trade Unions*, pp. 5–6.

The revisionists did succeed in breaking away from the CTUF a few of the tea export firms and a few of the smaller unions. They were able to do this only through the use of communalism and by throwing their entire national leadership, including all their members of Parliament, into the fight.[50]

Both federations have claimed victory in the contest. The new CFTU claimed that it had won between 70 and 80 percent of the former CTUF members in the opening months of the campaign and by 1965 asserted the federation included more than 60,000 members.[51] A year later the CFTU claimed the astounding total of 110,000 members.[52] Leaders of the CTUF, however, sharply dispute the claims. Sanmugathasan has described the new federation as a "splinter" organization,[53] and in 1965 claimed 84,531 members for the CTUF.[54] In 1963, the undivided federation had reported a membership of 68,000 to the Commissioner of Labour.

While the question is hotly disputed, non-Communist trade unionists and politicians generally accept the claim that the new federation succeeded in capturing a majority of the old CTUF members. Sanmugathasan and the CTUF, however, reportedly retained most of the federation's cadre of trade union activists.[55] CTUF reverses were most marked among workers in the tea and rubber processing industries concentrated in the Slave Island district of Colombo and in the port. The major remaining area of CTUF strength, and one in which the federation reportedly is increasing its membership, is among the Indian Tamil laborers on the estates.

Three major factors are commonly cited in explanation of the relative success of the new CFTU and the "regular" Communists. First, most CTUF members outside the estates were Sinhalese and when the contest occurred many were unwilling to follow Sanmugathasan, who is a Tamil. Sanmugathasan frequently has charged that communal appeals were used against him.[56] Irrespective of the extent to which deliberate use

[50]*The History of 25 Years of Proud Service* ..., p. 45.
[51]M. G. Mendis, "The Communist Party and the Workers," *Forward* (Colombo), July 2, 1965, p. 5.
[52]Mendis, *Ceylon Federation of Trade Unions*, p. 8.
[53]Author's interview, July 1, 1967.
[54]N. Sanmugathasan, *17th Congress Session of the CTUF (Colombo, November 1965) : Report by General Secretary* (Colombo : Ceylon Trade Union Federation, 1965), p 21.
[55]This was the almost universal judgment of trade unionists, party officers, and others connected with labor affairs but not involved with either contending federation who were interviewed by the author in 1965 and 1967. It was also the conclusion of the Employers' Federation of Ceylon, which presumably was neutral in the fight. See Employers' Federation of Ceylon, *Annual Report and Accounts, 1963–64* (Colombo : Employers' Federation of Ceylon, 1964), pp. 16–17. The CTUF's retention of a major part of the federation cadre was conceded by some "regular" Communist officials interviewed by the author.
[56]E.g., Sanmugathasan, *17th Congress Session of the CTUF*, p. 4; author's interview, July 1, 1967. See also the CTUF statement on the "regular" Communists' campaign against it, quoted above.

was made of communal appeals, the lingering strength of communal indentification and solidarity, even among the urban working class, suggests that this was very probably a factor of considerable significance. A second factor was the support given the new federation by workers who were neither members nor close supporters of the party, including members or sympathizers of other parties. Pro-LSSP workers who belonged to CTUF unions in the absence of an LSSP-sponsored union in their work-place were instructed to support the new CFTU because at that time the LSSP and the "regular" Communist Party were associated in the United Left Front.[57] Due to the political isolation of the "left" Communists, it is likely that sympathizers of other parties also followed this course. Keuneman noted that "many non-Party workers joined actively in the struggle against the splitters."[58]

A third factor frequently cited is that the principal loyalty of the rank-and-file union members was to the veteran party leaders such as Keuneman and Dr. S. A. Wickremasinghe, who remained at the head of the "regular" party, rather than to the activists and officeholders of their own labor organizations. Although the evidence is not conclusive, this explanation implies a highly significant characteristic of the attitudes and loyalties of trade union members. The long-standing close connection between the party and the federation may have obscured the distinction for many workers. While neither Keuneman nor Wickremasinghe has been actively engaged in day-to-day trade union affairs for many years and immediately prior to the split did not formally head the federation, both had held posts in the federation in the past and have been continually involved in May Day and other labor rallies and demonstrations and major strikes. They may have been more familiar and prestigious figures to many workers than the federation functionaries. The significance of party identification and loyalty is implied in Keuneman's description of the campaign for the federation's membership to a party congress in 1964:

> When we went from factory to factory, work place to work place, explaining the issues to the workers, they rallied to the support of their Party.
>
> The workers of one work-place after another passed resolutions condemning the splitters and proclaiming their support of the Party.[59]

The party schism, thus, cost the "regular" Communists the labor federation which they had cultivated for more than two decades, although

---

[57]Author's interview with LSSP secretary Leslie Goonewardene, August 3, 1965. Sanmugathasan also has referred to LSSP assistance given his opponents. Sanmugathasan, *17th Congress Session of the CTUF*, p. 4.

[58]Keuneman, *Under the Banner of Unity*, p. 46.

[59]*Ibid.* M. G. Mendis attributed the success of the CFTU to the "political consciousness" of the union members. Author's interview, August 15, 1967.

they were subsequently able to salvage a considerable portion of the federation's membership. The Communists' experience illustrates the threat to the party's control of its trade unions posed by the defection of party members who head the unions, particularly when they have been long associated with the party's labor activities and have built up a following among the lower-level officers and activists. However, the episode also suggests the multiplicity and strength of links between the party and its labor following, including, presumably, relatively widespread rank-and-file identification with the party and loyalty to the party's leaders, even in opposition to the leaders of the labor organization.

VI

PROFILES OF PARTY-ORIENTED
TRADE UNIONS

Many trade unions are consistently aligned with a political party on political questions and regularly associated with the strikes, demonstrations, and rallies staged by the party despite the absence of an acknowledged commitment to the party or organizational links with the party's federation. While accepting party guidance on political issues and action, these unions ordinarily function without reference to the party in their immediate day-to-day trade union tasks. Most are relatively strong organizations which presumably do not require the close support and assistance customarily provided to party-sponsored unions. They were not formed by the initiative of the party, but came under party influence through the assumption of leadership by the party's members or supporters.

The leaders of party-oriented unions are invariably party activists or devoted sympathizers, who are able to secure union support for most party positions and activities by their hold on union offices and influence with the membership. The partisan alignment of some unions seems determined by the political loyalties of a single leader or a few top officers. In other organizations, the political sympathies of the leaders are shared more broadly, possibly by a significant segment of the membership. The leaders are usually able to mobilize considerable, if not unanimous, rank-and-file support for actions proposed by the party. Thus, the overt political behavior of the party-oriented unions may not differ substantially from that of unions under more direct and avowed party control. The party-oriented union, in fact, may be more enthusiastically partisan because it often has a more politically conscious and articulate membership. The relationship between party and union, however, is typically less intimate, and the party cannot always depend on automatic acquiescence in the course of action it proposes.

A delicate balance often seems to exist between the leaders' political loyalties and their concern for the organizational strength and cohesion of the union. Many party-oriented unions are composed of white-collar or other relatively educated, sophisticated, and politically articulate members who are likely to possess strong partisan sentiments, but also are less prone than uneducated, unskilled laborers to accept without question or objection the political alignment determined by the leadership. The officers of a number of the party-oriented unions are drawn from the membership of the union and, lacking the deference or the claim to superior skills or knowledge enjoyed by "outsiders" leading unskilled workers' organizations, they occasionally face serious competition for control of the union. The membership and perhaps some elements of the leadership frequently include supporters of several different parties. While the leaders generally have some latitude in determining the political orientation and actions of the union, many must be concerned with retaining the support of the unions' executive committee and, ultimately, of the general membership, and apparently fear that too overt or close a partisan alignment would create dissension which might weaken the union or jeopardize their control.

Conspicuous among the party-oriented unions are organizations of public servants. The restrictions which prohibit public servants' unions from having political objectives or links with political organizations and which limit officers to members of the public service[1] have not prevented some unions from developing very close, if unavowed, ties with parties. It is widely known, for example, that the Ratmalana Railway Workers' Union was formed by the Samasamajists in 1937 and has remained staunchly aligned with the LSSP for more than thirty years. Nonetheless, the legal restrictions make close party-union relations difficult and, although some public servants are covert party members, the prohibition on "outsiders" as officers of public servants' unions restricts one of the principal avenues by which party influence is transmitted to labor organizations. Also, privileges granted public servants' unions, particularly the check-off of union dues and the release of officers for fulltime trade union work, probably enhance the organizational self-sufficiency of the unions, thus reducing the need for party assistance. Public servants, however, tend to display a high degree of political awareness and concern, which undoubtedly has contributed to the tendency of public servants' unions to develop informal associations with or leanings toward political parties.

The unions classified as party-oriented vary considerably in composition and characteristics, and in the intimacy and durability of their partisan alignments. A series of brief profiles of four party-oriented organizations

[1]Under the Trade Unions (Amendment) Act, No. 15 of 1948, public servants' trade unions may not include as officers or members persons who are not public servants, have political objectives, or participate in political strikes. Furthermore, rules 246 and 247 of the public service regulations prohibit a public servant from belonging to "any political association" or any trade union which permits membership by non-public servants, and restrict public servants to membership in associations "which do not have political objects and which are not associated directly or indirectly with any political party or organization." *The Ceylon Government Manual of Procedure* (4th ed.; Colombo: Government Press, 1957, with correction slips through no. 26, dated April 19, 1967), pp. 43–44.

follows. Two of the organizations are composed of white-collar government employees, a third primarily of clerks in the private sector, and the fourth is a large federation composed of members of the lower grades of the public service. The range of partisan links displayed by the four organizations suggest the diversity of political circumstances existing among the party-oriented unions.

1. Government Clerical Service Union

The Government Clerical Service Union is among the oldest and most prominent public servants' unions in Ceylon. With 12,595 members in 1969,[2] the union included about two-thirds of the members of the General Clerical Service. The GCSU represents the articulate, politically conscious, and at times volatile government clerks, and there is possibly no more aggressive and combative union in Ceylon. The GCSU was a leading participant in the general strike of 1947, during which police fired on demonstrators and killed a GCSU member, creating one of the best known martyrs of the Ceylonese labor movement. Every year for more than two decades, the union, in cooperation with other labor organizations, has observed Kandasamy Commemoration Day in honor of the clerk killed in the strike. The union undertook and won a spirited battle with the Government in 1962, when the Cabinet decided to requisition for public use a headquarters building the union was constructing. The GCSU responded with a vigorous campaign, including the staging of a public protest rally and lobbying with members of Parliament, both in the Government and the opposition.[3] A considerable portion of the labor movement and virtually the entire political opposition quickly lined up in support of the GCSU. Government M.P.'s began to announce their opposition to the move and eventually the Government parliamentary group voted unanimously to recommend reversal of the decision.[4] A month after the battle began, the Cabinet reversed its earlier decision to take over the building and extended a loan to the GCSU for its completion.[5]

For at least a decade most officers of the GCSU have been known to be sympathetic toward the Lanka Sama Samaja Party, and the union has been an enthusiastic participant in the general strikes, demonstrations, and campaigns initiated by the LSSP. The GCSU joined the LSSP-led political strike of 1959 protesting amendment of the Public Security Act

[2]Government Clerical Service Union, *48th Annual and Finance Reports, 1968–1969* (Colombo: Government Clerical Service Union, 1969), p. 37.

[3]Author's interview with GCSU president I. J. Wickrema, June 28, 1967.

[4]See Ceylon, House of Representatives, *Parliamentary Debates (Hansard)*, vol. 46, col. 5620 (May 23, 1963); *Ceylon Observer*, May 24, 1962, and June 6, 1962; and *Ceylon Daily News*, June 1, 1962, and June 6, 1962.

[5]I. J. Wickrema, "A Great Leap Forward," *Ceylon Daily News*, April 2, 1966, p. 13.

and a general strike in January, 1961, in support of striking port workers. It also participated in a half-day strike and demonstration in December, 1964, called to protest the parliamentary defeat of the SLFP-LSSP coalition Government, and in a coalition-sponsored political strike in January, 1966, attacking proposed official language regulations. The GCSU's 1965 annual report remarked of the LSSP entry into the Government in 1964: "The formation of the Coalition Government was hailed by major sections of the working people as a progressive step. They saw some of their leaders sharing governmental power for the first time"[6] The GCSU was a founder of the Joint Committee of Trade Union Organisations formed in 1963, and after the split in the original grouping joined in the JCTUO reconstituted in 1965 to include the labor organizations closely aligned with the SLFP-LSSP-Communist coalition.

The union's LSSP orientation was emphasized and publicized by a 1965 leadership struggle which resulted in victory for the pro-LSSP candidates for the major offices. In the election for president of the union, the pro-LSSP candidate, I. J. Wickrema, received 461 delegates' votes to 204 obtained by his principal opponent, who was thought to be in sympathy with the Lanka Sama Samaja Party (Revolutionary), which had split from the LSSP the preceding year.[7] Persons believed to be LSSP sympathizers also won most of the other union offices. The same leadership was returned to office in each of the four succeeding years, despite challenges from dissidents. The 1965 GCSU election did not, however, mark a major change in the union's leadership or political orientation. The former president, who had held the post since 1958, had resigned shortly before the annual conference to take a position abroad, and the new president and general secretary had both served earlier as officers and central executive committee members.

Although support for the LSSP has appeared to be considerable not only among the leaders but also among the rank and file, factions sympathetic toward other parties have existed within the union membership. Since the 1964 split in the LSSP, a pro-LSSP(R) faction has commonly been identified. In addition, the GCSU for many years has contained a pro-Communist faction. The 1968 election of union officers produced a clear contest between two slates of candidates. The pro-LSSP incumbents were challenged by a slate considered pro-Communist, which included candidates for every post on the central executive committee.[8] The

[6]Government Clerical Service Union, *44th Annual Report (Part I), 1964–65* (Colombo: Government Clerical Service Union, 1965), p. 3.

[7]The results of the election are reported in *Ceylon Daily News,* May 31, 1965, p. 1. On the election's partisan implications, see *ibid.,* May 28, 1965, p. 1, and May 29, 1965, p. 1.

[8]For an analysis of the 1968 leadership contest, together with a plea that the pro-Communist members "stop their splitting and cooperate with the other progressives," by a former GCSU general secretary, see K. Vaikunthavasan, "Coalition Splinters within the GCSU," *Ceylon Daily News,* June 2, 1968, p. 11.

contest occurred although the Samasamajists and the regular Communists were allied in the opposition coalition and party leaders were attempting to discourage clashes between their supporters in the trade unions. The pro-LSSP slate won every post by a majority of about 200 of the 700 delegates' votes.[9]

The union's involvement in politics is considered virtually inevitable by the organization's leadership. Wickrema has contended that GCSU members, and other public servants, are particularly conscious of politics and inevitably concerned with political matters because their daily conditions of work are affected by political decisions. As they observe changes of Governments, they feel the effects of different policies directly and consequently they develop partisan preferences. For example, Wickrema felt the GCSU members could have profited considerably by the continuation of the SLFP-LSSP coalition Government because it was sympathetic to the aspirations and receptive to the demands of the union. In contrast, the post-1965 National Government had shown indifference to public servants' grievances and had engaged in extensive "victimization" of union officers and activists. The GCSU's orientation toward the LSSP, Wickrema argued, resulted from the fact that the party has a large labor following and is deeply concerned with trade union questions. Furthermore, it is not encumbered by international ties and directives from abroad, as is the Communist Party. GCSU members tend to possess a strong trade union *elan* and consequently find their attitudes in agreement with the policies of the LSSP.[10]

Nonetheless, GCSU leaders seek to avoid too close or conspicuous an alignment of the union with a single political party. The GCSU seeks universality of membership within the General Clerical Service, and a political test for membership is rejected as conflicting with the aspiration for universality. It is claimed that, because supporters of a number of political parties are found among the members, an avowed partisan commitment would jeopardize the solidarity of the union.[11] GCSU spokesmen often distinguish between organizational activities and the actions of union members as individuals. Participation in May Day rallies, which are invariably arranged along partisan lines, has been explained as the acts of the individuals rather than of the GCSU as an organization. GCSU participation in strikes and demonstrations with strong political overtones has been described as intended to defend trade union rights or protect occupational interests of the membership, rather than as an expression of political sentiments.

While the 1965 GCSU conference did not mark a change in the partisan

[9]*Ceylon Daily News,* June 4, 1968, p. 1.
[10]Author's interview with I. J. Wickrema, June 28, 1967.
[11]Author's interview with GCSU general secretary K. M. Karunarathna, August 4, 1965.

orientation of the union, it highlighted the political discord within the union and perhaps indicated a trend toward stronger partisan alignment. The apparently heightened dissension and partisanship seem largely produced by political circumstances outside the union. The conference followed by only two months the parliamentary election of March, 1965, in which the governing SLFP-LSSP coalition was defeated by the supposedly anti-labor UNP and its allies. The hard-fought election inflamed partisan sentiments throughout the society, and the coalition defeat was a bitter disappointment for many trade unionists. The coalition defeat not only sharpened the longstanding antagonisms between the UNP and the parties forming the coalition, but engendered considerable bitterness against the LSSP(R) on the part of sympathizers of the LSSP and other coalition parties. The two M.P.'s belonging to the LSSP(R) had voted against the coalition Government in a critical parliamentary test in December, 1964, which resulted in the defeat of the Government by one vote and led to the premature dissolution of Parliament and an election at a time many coalitionists thought disadvantageous to the coalition. The 1965 conference of the GCSU was the first held since the LSSP split in June of the preceding year and reflected the conflicts involved in the party schism.

The fight over the "twenty-one demands" in the latter half of 1964 had tended to polarize the GCSU leadership into pro-coalition and anti-coalition camps. The GCSU originally was a vigorous champion of the twenty-one demands and even after the formation of the SLFP-LSSP Government, which produced a plea for postponement of the demands by the LSSP, the GCSU continued to press for immediate presentation of the demands to the Government and to private employers. In October, 1964, the issue came directly before the central executive committee, and by a ten-to-eight vote the committee reaffirmed its support for the immediate presentation of the demands, the position strongly advocated by the LSSP(R). Less than two weeks later, a special meeting of the committee reconsidered the question and voted twelve-to-ten to reverse its earlier decision.[12] The reversal on the twenty-one demands was the principal issue in the 1965 leadership contest and remained a major source of contention between opposing candidates for union offices for several years. The officers elected in 1965 and subsequently re-elected had opposed presentation of the demands in both votes while their rivals for office had taken the opposite position.

Another political development created further dissension within the union. Following the 1965 election, the SLFP-Marxist coalition concentrated on appeals to the Sinhalese, Buddhist majority and denounced

[12]GCSU, *44th Annual Report*, pp. 8–10. On the fight over the twenty-one demands, see Chapter IX.

Government concessions to the Tamil minority. The GCSU's pro-coalition stand and particularly its participation in the coalition-sponsored political strike on January 8, 1966, protesting regulations providing for the official use of the Tamil language, created communal discord within the union and cost it many of its Tamil members. A Tamil who had been a GCSU officer for a decade left the union with an angry blast at the pro-Marxist leaders for succumbing to communalism and converting the GCSU into "a complete stooge Union to their political masters."[13] Resignations from the union following the 1966 strike were sufficiently serious to be cited by the GCSU treasurer as contributing to the union's financial difficulties in 1967.[14]

The eruption of communal issues in politics created particularly grave problems for the GCSU because it produced a conflict between the union's partisan allegiance and its multi-communal composition and ethos of hostility toward communalism. The union contains a sizable non-Sinhalese membership. In 1967, when some Tamils who had resigned earlier were claimed to be returning to the union, the GCSU was reported to include about 3,500 Tamil members, almost one-third of its membership and more than half the estimated 6,000 Tamil clerks in the General Clerical Service.[15] The GCSU had for years disparaged communal sentiments and appeals, which were held to threaten the solidarity of the union and the labor movement. The union's 1965 annual report condemned "attempts to raise communalism and thereby disrupt the working class and the Trade Union movement," and urged that the GCSU "should show itself as a model organisation where members belonging to various communities, professing different religious beliefs and holding divergent political views, carry on their activities smoothly."[16] The GCSU's two principal rivals for members among the government clerks are the Samastha Lanka Rajaye Lipikaru Sangamaya, which appeals to and consists almost exclusively of Sinhalese clerks, and the Arasanka Eluthuvinargnar Sangam, which seeks explicitly and solely to represent the Tamils in the General Clerical Service. The GCSU leaders have denounced communal-based unions and ardently claimed to desire to attract and hold Tamil as well as Sinhalese members.[17]

---

[13]*Ceylon Daily News*, December 20, 1965, p. 1. Dissension within the GCSU, and other pro-coalition unions, was given much publicity by the coalition's opponents. The UNP weekly newspaper, for example, intimated after the 1965 GCSU conference that the union was on the verge of collapse and claimed that the GCSU's difficulties "should open the eyes of the workers to the perfidy of these Marxist political opportunists masquerading as the champions of the working class." *Siyarata*, June 25, 1965, p. 1.

[14]Government Clerical Service Union, *46th Annual Report and Statement of Accounts, 1966–1967* (Colombo : Government Clerical Service Union, 1967), p. 50.

[15]Author's interview with I. J. Wickrema. Estimates by other informed persons frequently attributed a somewhat smaller Tamil membership to the GCSU but did not differ substantially.

[16]GCSU, *44th Annual Report,* p. 75.

[17]In interviews by the author in 1965 and 1967.

The dilemmas confronting the union with the reappearance of the official language controversy stemmed not only from the partisan association of the union, but also from its changing composition. A decade earlier, the entire membership had been recruited on the basis of competence in the English language. By 1967, however, many government clerks who were educated in Sinhalese had been recruited. The GCSU for years had agitated for the protection of the so-called "old entrants" — public servants recruited before the adoption of Sinhalese as the official language in 1956, who were educated in English and whether Sinhalese or Tamil usually were unable to perform their duties in any language except English.[18] After a decade of recruitment of the Sinhalese-educated, the union felt a responsibility for their interests as well. The leadership may also have considered that within the next decade almost the entire service would presumably be proficient in Sinhalese. A failure to identify with and champion the interests of the Sinhalese-educated clerks might spell the future decline of the organization. According to union officers, the regulations promulgated in January, 1966, compromised the position and prospects of the Sinhalese-educated clerks. A GCSU statement on the official language question in 1967, while attempting to protect the interests of members recruited through examinations in Sinhalese, Tamil, and English, sharply attacked an alleged return to the use of English, which was "motivated by Capitalistic and Imperialistic considerations and bureaucratic tendencies."[19]

The GCSU reacted vigorously and belligerently to Government moves after 1965 which were viewed as threats to the union. Soon after the 1965 election, the GCSU complained of wholesale transfers of GCSU activists,[20] but the volume and intensity of charges against the Government climbed steeply following the January, 1966, political strike. As a result of the strike, 104 union members, including all the major officers, were suspended pending disciplinary proceedings. In addition, a large number of GCSU activists, principally officers of the union's branches, were transferred from one location to another. The union accused the Government of mass "victimization" and a concerted effort to disrupt and weaken the GCSU and other pro-coalition unions.[21] In 1967 a demand that disciplinary action resulting from the strike be withdrawn was coupled with a demand for long-sought salary increases in the clerical grades. The linking of the

[18]E.g., see Government Clerical Service Union, *43rd Annual Report and Statement of Accounts, 1963–1964* (Colombo : Government Clerical Service Union, 1964), pp. 12–14; GCSU, *44th Annual Report,* pp. 38–41.

[19]*Red Tape,* January–February, 1967, p. 7. *Red Tape* is the official organ of the GCSU.

[20]E.g., Government Clerical Service Union, *Onslaught Against Trade Unions?* (leaflet; Colombo, July 23, 1965); *Red Tape,* June, 1965, p. 1.

[21]Author's interview with I. J. Wickrema. GCSU grievances are summarized in a letter from the union's president to the Prime Minister, published as a supplement to *Red Tape,* November, 1966.

popular salary demand with the protest over strike punishments may have been intended to unite the union behind the leadership and strengthen rank-and-file support for the union's position on the controversial 1966 strike. The campaign for the two demands, in which the GCSU was joined by other pro-coalition public servants' organizations, culminated in a twenty-five day strike in late 1968.[22]

2. Public Service Workers' Trade Union Federation

The Public Service Workers' Trade Union Federation has functioned openly and with quasi-official recognition for more than a decade although public servants' unions are prohibited by statute from forming federations. The PSWTUF, in fact, maintains a headquarters adjacent to the old Secretariat building housing many of the major offices of the bureaucracy. The federation grew out of a grouping called the All-Island Conference of Public Service Trade Unions formed in 1954. The conference was converted into the PSWTUF in late 1957 and within a few months had launched a major strike demanding a Rs. 17.50 per month living allowance and relief of a number of public servants' grievances. The strike followed by a decade the general strikes of 1946 and 1947 led by public servants' unions and was claimed to have surpassed the earlier strikes in the number of public servants involved.[23] It rapidly assumed strong political overtones and led to the declaration of a state of emergency.

The PSWTUF is composed of government employees in the lower grades, below the clerical level, called "minor employees" and consisting of office peons, drivers, watchers, laborers, quasi-industrial workers, and other subordinate personnel. Several white-collar unions which originally belonged to the federation withdrew soon after the 1958 strike. The federation in 1967 claimed 95,700 members in ninety-two affiliated unions. Among the largest of the constituent unions are the All-Ceylon Post and Telegraph Workers' Union with about 15,000 members, the 10,000-member Rajaye Podu Sevaka Kamkaru Sangamaya (Government Minor Employees' Union), and the All-Ceylon Railway Engineering Workers' Union with about 8,000 members.[24]

Despite prefunctory disclaimers, the PSWTUF's orientation toward the Communist Party is thinly disguised and widely recognized. The federation is a member of the Communist-led World Federation of Trade Unions, and has consistently taken positions on major issues coinciding with those

[22]*Red Tape*, June, 1968, pp. 1, 7; and July, 1968, pp. 1–2; and GCSU, *48th Annual and Finance Reports*, pp. 15–31. The 1968 public servants' strike is discussed further in Chapter VIII.
[23]Public Service Workers' Trade Union Federation, *Fifth Congress Report—From 1965 to 1967* (Colombo: Public Service Workers' Trade Union Federation, 1967), p. 9.
[24]Author's interviews with PSWTUF president Piyadasa Adipola, July 27 and August 14, 1967.

of the Communist Party and since the 1963 party split of the "regular" party. In the 1958 strike, the federation was joined by the CTUF and supported by the Communist Party. The federation did not, however, take part in the political strike called by the LSSP, but opposed by the Communist Party, the following year. Consistent with the attitude of the Communist Party, the PSWTUF was critical of certain features of the 1960–1964 SLFP Government, but claimed that in its "progressive" policies, "our Federation supported the Government in every possible way."[25] In the 1965 election, which found the Communist Party allied with the SLFP-LSSP coalition in opposition to the UNP, the federation's central executive committee adopted a resolution urging support for the "anti-imperialist and progressive camp." The federation subsequently claimed "all Unions affiliated to our Federation acted accordingly."[26] The PSWTUF supported the coalition parties in political strikes called in December, 1964, to protest the defeat of the coalition Government in Parliament, and in January, 1966, in opposition to the introduction of official language regulations by the UNP-dominated Government then in power. The federation has been a member of the pro-coalition Joint Committee of Trade Union Organisations since 1965, and participated in a major coalition-supported strike of public servants in late 1968.

The PSWTUF was openly hostile to the post-1965 Government formed by the UNP and its allies. As the federation's fifth congress report stated :

> With the defeat of the coalition government at the March 1965 General Election reaction reared its head again. The UNP with the Federal Party and five other reactionary parties formed the present government. With the formation of the government the workers of this country were faced with an era of misfortune.[27]

PSWTUF president Piyadasa Adipola has contended, however, that the federation has opposed and fought all Governments in the interests of its membership. Public servants have accumulated many grievances in the past decade during which their wages have lagged behind a steadily rising cost of living. The federation fought aggressively for workers' demands against the S. W. R. D. and Sirimavo Bandaranaike Governments in power between 1956 and 1965, won many concessions, and suffered no "victimization" as a result of its strikes. During the 1965 election campaign, the UNP had promised to preserve trade union rights and refrain from acting against political opponents. However, Adipola argued, after the 1965 election the Government attempted to crush the labor movement by

[25]PSWTUF, *Fifth Congress Report*, p. 12.

[26]*Ibid.*, p. 17. As a minor indication of the political links of the PSWTUF, it could be noted that the federation's latest report was printed at the Communist Party's Lanka Press, located at the party headquarters at 91, Cotta Road, Colombo.

[27]*Ibid.*

massive "victimization" of public servants, first for political activity during the election and later for participation in the January 8, 1966, strike. About 600 members of the federation's unions were suspended following the 1966 strike. Government actions, Adipola claimed, had pushed labor organizations into politics by repressive moves against the trade unions.[28]

Although the orientation of the PSWTUF toward the Communist Party has been clear, it has not been as complete and unquestioned as the alignment of the CFTU. Communist Party members[29] have always been active in the federation. The first president of the federation, J. A. K. Perera, resigned from the public service in 1960 to contest a parliamentary seat as a Communist candidate. He later became an officer of the Communists' CTUF and since the 1963 split has been a vice president of the CFTU. Other federation activists and officers of affiliated unions, however, have been neither Communist Party members nor sympathizers. The GCSU was a prominent affiliate in the early days of the federation, and its withdrawal in 1958 may have reflected partisan tensions between the growing Communist influence in the federation and the pro-LSSP orientation of the GCSU.

Varying political currents within the federation produced a clash within the leadership in 1964 and resulted in the resignation of the federation's general secretary, Wilfred Perera, and the withdrawal from the federation of the Union of Post and Telecommunication Officers, which he heads. The dispute erupted over the issue of the "twenty-one demands" formulated earlier in the year by the Joint Committee of Trade Union Organisations, to which the PSWTUF belonged. After the SLFP-LSSP coalition Government was formed, the coalition asked that agitation for the demands be suspended. The request for restraint was opposed by the pro-Peking Communists and the Trotskyists of the LSSP(R), as well as other trade unionists. The "regular" Communist Party took an intermediate position, asking a carefully qualified presentation of the demands. The PSWTUF along with the CFTU and Sri Lanka Jathika Guru Sangamaya were the only labor groups adhering to the Communist position. However, as noted in the subsequent PSWTUF report, "some confusion was created among certain unions of the Federation." The central executive committee supported the position of the president, Adipola, against the general secretary's argument that the demands should be presented without qualification.[30] Perera later claimed that the federation's president

[28]Author's interview, July 27, 1967.
[29]As public servants they may not be avowed members of a political party, but little effort is made to hide the fact that some PSWTUF officers, as well as officers of other public servants' organizations, are covert party members. One high PSWTUF officer is reliably reported to be a member of the Communist Party central committee.
[30]PSWTUF, *Fifth Congress Report*, pp. 15-16.

told him he had been directed by the Communist Party central committee to back the position taken by the party on the issue.[31]

Following the fight over the twenty-one demands and the withdrawal of Wilfred Perera and his union, the PSWTUF has probably moved into closer alignment with the Communist Party. Nonetheless, the numerous heterogeneous unions within the federation undoubtedly contain both elements of support for other parties and a sizable body of members who are indifferent to the Communist Party, as is claimed by the federation's president.[32] The diversity of partisan sympathies among the members and activists of the federation appears to be the chief obstacle to more pronounced and open links between the party and the federation, perhaps reinforced by the restrictions on public servants' political activity or membership in organizations affiliated with political parties. The general secretary of the Communist Party, while readily conceding that the federation contained a number of Communist supporters among its activists, described the party's relations with the PSWTUF as considerably less close and direct than its ties with the CFTU, and probably not as close as the LSSP's links with the other large federation of public servants' unions, the Government Workers' Trade Union Federation.[33]

3. Sri Lanka Jathika Guru Sangamaya

The largest individual union of public employees in Ceylon is the Sri Lanka Jathika Guru Sangamaya (Ceylon National Teachers' Union), which in 1967 claimed 44,000 members.[34] The union was formed in 1960 by a merger of two unions representing teachers in the government schools and the private schools. The merger coincided with the government's takeover of the "assisted" schools which were privately owned and operated, mostly by religious bodies, but largely supported by public funds. The membership is almost entirely composed of teachers in Sinhalese-language schools and has been described as "98-percent Sinhalese." Teachers in the Tamil-language schools are organized in a separate union, but cooperation between the two is common. A number of very small unions of teachers also exist.

The SLJGS abruptly became enmeshed in acute political controversy during and after the 1965 election campaign. Accusations were made that large numbers of SLJGS members played an active role in the campaign, although teachers in government schools, like other government

---

[31]Author's interview with Wilfred Perera, July 1, 1967.
[32]Author's interviews with Piyadasa Adipola.
[33]Author's interview with Pieter Keuneman, August 3, 1967.
[34]Unless otherwise indicated, information in the following two paragraphs is based on several interviews by the author with SLJGS general secretary L. Ariyawanse between June and September, 1967.

employees, are prohibited from participation in politics. Shortly after the election, 239 union members were suspended from their jobs for political activity, about 140 of whom were later dismissed by the Education Department. In addition, a large number of teachers were transferred to different assignments, according to the union, as punishment for political activity. By August, 1966, about 3,000 members of the union were claimed to have suffered "victimization" on political grounds.[35] Of thirty-one members of the union's working committee, all but three had been dismissed or transferred by 1967. Among those dismissed were the general secretary and president of the union. Virtually all teachers against whom action was taken were charged with aiding the coalition parties against the UNP and its allies.[36] In addition to the action against its members, the SLJGS charged the government with attempting to undermine the union by bringing pressure on members to cancel authorization for the deduction of union dues from their pay and unreasonable delay in forwarding to the union the dues collected.[37] The union attempted to rally public opinion behind the demand for political rights for teachers and removal of punishments for political activity through agitation in the countryside.[38]

The disciplinary action against teachers was made a major issue by the opposition coalition and was condemned by most trade unionists, including a number who did not support the coalition politically. A mass rally staged by trade unions associated with the coalition in June, 1965, to protest the measures against the teachers was among the first major anti-Government demonstrations after the 1965 election. A motion of no confidence was moved in Parliament against the Minister of Education by the coalition parties on the issue. Mrs. Bandaranaike, in a speech at an SLFP conference two years later, promised that on the coalition's return to power the dismissed teachers would be restored to their positions with compensation.[39]

Teachers were conceded by SLJGS leaders to have actively participated in the 1965 election campaign.[40] Although most worked on the side of the coalition parties, it is claimed that some teachers openly supported every

[35]Sri Lanka Jathika Guru Sangamaya, *1965–66 Varshaya Sambandayen Idiripath Karanalada Pradhana Lēkam Mahathāgē Avurudu Vārthāva* [Annual Report of the General Secretary Presented for the Year 1965–66] (Colombo : Sri Lanka Jathika Guru Sangamaya, 1966), p. 1.

[36]Soon after the action was commenced, the Education Department announced that of eighty-seven suspended teachers, one had allegedly worked for the UNP. *Ceylon Observer,* July 23, 1965, p. 1. The Minister of Education claimed that 40,000 teachers had taken part in the campaign and that disciplinary action was taken only against those who most flagrantly defied the prohibition against political activity. *Sunday Times of Ceylon,* June 27, 1965, p. 1.

[37]SLJGS, *1965–66 Varshaya ... Avurudu Vārthāva,* pp. 13–14.

[38]"Sri Lankā Jāthika Guru Sangamayē Pasvāni Avurudu Maha Sabhāva Vetha Idiripath Kerena Lēkam Mahathāgē Vārthāvayi [General Secretary's Report Presented at the Sri Lanka Jathika Guru Sangamaya's Fifth Annual Conference]" (mimeographed; Colombo, August 3, 1967), pp. 1–2.

[39]*Ceylon Observer,* July 20, 1967, p. 10.

[40]The following is based on the author's interviews with L. Ariyawanse.

party but that disciplinary action was taken almost exclusively against those who aided the coalition parties. The political activity of teachers was explained as resulting from the belief that, although technically prohibited, no Government would attempt to block their participation. Teachers in the private, "assisted" schools had had unrestricted political rights and had been very active in politics prior to 1960. At the time of the government's takeover of the "assisted" schools, the argument was made that many thousands of teachers would abruptly be deprived of the political rights they had previously enjoyed. The Government of Sirimavo Bandaranaike reportedly responded by indicating that no measures would be taken to curb political activity by teachers even though they had been transformed into public employees, and between 1960 and 1965 the teachers in government schools had in practice been allowed political rights. Further, it was asserted that the Minister of Education in the coalition Government encouraged teachers to work in support of the coalition during the 1965 campaign, with the implied threat of reprisals if they did not do so. Consequently, teachers believed they were participating in the campaign with the knowledge and support of the Government then in power. The massive and severe action taken by the Government formed after the election came as a surprise to the SLJGS leaders, since the UNP had promised during the campaign not to engage in retaliation against its opponents if it returned to power.

The unions which eventually formed the SLJGS were reportedly always politically oriented, recognizing that for the most part their goals could only be obtained in the political field. According to the SLJGS general secretary, the union has "always argued that it is a political fight; we can't win our demands otherwise." The "victimization" after 1965, he contended, has further politicized the union by dramatizing the necessity to defeat the National Government in order to win back the position it previously enjoyed and recover from the repression it had suffered.[41]

Admittedly politically inclined and driven by the developments of 1965 into ardent hostility toward the Government then in power, the SLJGS nonetheless is claimed by its leadership to lack ties with any political party. Observers outside the union, however, contend that it has long been identified with the Communist Party and since the Communist split has been oriented toward the "regular" party. The Communist Party newspaper seemed to support this contention in asserting of the SLJGS: "All progressives are well aware of the role played by the Communists in the formation of this union and the struggles conducted by it."[42] The SLJGS was the only union belonging to the Joint Committee of Trade Union Organisations other than the Communists' CFTU and the strongly

[41]Author's interview with L. Ariyawanse, July 19, 1967.
[42]"The C.P. in the Struggle for Teachers' Rights," *Forward* (Colombo), July 2, 1965, p. 8.

Communist-oriented PSWTUF to support the party's position in the 1964 fight over the "twenty-one demands."[43] The union is one of eleven labor organizations comprising the pro-coalition JCTUO formed after the fight over the twenty-one demands had split the earlier, more inclusive Joint Committee in 1964. A former union activist, B. Y. Tudawe, was elected to Parliament in 1965 as a Communist Party candidate. Although the union did not strike on January 8, 1966, over the official language regulations, its members participated in the coalition-sponsored demonstration.[44] The 1966 general secretary's report suggested that the union members had incurred the wrath of the Government not simply because they participated in politics, but because they worked politically for the benefit of the disadvantaged in opposition to the privileged classes.[45]

4. Ceylon Mercantile Union

The Ceylon Mercantile Union is unquestionably among the most powerful labor organizations in Ceylon, and is generally conceded to be the most successful Ceylonese union in performing the conventional "economic" functions of trade unions through collective bargaining on issues of wages and employment conditions.[46] Founded in 1928 by A. E. Goonesinghe, the CMU is one of the oldest Ceylonese unions still in existence. Its size and influence remained very small, however, until the growth of labor militancy at the conclusion of the Second World War. In 1948, the old leadership was overthrown and Bala Tampoe became CMU general secretary, a post he has retained to the present time. In the 1950's, the strength of the union began to grow, and during the past decade its membership has been increasing at an astonishing rate, undoubtedly as a result of the prestige the union has acquired in a long series of victories in industrial disputes. CMU membership, which stood at 5,256 in 1955, had climbed to 16,867 by 1965 and in 1969 reached 33,031.[47]

For most of its history, the CMU was a white-collar union composed of clerical employees of privately owned commercial firms, principally located in Colombo. A large proportion of its members were employed by firms belonging to the Employers' Federation of Ceylon, probably the most active and influential association representing business interests on the

[43] *The C.F.T.U. and the Working Class Movement* (Colombo: Ceylon Federation of Trade Unions, 1966), p. 36.

[44] Author's interviews with L. Ariyawanse.

[45] SLJGS, *1965–66 Varshaya ... Avurudu Vārthāva*, p. 5.

[46] The CMU, for example, was cited as one of the unions in the developing countries which ably and successfully functions in the manner associated with trade unionism in the more industrialized Western countries by Everett M. Kassalow, "Trade Unionism and the Development Process in the New Nations: A Comparative View," in Solomon Barkin *et al* (eds.), *International Labor* (New York: Harper & Row, 1967), p. 77.

[47] Information supplied by the CMU headquarters.

island. With the establishment of state-owned public corporations during
the past decade, the CMU commenced to organize clerks in the public
corporations as well as in the private firms. In the last few years the composition of the CMU has begun to undergo another change. Its membership
has expanded to include manual workers in firms in which the CMU
previously represented the clerks. This is particularly significant in the
ports of Colombo and Trincomalee, where the union originally obtained
a foothold by organizing tally clerks and other white-collar employees,
but has begun also to represent large numbers of stevedores and other
dock workers. In 1966, the CMU organized branches for stevedore and
wharf labor in the Colombo port and by the following year the union
reported nearly 5,000 workers were organized into eleven CMU branches
in the Port (Cargo) Corporation, which became the largest single employer
of CMU members.[48] The CMU in 1969 included about 12,000 members
in Employers' Federation firms, more than 6,000 in the Port (Cargo)
Corporation and nearly 5,500 in other public corporations, 5,000 in
private industrial establishments, and 4,000 in miscellaneous privately
owned shops and small business.[49] The CMU thus has been rapidly
changing in character from a union exclusively composed of white-collar
office employees of private commercial firms to a mass organization
encompassing all grades and levels of employees of commercial firms and
reaching out into publicly owned industrial, transport, and service
enterprises.[50]

The CMU has carried on and won a number of hard-fought struggles
with private employers and government corporations in recent years.
A 1961 collective agreement between the Employers' Federation and the
CMU was the first major collective agreement and the most comprehensive
ever negotiated in Ceylon. A renewal of the agreement in 1967, which
followed nearly two years of hard negotiating and a strike and port
boycott against federation firms, provided for the checkoff of union dues
for the first time in the private sector, in addition to conceding wage and
other demands of the union. A notable CMU victory occurred in a port
strike extending from November, 1963. to January, 1964. For several
years previously, during a number of strikes in public corporations, the
SLFP Government had maintained the position that it would not negotiate

[48]Ceylon Mercantile Union, "Ninth Annual Delegates Conference, 16th and 17th April
1967 : General Secretary's Report" (mimeographed; Colombo, April 14, 1967), pp. 8, 28.
Employees of public corporations are not considered members of the public service and,
hence, are not subject to the restriction which prohibits public servants from joining unions
containing members from outside the public service.

[49]*CMU Bulletin*, July, 1969, p. 2.

[50]The union's constitution indicates that membership is open to "any person" employed
by "Mercantile, Commercial, Industrial and other non Government establishments in
Ceylon." Ceylon Mercantile Union, *The Constitution* (Colombo : Ceylon Mercantile Union,
n.d.), pp. 1–2.

while a strike was in progress. The CMU port strike continued for seventy days and eventually led to an all-union sympathy strike. Finally, the Government retreated from its stand and agreed to negotiate without insisting that the strike first be terminated.[51] A forty-two day port strike by the CMU, supported by a month-long strike of the entire union membership, in 1968 threatened to become a major test of wills between the union and the Port (Cargo) Corporation but finally ended in a compromise settlement.[52]

The CMU's political position is one of some complexity. The leadership disclaims any partisan alignment for the union and the members are conceded by both CMU officials and outside observers to be divided in their political allegiances. The interest and attention of the members and leaders seem focused on winning immediate job-related gains through collective bargaining, to the neglect of political battles and causes. Nonetheless, the CMU has played a prominent role in politics and maintained discernible partisan leanings for two decades. A loose and informal association linked the CMU with the LSSP for many years. More recently a connection has existed between the union and the LSSP(R).

As is usual with party-oriented unions, the CMU's partisan leanings have been primarily the product of the political sympathies of its leadership. For two decades, Bala Tampoe has been general secretary and unchallenged head of the organization. While leading the CMU and building a reputation as probably the most able trade unionist on the island, Tampoe has been a prominent political activist. Until the 1964 LSSP split, he was a leading Samasamajist and member of the party's polibureau. He left the LSSP with the orthodox Trotskyists who founded the LSSP(R) in 1964 and a year later became the secretary of that small party. He contested parliamentary seats in 1956 and 1960 as an LSSP candidate and in 1965 as a candidate of the LSSP (R). An irrepressible political orator, he has been a frequent speaker at party meetings and rallies.

Although the association between the CMU and the LSSP was more ambiguous and uncertain than that linking the party with the CFL or even the more obviously LSSP-oriented unions, a marked degree of harmony existed between the CMU and the LSSP. CMU members regularly participated in LSSP rallies and demonstrations, including May Day rallies (always a test of partisan sympathies). A number of CMU activists were members of the LSSP, and probably many CMU members were LSSP sympathizers. The CMU joined in the 1959 political strike protesting amendment of the Public Security Act, which was sponso-

[51]See Ceylon Mercantile Union, "Annual Delegates' Conference, 1st November, 1964: General Secretary's Report" (mimeographed; Colombo, November 1, 1964), pp. 1-2; Ceylon, House of Representatives, *Parliamentary Debates (Hansard)*, vol. 55, cols. 975 978 (January 7, 1964).

[52]*Ceylon Daily News*, March 29, 1968, p. 1, and April 30, 1968, p. 1.

red by the LSSP and opposed by other parties active in the labor movement. The union also took part in the January, 1962, general strike which included the labor following of all the Marxist parties.[53] The CMU was an enthusiastic member of the generally pro-Marxist Joint Committee of Trade Union Organisations until the grouping broke up in 1964.

LSSP leaders, reflecting on the relationship between the party and the union prior to 1964, recognized that they did not "control" the CMU, but felt the party was "influential" with the union. The union contributed support to party rallies and provided some party activists and members. In the few dramatic moments when trade union strength was mobilized for relatively direct political purposes, the Samasamajists believed they could count on CMU backing. At the least, they could be confident that their political opponents would not have CMU support for action opposed by the LSSP. The loss of Tampoe by the party was considered a loss of influence in the CMU and, consequently, a weakening of party influence in the labor movement.[54]

Since Tampoe left the LSSP, the CMU has repeatedly taken positions in opposition to those of the LSSP. In the fight over the "twenty-one demands" immediately after the party schism, the CMU adhered to the LSSP(R) position of insisting on the immediate presentation of the demands, despite LSSP pleas for postponement. Since the 1965 election, the CMU has remained aloof from the labor groupings assembled both by the coalition and by the parties supporting the National Government. Although it had participated in the 1959 and 1962 strikes, the CMU refused to join the coalition-sponsored political strike in January, 1966, and boycotted a massive trade union meeting in August, 1967, called by the pro-coalition labor organizations to consider a general strike. In 1968, the CMU and the LSSP clashed bitterly over a labor dispute in the port of Trincomalee.[55]

Influence with the CMU, earlier considered by politicians to be an important asset of the LSSP, since 1964 has been regarded as the principal—almost the only—strength of the LSSP(R). Reversing the usual party-union relationship, the CMU seems to have bolstered and lent prestige to the small and weak LSSP(R). The party conducts its publishing and

[53]The 1959 strike was described by Tampoe as the only political strike in which the CMU had ever participated, and even it was claimed to have had implications for trade unionism because of provisions for the use of emergency powers to end strikes in the proposed legislation. The 1962 general strike was described as a defense of trade unionism, as it was called to protest the use of military personnel to operate the Colombo harbor during a port workers' strike. Author's interview, June 25, 1967.

[54]Based on the author's interviews with Samasamajist leaders between 1965 and 1969. Their assessments of CMU–LSSP relations did not differ substantially from those of LSSP(R) activists with whom the author discussed the question.

[55]The clashes between the CMU and the LSSP after 1964 are discussed further in Chapter IX.

other activities in a room which shares one floor of an office building with the CMU headquarters and appears to be administratively dependent on the union. The relationship between the CMU and the party became a major issue in an LSSP(R) schism in 1968. A small band of dissidents led by Edmund Samarakkody, long considered to be the most doctrinaire and orthodox of the Trotskyists, broke with the LSSP(R) and formed a Revolutionary Samasamaja Party with an angry blast at Tampoe and the CMU. A statement issued by the dissidents claimed the party was being converted into "an appendage of the CMU" and charged that at a party conference a few days earlier Tampoe had "mobilised the members of the Ceylon Mercantile Union in the party some of whom were paid officials or employees of the CMU, to back his leadership of the party at the conference." While denouncing the influence of the CMU in the party, the dissidents also attacked Tampoe for refusing to take trade union action on a series of issues which would have pitted the union against the Dudley Senanayake Government.[56]

Tampoe's ability to swing the CMU abruptly from co-operation to conflict with the LSSP with little evident internal dissent probably was aided by circumstances within the union and concurrent political developments. The connection between the CMU and the party was never extremely close and existed largely at the top. The CMU is generally believed to have always contained a large body of members who were not in sympathy with Marxism but accepted Tampoe's leadership, including occasional cooperation with the LSSP, because of the effective leadership he provided and the occupational gains he was able to secure. Tampoe's considerable prestige as a trade unionist and longstanding control of the CMU make unlikely a serious challenge to his position, and the CMU's stress on non-political occupational issues may make the loose political orientation of the union of slight significance to the rank and file. Nonetheless, especially since 1964, Tampoe has emphasized that many different political persuasions exist within the union's membership and has claimed that avoidance of internal partisan conflict is essential to the organization's strength and cohesion.[57] He has conceded that the CMU general council contains supporters of several political parties, but has argued that political disputes have not disrupted the union because the general council members are confident that he will not compromise the union's interests for partisan reasons, despite his personal political activities.[58]

Furthermore, the support which the Marxist parties, particularly the

[56]The text of the dissidents' statement appears in *Ceylon Daily News*, May 1, 1968, p. 13.
[57]See, for example, Tampoe's 1965 May Day speech, reported in *CMU Bulletin*, May, 1965, p. 2.
[58]Author's interview, June 25, 1967.

LSSP, once appeared to enjoy among the private-sector clerks is thought
to have eroded appreciably by the mid-1960's. One explanation for the
mercantile clerks' declining political radicalism and activism lies in the
successes of the CMU in recent years and the resulting realization of some
immediate occupational objectives, which may have stimulated hopes for
additional gains through economic trade unionism at the expense of faith
in political action. Clerical employees in the private sector have fared much
better in wage gains than either government clerks or school teachers,
the other major categories of organized white-collar employees.[59] In
addition, old loyalties to the LSSP were shaken by the 1964 party split
and fight over the twenty-one demands, and possibly more profoundly
by the reappearance of communal controversy after the 1965 election.
Clerks in the private commercial firms are educated in the English language
and a large proportion of them are of Tamil, Burgher, and Christian
origin.[60] The LSSP's coalition with the SLFP and the coalition's appeal
to the Sinhalese, Buddhist majority and demands for expanded opportunities for the Sinhalese-educated seemed to threaten the precarious status
of the English-educated clerks, particularly those belonging to the ethnic
and religious minorities. Both as a labor leader and as a politician, Tampoe
was an outspoken critic of the exploitation of language and other communal
issues by the coalition parties.[61]

CMU political behavior probably reflects to a considerable extent
Tampoe's own evolving political attitudes. Philosophically committed to
orthodox Trotskyism, Tampoe split with the LSSP because of the party's
coalition with a "bourgeois" party and growing preoccupation with
parliamentary activity.[62] He rejects concentration on parliamentary

[59]Until late 1967, virtually no change had occurred in the real wages of government
clerks in ten years and the real wages of government school teachers actually declined in
this decade. Central Bank of Ceylon, *Annual Report of the Monetary Board to the Minister of
Finance for the Year 1967* (Colombo : Central Bank of Ceylon, 1968), pp. 139–140. The CMU
was said to have won salary increases for its members ranging from 61 to 130 percent during
this period. Wilfred Perera, "Presidential Address of Mr. Wilfred Perera at the U.P.T.O.
Conference of Delegates Held on 28th and 29th June, 1967" (mimeographed; Colombo,
1967), p. 6.

[60]The concentration of non-Sinhalese and non-Buddhists (including Sinhalese Christians)
in clerical occupations is universally recognized, but the exact proportions are not known.
As an indication of the ethnic composition of employees in the private sector, a survey of
844 import and export firms found that Sinhalese comprised 54 percent, Tamils 17 percent,
Moors and Malays 11 percent, and Burghers 10 percent of all administrative, technical,
and clerical employees (the vast majority of whom were undoubtedly clerks). By way of
comparison, Sinhalese accounted for 77 percent, Tamils 8 percent, Moors and Malays
9 percent, and Burghers 2 percent of all other employees of the firms surveyed. Ceylon,
Department of Census and Statistics, *Census of Commerce, 1961* (Colombo: Government
Press, 1964), p. 51.

[61]Tampoe is himself of Tamil Christian background, although he broke with the LSSP
on the issue of alleged class collaboration and betrayal of the working class, before the lines
of renewed communal controversy had emerged.

[62]The following is based on a number of interviews and informal conversations with
Tampoe between 1965 and 1969.

politics since he contends that the working class is inevitably a minority which can never come to power through elections and the capture of Parliament. He feels that an eventual proletarian revolution is necessary to sweep away the institutions of bourgeois society. However, in the present circumstances of Ceylon, the proletarian revolution is in the very distant future. Therefore, the most effective immediate course is to work in the trade union movement, winning the demands and improving the circumstances of workers and strengthening trade unionism. The class struggle in contemporary Ceylon, Tampoe argues, can be carried on with greatest effect by using the economic weapons of a strong and aggressive labor movement against the bourgeoisie. Thus, somewhat paradoxically, the most militant and uncompromising revolutionary creed justifies emphasis on the immediate and non-political functions of trade unionism. Tampoe has remained politically active and has continued to use the rhetoric of revolutionary Marxism,[63] but the frustrations which the Marxists have experienced in politics and his own successes in trade unionism seem to have produced increasing disenchantment with conventional political action and concentration on economic trade unionism. Tampoe complained to a recent CMU conference that

> important sections of the trade union movement continue to be led by political parties which seek to subordinate the interests of the working-class to their sectarian interests in the arenas of Parliamentary and Local Government politics, and to foster in the working-class the illusion that its interests can best be served through Parliament, rather than by the building up of its own organised strength outside Parliament, for struggle in its interests, on economic as well as political issues affecting the working-people.[64]

CMU hostility toward restraints on unfettered trade unionism, consistent with the union's reliance on its own bargaining strength, has been an important cause of political involvement by the union. The political strikes in which the CMU participated were justified as intended to protect the free exercise of trade union power. Although opposed to the political strike of January, 1966, Tampoe vigorously condemned the disciplinary action taken against strikers in the public service and public corporations, on the grounds that "workers have a right to strike in protest

[63]In 1969, for example, Tampoe circulated among LSSP members a lengthy letter criticizing LSSP collaboration in the coalition and concentration on parliamentary politics, and concluding with an appeal to "go forward once again under the revolutionary Socialist banner of the Fourth International!" "Open Letter to the Members of the Lanka Sama Samaja Party from the Lanka Sama Samaja Party (Revolutionary)" (mimeographed; Colombo, August 9, 1969).

[64]Ceylon Mercantile Union, *Tenth Delegates' Conference, 17th & 18th March 1969 : General Secretary's Report & Conference Resolution* (Colombo : Ceylon Mercantile Union, 1969), p. 4.

on any matter that they judge, even wrongly, to be adverse to their interests, as they understand them."[65] A resolution approved at the 1967 CMU conference declared the union's determination "to resist by all necessary means, inclusive of a continuous General Strike, any attempt on the part of the Government or by any employer . . . to suppress or to restrict the existing democratic rights of association and action of workers. . . ."[66]

The CMU has been conspicuously successful relative to other Ceylonese labor organizations in obtaining its objectives by its own bargaining power in direct confrontation with employers. The long CMU restriction to the private sector where the major conflict was between the worker and the individual private employer may have contributed to the development of the union's emphasis on collective bargaining rather than political action.[67] A membership composed until recently of educated, urban, lower-middle-class clerks may have been conducive to concentration on immediate occupational demands because the membership's needs and aspirations were generally capable of satisfaction by incremental improvements in salaries, pensions, and conditions of employment.

Changes which the CMU is presently undergoing could create a tendency away from economic trade unionism and toward increasing reliance on political action. Growing involvement with public corporations is almost certain to heighten concern with political decisions and multiply opportunities for conflict with governmental agencies. As the union is drawn into contests with public corporations, it may find that economic bargaining power is ineffective against an enterprise backed by the government and be required to seek political solutions. A growing proportion of members who are unskilled laborers with little education, a weak bargaining position, and desolate economic circumstances could also tempt the union toward greater political action. The laborers are more desperately in need of improved housing, schools, medical facilities, and other changes in the social environment which the state alone can bring about. Furthermore, the weak bargaining position of unskilled laborers is likely to suggest resort to governmental intervention through legislation and regulation to improve wages and working conditions. It is far from certain, however, that the changes in membership composition will significantly affect the future political involvement of the CMU. The habits, perspective, and style of the union may be sufficiently established to resist the influence

[65]CMU, "Ninth Annual Delegates' Conference," p. 24.

[66]Ceylon Mercantile Union, "Draft Resolutions for the 9th Annual Delegates Conference of the Ceylon Mercantile Union" (mimeographed; Colombo, April 2, 1967), p. 1. CMU concern with political issues and governmental actions affecting trade unionism is indicated in an open letter from Tampoe on behalf of the union to the Prime Minister, entitled *Democratic Freedoms and Industrial Relations* (leaflet; Colombo, March 27, 1967).

[67]This was cited by Tampoe as a major factor in causing the CMU to be less preoccupied with politics than public servants' organizations, whose members are directly and obviously affected by political decisions and are conscious of changes in their occupational circumstances produced by transfers of governmental power. Author's interview, June 28, 1965.

of these recent changes. Successful economic trade unionism seems to have generated considerable momentum. As the new members are introduced to successes in collective bargaining they may accept and reinforce the union's commitment to economic trade unionism.

VII

PROFILES OF UNCOMMITTED TRADE UNIONS

Few Ceylonese trade unions possess both the capacity and the desire to play a significant role in politics independent of close and durable connections with a political party. Some organizations which presumably possess the capabilities, such as the Ceylon Mercantile Union or the Government Clerical Service Union, have chosen partisan alignment. A relatively small number of unions, however, are clearly concerned with politics and frequently involved in political activities and controversies, but have avoided the kind of close partisan association and predictable political behavior which is typical of party-oriented unions.

The politically uncommitted unions commonly co-operate with or oppose parties in specific circumstances, since it is the political parties which usually define the issues and propose the actions of concern to trade unions, whether related directly to the labor movement or more generally to the political, economic, and social environment within which unions function and their members live and work. However, in contrast to the party-oriented unions, the uncommitted unions preserve a political identity independent of and separate from that of any political party and act with some degree of autonomy in responding to political issues and participating in political activities. The leaders of uncommitted unions in some cases have personal partisan sentiments and loyalties, but they are not party activists conspicuously identified with the leadership of a party and regularly immersed in party affairs. In other unions, the leader may be personally active in politics, as is Democratic Workers' Congress president A. Aziz, but not within an individual political party.

Although the unions classified as uncommitted lack firm and durable links to individual parties, they are not necessarily neutral in partisan matters. For most uncommitted unions, ideological considerations or the partisan sympathies of the leadership sharply narrow the range of parties with which co-operation or temporary alliance may be sought. Few prominent unions appear to possess the ideological flexibility to bargain between the principal opposing political groups for specific concessions and advantages. The Ceylon Workers' Congress, discussed below, has been the one major labor organization which has successfully played this role. Nor do most uncommitted unions totally reject partisan politics. This attitude has, however, been adopted by one union, the Union of Post and Telecommunication Officers, which in recent years has been uncompromisingly hostile to all partisan influences in the labor movement. The UPTO president, Wilfred Perera, pulled the union out of the Public Service Workers' Trade Union Federation when the federation shifted position on the "twenty-one demands" to conform with the altered stand of the "regular" Communist Party in 1964.[1] Subsequently, Perera has been an outspoken critic of trade union subordination to political parties. Soon after the union's split with the PSWTUF, he called upon the UPTO membership "to insulate our Union from party politics,"[2] and at a 1967 UPTO conference he declared, "We do not want to be pawns in any political game nor are we prepared to pull the chestnuts out of the fire for any political party or politically committed trade union."[3]

While movement into or out of the party-sponsored category is quite rare, movement between the party-oriented and uncommitted categories is less difficult and probably more common. The Ceylon Mercantile Union, considered in the last chapter, although unambiguously party-oriented until 1964, may be in the process of transition to the uncommitted category. The Samastha Lanka Rajaye Lipikaru Sangamaya, discussed below, is another borderline case, possibly in the process of moving from the uncommitted to the party-oriented ranks.

Sketches of four uncommitted or weakly committed unions are presented in this chapter. The four unions range in size from more than 350,000 to under 5,000 members. Two are very large estate workers' organizations which are distinctive both because of their considerable size and because of the particular occupational and communal problems of their members. The other two unions are relatively small organizations representing white-collar office employees, one consisting of government clerks and the other primarily of employees of privately owned banks. The four unions differ in their political involvement scarcely less than in their size and composition, ranging from considerable autonomous political influence and standing to a posture which borders on that of the party-oriented unions.

1. *Ceylon Workers' Congress*

The Ceylon Workers' Congress has been the largest labor organization in Ceylon for nearly three decades. With more than 350,000 members

[1]Author's interview with Wilfred Perera, July 1, 1967.
[2]*Ceylon Observer*, June 27, 1965, p. 1.
[3]Wilfred Perera, "Presidential Address of Mr. Wilfred Perera at the U.P.T.O. Conference of Delegates Held on 28th and 29th June, 1967" (mimeographed; Colombo, 1967), p. 1.

in 1967, the CWC dwarfs all other Ceylonese trade unions and includes more than one-quarter of all union members and almost half of all organized agricultural workers on the island.[4] The membership of the union consists almost entirely of Indian Tamils employed on tea and rubber estates. Although it is not organized as a federation, a considerable degree of decentralization exists within the union. Many union functions are performed by six regional offices, representing the estate areas in which the CWC is strong and Colombo, and forty district offices which operate under the regional offices.[5] The CWC is a member of the International Confederation of Free Trade Unions, and its leaders regularly represent Ceylonese organized labor at international labor conferences.

The CWC is an outgrowth of the Ceylon Indian Congress, a political organization formed in 1939 to defend the interests of the Indian Tamil community. The Ceylon Indian Congress Labour Union was created the following year and began the first successful attempts at organizing estate labor, combining in its appeal the estate workers' communal solidarity and concern with employment problems. In 1950, the labor organization's name was changed to the Ceylon Workers' Congress, and by the following year it included nearly 135,000 members from a total membership of all workers' unions of about 235,000.[6]

The CWC in recent years has sought to escape its exclusive identification with the Indian Tamil estate workers. The 1964–1965 CWC report claimed the organization contained Sinhalese and Muslim as well as Tamil members and had extended its activities to a number of industries outside the estates.[7] However, the enlargement of the communal or

---

At the time of the 1968 public servants' strike, Perera was accused by coalition supporters of being a tool of the UNP. Ceylon, House of Representatives, *Parliamentary Debates (Hansard)*, vol. 83, col. 413 (December 7, 1968).

[4]Although conflicting claims and uncertainties are particularly marked regarding membership figures for estate workers' unions, it is universally agreed that the CWC has by far the largest membership. The other major estate workers' unions are the Democratic Workers' Congress, the CTUF-affiliated Ceylon Plantation Workers' Union, the CFL-affiliated Lanka Estate Workers' Union, and the National Union of Workers. A survey of trade union membership on 564 member companies' estates conducted by the Ceylon Estates Employers' Federation at the end of 1963 produced the following results: CWC, 157,667; DWC, 71,556; LEWU, 35,921; CPWU, 13,564; and Lanka Jathika Estate Workers' Union, 11,673. Ceylon Estates Employers' Federation, *XXth Annual Report and Accounts, 1963–1964* (Colombo: Ceylon Estates Employers' Federation, n.d.), p. 11. Curiously, the reported membership in the Lanka Jathika Estate Workers' Union is more than twice the membership claimed by the union at that time, possibly resulting from a bias on the part of the reporting estates or a belief among the workers surveyed that their supervisors would prefer to be told they belonged to the pro-UNP union.

[5]*Ceylon Workers' Congress Report, 1964–1965* (Colombo: Ceylon Workers' Congress, 1965), p. 2.

[6]*Administration Report of the Commissioner of Labour for 1951* (Colombo: Government Press, 1952), p. 16.

[7]*Ceylon Workers' Congress Report*, pp. 2–3, 6.

occupational groups represented appears to be little more than a gesture,[8] and the circumstances of the Indian Tamil estate workers have clearly remained the overwhelming concern of the CWC in both politics and labor relations.

The estate workers suffer from many obstacles to vigorous and effective collective bargaining. The Indian Tamil workers generally live in "coolie lines" on the estates, where they are regimented into the unique patterns of estate life and are largely isolated from interaction with the surrounding Sinhalese villagers by differences in language, religion, social organization, and circumstances of daily life and work.[9] Their dispersal among a large number of estates, relatively low education levels, meager pay, general poverty, and social and political isolation undoubtedly limit the aggressiveness and success of estate workers' unions in labor-management relations as well as politics. The estate workers' unions, furthermore, are faced by strong and highly organized employers, many of which are British companies. About 400 of the most important estate companies, operating more than 600 individual estates, are members of the Ceylon Estates Employers' Federation.[10] The CWC has been able to overcome these difficulties to some extent because of its immense size and organizational strength and has won a few recent victories in collective bargaining, the most notable of which was a collective agreement concluded with the Ceylon Estates Employers' Federation in 1967.

For almost two decades, the CWC tended to remain aloof from the industrial and political activities of the rest of the labor movement, probably reflecting the Indian Tamil estate workers' unique circumstances and communal solidarity, which have separated them from the largely urban, Sinhalese or Ceylon Tamil commercial and industrial employees and public servants who comprise most of the labor movement outside the estates. The CWC, however, was an original member of the Coordinating Committee of Trade Union Organisations formed by the unions which supported the 1959 LSSP-led political strike, and of the successor Joint Committee of Trade Union Organisations formed in 1963. Subsequently, the CWC was highly critical of the LSSP and Communist leaders

[8]All the sixty-two officers and executive committee members listed in 1965 appear to have Tamil names. *Ibid.*, p. 5.

[9]Sinhalese, who increasingly have been finding employment on the estates in recent years, usually live in nearby villages and go to and from the estates for work each day. Consequently, the circumstances of Sinhalese estate workers vary considerably from those of the Indian Tamils. On the social organization of the Indian Tamil estate workers, see R. Jayaraman, "Caste and Kinship in a Ceylon Tea Estate," *Economic Weekly* (Bombay), XVI (February 22. 1964), 393-397.

[10]Among the objectives of the federation is : "To secure mutual support and co-operation in dealing with demands made or action taken by employees or any class or classes of employees or by any Trade Union on all matters or questions affecting the general or common interests of [the federation's] members." Ceylon Estates Employers' Federation, *Rules* (Colombo : Ceylon Estates Employers' Federation, 1948), p. 2.

for shelving the JCTUO's "twenty-one demands."[11] The CWC held its own May Day rallies in the estate areas until 1965, when it participated with other labor organizations aligned with the National Government in a rally held in Colombo. Perhaps indicative of an increasing involvement in wider issues of the labor movement and politics, CWC president S. Thondaman played a leading role in forming a pro-Government grouping of labor organizations called the Ceylon National Trade Union Confederation in 1966.

The CWC was established as the labor arm of a political party, but unlike other similarly formed unions, overshadowed and eventually swallowed the political party which created it. In the 1947 election, the Ceylon Indian Congress won seven parliamentary seats from the estate areas.[12] However, shortly after independence, statutes were enacted excluding most Indian Tamils from Ceylonese citizenship and the franchise. Because they were not automatically accepted as citizens of India, a large majority of the Indian Tamils became stateless. With most of its clientele unable to vote, the political party atrophied and the efforts of the Indian Tamil leaders shifted to the trade union. The CWC became not only the labor organization but the general spokesman of the Indian Tamil community in public affairs.[13] After lying dormant for a dozen years, the party, renamed the Ceylon Democratic Congress in 1954 to escape the communal connotations of the original name, offered three candidates for parliamentary seats in March, 1960, but with a pronounced lack of success. Following the election the party was disbanded and replaced by a political section of the CWC.[14]

The role and influence of the CWC in politics have not been as great as the union's tremendous size might suggest. The organization, representing a vulnerable and politically weak minority, has been almost exclusively concerned with issues relating to the status of the Indian Tamil community. The overriding political concern of the Indian Tamils has been with the related questions of citizenship and repatriation to India. In 1946, the Ceylon Indian Congress had organized a hartal involving a work stoppage by 290,000 estate laborers and 51,000 other workers in protest against proposed constitutional changes leading to independence,[15] and in 1952 the

[11]E.g., *Ceylon Workers' Congress Report*, pp. 35–36.

[12]At least five of the seven Ceylon Indian Congress members elected to Parliament had been active in organizing estate labor and a sixth was a former member of the Board of Indian Immigrant Labour. Ceylon Daily News, *Parliament of Ceylon, 1947* (Colombo: Associated Newspapers of Ceylon, Ltd., n.d.), pp. 56–63, 81–83.

[13]CWC president S. Thondaman, for example, reportedly once claimed that the CWC functioned not only as a trade union but also as a more general protector of estate workers' rights. *Ceylon Daily News*, November 24, 1961, p. 13.

[14]Author's interview with S. Thondaman, July 16, 1967.

[15]*Administration Report of the Commissioner of Labour for 1946* (Colombo: Government Press, 1947), p. 18.

CWC conducted a one-hundred-day *satyagraha* campaign to protest the denial of citizenship to the Indian Tamils.[16] The CWC has made efforts to secure citizenship for all Indian Tamils who can qualify by assisting in legal matters and engaging in propaganda urging all those able to do so to register as citizens. By 1964, 134,000 Indian Tamils had received Ceylonese citizenship and 51,000 had registered as Indian citizens.[17]

For a number of years, the CWC cooperated informally with the Federal Party, which represents the Ceylon Tamils of the North. The union staged a one-day token strike in April, 1961, as an expression of support for a *satyagraha* campaign being conducted by the Federal Party in the North on the official language issue. By the following year, however, hostility developed between the CWC and the Federal Party, perhaps reflecting CWC resentment over Federalist attempts to champion the interests of all Tamil-speaking peoples in Ceylon and belief that the Federalists had little fundamental concern with the specific problems of the Indian Tamils. In late 1962, Federal Party branches were organized in the estate areas and an estate workers' union was formed by the party in a clear attempt to bypass the CWC and establish direct links with the Indian Tamils on the estates. Following the 1965 election, both the Federal Party and the CWC supported the National Government and public recriminations were avoided, but relations between the two organizations remained strained.[18]

The Indian Tamils possessing citizenship and the vote are scattered among constituencies with majorities of Sinhalese voters which have not been contested by candidates of the Federal Party or, with a few exceptions in 1960, of the Ceylon Democratic Congress. The CWC supported the SLFP-led coalition which won the 1956 election and worked for the SLFP among estate workers who held Ceylonese citizenship in July, 1960. But the support was rendered quietly, without public endorsements and pronouncements which it was assumed would hurt the endorsed party among Sinhalese voters.[19] CWC president S. Thondaman claimed that at each parliamentary election through 1960, most CWC members able to vote had supported "the SLFP as against the UNP, in the hope that the SLFP would do justice to the plantation workers."[20] Disillusionment, however, followed the union's support for the SLFP both in 1956 and 1960.[21]

[16]*Ceylon Workers' Congress Report*, p. 2.

[17]*Ceylon Today*, XIII (February, 1964), 19.

[18]Author's interviews with CWC and Federal Party leaders during 1962, 1965, and 1967.

[19]Author's interview with S. Thondaman, July 16, 1967.

[20]S. Thondaman, *Presidential Address, Ceylon Workers' Congress, Twenty-First Sessions* (Colombo : Ceylon Workers' Congress, 1965), p. 2.

[21]Ceylon Workers' Congress, "Report of the Seventh Annual Sessions of the Ceylon Workers' Congress, Held at 'Sarvodhaya Sadukkam,' Nuwara Eliya on 28th September, 1958" (mimeographed; Colombo, 1958), pp. 17–19; Thondaman, *President Address*, pp. 3–4.

In 1965, the CWC for the first time publicly endorsed and openly worked for a major political party. The CWC executive committee in early 1965 unanimously approved a resolution calling on CWC members with Ceylonese citizenship to vote for the UNP.[22] Thondaman announced that all union branches had been directed "to give wholehearted support to the United National Party candidates," and appealed beyond the CWC membership to all citizens of Indian origin to vote for the UNP.[23] Following the election, CWC spokesmen pledged their firm support for the National Government formed by the UNP, Federal Party, and several other parties.[24]

The CWC redirected its partisan sympathies and plunged openly into the 1965 election contest because of developments on the citizenship and repatriation questions preceding the election. After intermittent talks extending over a decade, in October, 1964, an agreement was reached between the governments of India and Ceylon providing for the repatriation to India of 525,000 Indian Tamils over a fifteen-year period and the granting of Ceylonese citizenship to 300,000. The fate of an additional 150,000 was left for future decision.[25] The CWC passionately attacked SLFP Prime Minister Sirimavo Bandaranaike's interpretation of the agreement as providing for compulsory repatriation and her proposal that Indian Tamils who received Ceylonese citizenship be placed in separate electorates.[26] The National Government formed after the 1965 election renounced the use of compulsion in securing repatriation to India and pledged to confer Ceylonese citizenship immediately on all the Indian Tamils who were to receive citizenship, rather than matching the grant citizenship to the pace of repatriation over a period of fifteen years. Implementation of the Indo-Ceylon agreement became one of the major issues dividing the National Government and the opposition SLFP-Marxist coalition.

Despite the political disabilities of the Indian Tamils, the CWC has been able to play a political role by bargaining among competing Sinhalese parties with the offer of its endorsement and support. The votes of the 134,000 Indian Tamils possessing citizenship are considered marginally important in at least half a dozen hill-country constituencies. An indication of the electoral role played by the CWC is contained in the following passage from the union's 1964–1965 report :

The Maskeliya electorate has 8,810 votes from the estates, and the victory of the U.N.P. candidate in the last [1965] General Elections

[22]*Ceylon Workers' Congress Report*, p. 44.
[23]*Ceylon Daily News*, March 18, 1965, p. 1.
[24]*Ibid.*, May 7, 1965, p. 3; Thondaman, *Presidential Address*, pp. 2–3.
[25]*Ceylon Today*, XIII (November, 1964), 15–22.
[26]Thondaman, *Presidential Address*, pp. 3–7; *Ceylon Workers' Congress Report*, pp. 41–44, 61–63; *Times of Ceylon*, December 21, 1964, p. 9.

was in no small measure due to the support of the CWC['s] 6,319 voters who stood for democracy. In spite of active and largely extended propaganda by opposition political parties, rival unions and self seeking individuals, ... [the CWC's regional unit] helped to return to Parliament Mr. Edmund Wijayasooriya, the UNP candidate with an over whelming [sic] majority.[27]

The UNP won this constituency in 1965 by 3,173 votes after losing it to the SLFP in July, 1960 by 1,115 votes.

The CWC's ability to avoid permanent partisan attachments, and thus maintain its freedom to bargain among competing parties, rests in large measure on its size and organizational strength. While the union must ally itself with a major political party to achieve its political goals, it is not dependent on party support and assistance for the performance of its daily trade union activities or to represent it in dealings with employers or governmental agencies. While the numbers of CWC members who are able to vote is not large, the extensive organization of the union, reinforced by communal solidarity, probably allows the union to mobilize and direct their votes with considerable efficiency. Furthermore, the CWC's financial resources, produced by great size despite the poverty of individual members, provide it with an independent asset in politics. The CWC is one of very few unions in Ceylon which maintains a political fund of significant size. In the year ending March 31, 1965, expenditures from the political fund of slightly more than Rs. 66,000 (nearly $14,000) were reported.[28] For members opting to contribute to the political fund, Rs. 0.05 (less than $0.01) of the half-rupee monthly dues is allocated to the political fund.[29]

The fact that the CWC is almost entirely concerned with protecting the interests of a single minority community probably contributes to the union's bargaining flexibility, because the union need seek only concessions on the specific issues of direct concern to the community in exchange for its backing. The CWC seems to lack any strong ideological commitment which might narrow the range of possible political alliances. Its leaders do not appear to share the radical outlook on political and social questions which typifies the leadership of much of the labor movement. In addition, the CWC leadership apparently has firm control over union activities and is subjected to few rank-and-file pressures which might obstruct bargaining and the shifting of political support.[30]

[27]*Ceylon Workers' Congress Report*, p. 19.
[28]*Ibid.*, financial appendix, unpaged.
[29]"Constitution of the Ceylon Workers' Congress" (mimeographed; Colombo, September 1, 1965), p. 2. Under the Trade Unions Ordinance, union members individually must authorize allocation of part of their dues payments to the political fund, if one is maintained by the union.
[30]At the 1965 CWC conference, for example, Thondaman made reference to the major

Although the CWC does not function as a political party in that it does not itself nominate candidates for public office or offer a program covering a broad spectrum of governmental policies, it is widely regarded not only as a trade union but also as an autonomous political organization, with its own base of support and positions on the issues of particular concern to its clientele. Indicative of the quasi-party role of the CWC is the opposition's labeling of the National Government as the *hath havula* or coalition of seven, referring to six political parties and the CWC which initially supported the Government.[31]

The CWC's success in political bargaining has given the organization direct access to governmental leaders and the decision-making process through representation in Parliament since 1960. Following the election victory of the SLFP, with CWC endorsement, in July, 1960, Thondaman was named an appointed M.P. In 1965, after the CWC shift to the UNP camp and the UNP election success, both Thondaman and the financial secretary of the CWC, V. Annamalay, were among the six appointed M.P.'s. Parliamentary representation is regarded as of great importance to the CWC, although the union's representatives speak infrequently on the floor of Parliament and with rare exceptions have adhered to the Government whip in divisions.[32] Representation in Parliament provides CWC spokesmen with the opportunity to work within the Government Parliamentary Group and to participate in the early stages of policy formulation, when objections can be voiced and modifications suggested outside of public view. The value of behind-the-scenes access is highly appreciated by the CWC leadership because of recognition that public pronouncements by the CWC can create a communal reaction which would be detrimental to the interests of the union and its clientele.[33]

2. *Democratic Workers' Congress*

The Democratic Workers' Congress was created after a split in the Ceylon Workers' Congress in 1956, resulting from rivalry between two CWC leaders, S. Thondaman and A. Aziz. When Thondaman retained control of the CWC, Aziz left the organization with a number of followers to form the DWC. A tense and shaky reunification of the two groups was effected in 1960, but in March, 1962, they again split apart. Like the CWC,

---

decisions in connection with the Indo-Ceylon agreement and the election which the executive committee had made since the preceding conference. Thondaman, *Presidential Address*, p. 1.

[31]The six political parties with which the CWC was associated in the National Government were the UNP, MEP, Sri Lanka Freedom Socialist Party (consisting of former SLFP members), Federal Party, Tamil Congress, and Jathika Vimukthi Peramuna.

[32]Thondaman abstained on the crucial parliamentary vote in December, 1964, which overturned the SLFP-LSSP coalition Government.

[33]Based on the author's interviews with S. Thondaman, July 16, 1967, and other CWC officers, June 26, 1967.

the DWC is composed virtually entirely of Indian Tamil estate workers. Although leading a union of Tamil-speaking Hindus of recent South Indian origin, Aziz is a Muslim, originally from what is now West Pakistan, whereas Thondaman's family originally came to Ceylon from South India as *kanganies* (recruiters and overseers of estate labor), later becoming wealthy estate owners.

The rupture between Thondaman and Aziz is often attributed to personality clashes and conflicting personal ambitions, although political differences may have contributed to the breach.[34] Aziz has been much more inclined toward political activity on a wide range of issues than Thondaman and is considerably to the left of Thondaman in political outlook. Aziz has been deeply concerned with international affairs, particularly Middle Eastern politics and national independence movements, and travels widely to conferences of the Afro-Asian People's Solidarity Organization and other international groups. The more varied political interests of the DWC are suggested by the resolutions approved at the union's 1967 conference. Of six resolutions, the first dealt with the Indo-Ceylon agreement, the second with wages and working conditions on the estates, the third with education on the estates, and the final three with the Arab-Israeli conflict, Vietnam, and nationalist movements in Africa.[35]

Aziz is ideologically close to the Marxists, with whom he has often collaborated in labor and political activities. The DWC, however, has not become closely and predictably aligned with any party. Although Aziz is considered by some observers to have had closer affinities with the Communist Party than with the LSSP, the DWC supported the Samasama-jists on the 1959 political strike, which the Communists opposed, and belonged to the largely LSSP-led Coordinating Committee of Trade Union Organisations after 1959. Along with most other prominent labor organizations, the DWC was a member of the Joint Committee of Trade Union Organisations established in 1963. When the JCTUO was jolted by the formation of the SLFP-LSSP coalition Government and subsequent sharp disagreement over the fate of the JCTUO's twenty-one demands the following year, the DWC refused to accept either the position of the LSSP or that of the "regular" Communist Party. Together with the CWC and other JCTUO members not firmly committed to either of the two

[34]For an analysis of the split in terms of a power struggle and clash of ambitions between Aziz and Thondaman, see *Ceylon Observer*, March 9, 1962, p. 4. Aziz has implied that disagreement on political issues was a factor in the split. See A. Aziz, *Presidential Address of Mr. A. Aziz at the Annual Sessions of the Democratic Workers' Congress Held at Yatiyantota on the 17th of August, 1963* (Colombo : Democratic Workers' Congress, 1963), p. 1.

[35]Democratic Workers' Congress, "Resolutions of the Democratic Workers' Congress Passed at the Annual Sessions Held on the 28th of August 1967 at Yatiyantota" (mimeographed; Colombo, August 31, 1967).

major Marxist parties, the DWC continued to insist on immediate presentation of the demands.[36]

During the 1965 election contest, in which the CWC was allied with the UNP, Aziz actively worked for the opposing SLFP-Marxist coalition. Although the coalition position on the Indo-Ceylon agreement created a formidable obstacle to winning Indian Tamil support, he claimed to have held a few estate workers' votes for the coalition parties, including the margin by which LSSP leader N. M. Perera was returned to Parliament. Immediately after the election, Aziz broke with the coalition as a result of the coalition parties' attitudes on the Indo-Ceylon agreement and other issues affecting the minorities and increasingly enthusiastic advocacy of Sinhalese Buddhist claims.[37]

The DWC's identification with the coalition during the election weakened the union and is believed to have caused a serious loss of members. Shortly after the election and Aziz's disengagement from the coalition, the DWC accelerated a campaign for a Rs. 17.50 a month cost-of-living allowance for estate workers, culminating in a forty-five day strike in mid-1966. Although unsuccessful on the demand, the campaign and strike apparently helped the DWC to revive its sagging fortunes among the estate workers. Militancy on the Rs. 17.50 demand and other wage issues allowed the DWC to appear as the champion of the estate workers' occupational interests at a time when the CWC was fettered by political ties with the National Government. Thondaman has explained that he could not back the demand without risking a clash with the Government, which sought wage restraint in the interest of economic stability and growth. A break with the Government at that time, he contended, would have jeopardized the early granting of citizenship to the Indian Tamils, which he felt was more important to the Indian Tamil estate workers than the cost-of-living allowance. Consequently, although he approved of the demand, he sacrificed the allowance for citizenship.[38] By 1967, the DWC appeared to have largely recovered from its post-election reverses, due at least in part to the Rs. 17.50 demand.

Alienated by the coalition's attitudes toward the minorities and separated from the UNP and its allies by differences on a wide range of social and economic issues, Aziz chose to avoid association with either camp.[39] Soon after the election, Aziz commended the National Government for having "resolutely rejected chauvinistic and communal politics and ... forging national unity which had been shattered during the past few

[36]See Democratic Workers' Congress, *Administrative Report, 1963/64* (Colombo : Democratic Workers' Congress, 1964), p. 4.
[37]Author's interview with A. Aziz, July 7, 1965.
[38]Author's interview with S. Thondaman, July 16, 1967.
[39]Author's interview with A. Aziz, July 26, 1967.

years."[40] Within two years, however, he criticized the Government on a number of labor and economic issues and charged, "The many promises made by the Government to help the cause of the working class have yet to materialise."[41] With most political groups polarizing around the National Government or the SLFP-Marxist entente, the DWC gravitated toward the relatively few other trade unions and individuals not linked with either camp, many of whom were associated with the LSSP(R). In 1966, the DWC joined with the Ceylon Mercantile Union, Ceylon Bank Employees' Union, and Ceylon Estate Staffs' Union in forming the United Committee of Ceylon Trade Unions, but withdrew from the grouping the following year.

The DWC has not lacked the capacity to function autonomously in labor affairs, and to some extent in politics as well. Excluding the 1960 election, when it was reunited with the CWC and involved in the modest efforts of the Ceylon Democratic Congress, the DWC was not closely linked with a political party even before 1965. The union or Aziz cooperated with the LSSP and Communist Party on many occasions but maintained a separate political identity. As with most unions, the political position of the DWC is essentially a product of the attitudes and preferences of its principal leader, within the broad constraints of the basic interests of the membership. Although inclined toward the coalition on most issues, Aziz severed the union's previous partisan attachments when, as a result of coalition positions on questions of fundamental importance to the DWC membership, association with the coalition was no longer tenable. Since the DWC leadership held strong views not only on questions affecting the Indian Tamil minority but on a wide range of a social and political issues, the organization was prevented from forging new links with the principal alternative political grouping and was forced to withdraw to a largely ineffective political position, probably to await a shift in coalition policy on the minorities which would allow the union to re-establish the earlier alliance.

3. Samastha Lanka Rajaye Lipikaru Sangamaya

Although of modest size and relatively inconspicuous, the Samastha Lanka Rajaye Lipikaru Sangamaya (All-Ceylon Government Clerks' Union) is the second largest union representing members of the General Clerical Service, with a 1967 membership of 4,700. The SLRLS was founded by

[40]A. Aziz, "Presidential Address of Mr. A. Aziz at the Annual Sessions of the Democratic Workers' Congress Held at the Colombo Town Hall on 16th and 17th October 1965" (mimeographed; Colombo, 1965), p. 2.
[41]A. Aziz, "Presidential Address of Mr. A. Aziz at the Annual Sessions of the Democratic Workers' Congress Held at Yatiyantota on 27th and 28th August 1967" (mimeographed; Colombo, 1967), p. 2.

government clerks who split from the Government Clerical Service Union in 1956 (the year the Official Language Act designating Sinhalese as the sole official language was passed) for the express purpose of promoting and encouraging the change from English to Sinhalese as the language of administration.[42] Although the union concerns itself with such conventional considerations as salaries, pensions, and promotions, its officers still define its primary goal and *raison d'etre* as the promotion of the use of Sinhalese in the bureaucracy and the principal efforts of the organization have been directed toward this end.[43]

The union represents a new social element in the bureaucracy—the secondary-school graduates educated in the Sinhalese language who began to enter the clerical levels of the public service after 1956 and who tend to be more predominately rural and Buddhist in background than their co-workers educated in the English language. An estimated two-thirds of the union's members are clerks recruited to the public service since 1956 by examination in the Sinhalese rather than the English language,[44] and virtually the entire membership is Sinhalese. The union's president, G. S. Kumarasinghe, is himself an entrant through the Sinhalese medium who does not speak English. The SLRLS preoccupation with the language issue undoubtedly reflects the concern and insecurity of the Sinhalese-educated clerks whose careers are closely connected with the use of Sinhalese as the language of administration.

The language question has been an explosive political issue, and SLRLS concern with this question has ensnarled the union in partisan conflict. The encouragement of politicians who were active in the Sinhalese-only movement may have played a role in the formation of the union but the organization does not appear to have been closely linked with any political party, particularly prior to 1965. Although the SLFP was a vocal champion of Sinhalese-only and undoubtedly received the support of many SLRLS members, in 1963, while the SLFP was in power, the union denounced the pace at which the Official Language Act was being implemented and conducted a campaign intended to force a more rapid shift to the use of Sinhalese in the bureaucracy.

Shortly after the parliamentary election of 1965, a struggle for power within the SLRLS resulted in the defeat of the incumbent officers and their replacement by leaders considered sympathizers of the SLFP-Marxist coalition.[45] Whether as a result of the leadership change or of developments

---

[42]The expression "language of administration" is used here to refer to the language in which the daily work and internal communication of the public service is conducted. The meaning of the phrase "official language" is somewhat ambiguous and has been given varying interpretations.

[43]Author's interview with SLRLS president G. S. Kumarasinghe and other union officers, July 17, 1967.

[44]Estimate by the SLRLS president.

[45]*Ceylon Observer,* July 11, 1965, p. 1.

connected with the language issue, which included sharp coalition attacks on the UNP and its allies in the National Government for allegedly undermining the Official Language Act, the SLRLS began to move into open alliance with the opposition coalition and against the Government soon after the election. The union's increasing partisan alignment was demonstrated by its joining the reconstituted Joint Committee of Trade Union Organisations, formed as an openly pro-coalition grouping after the election, and participating in the coalition-sponsored political strike on the language issue in January, 1966. During 1965 the SLRLS joined in forming a "front" *(peramuna)* of trade unions, mostly small public servants' organizations, with the declared objective of protecting the Sinhalese language from the actions of the National Government. The front was claimed to have been instrumental, along with the JCTUO, in proposing the January, 1966, strike.[46] Forty-six members of the union were subjected to disciplinary action for participating in the strike.[47]

The union also carried on its own battle on the language question. A special SLRLS conference held in October, 1966, to consider what was regarded as a crisis in the language situation demanded the withdrawal of language provisions adopted for the public service during 1966 and immediate completion of the transition to Sinhalese as the language of administration. Early in the following year, after charging that the Government had ignored its demands, the union launched a "conduct public business in Sinhalese only" campaign in government offices. Eventually, grievances on the language question were taken by union representatives directly to the Minister of Finance and the Prime Minister.[48] Meanwhile, the union had undertaken a campaign in the rural areas to mobilize public support for its stand on the language question.[49]

Since the 1965 election, the SLRLS has become increasingly partisan. While its overt political behavior since 1965 has been scarcely distinguishable from that of the unions most firmly committed to the coalition parties, the SLRLS appears basically to be more an issue-oriented than a party-oriented organization. The union's vigorous stand on the language issue coincided with the position of the coalition, and the National Government's acts affecting the language of administration were viewed by the union as seriously threatening a fundamental interest of the membership. The union seems to have become ensnarled in political conflict less as an expression of partisan loyalty than as a reaction to a perceived threat to the basic interest of its members.

[46]Author's interview with G. S. Kumarasinghe.
[47]*Samastha Laṅkā Rajayē Lipikaru Saṅgamaya 1966/67 Vārshika Vārthāva* [Samastha Lanka Rajaye Lipikaru Sangamaya 1966/67 Annual Report] (Colombo : Samastha Lanka Rajaye Lipikaru Sangamaya, [1967]), p. 7.
[48]*Ibid.*, pp. 13–19, 30–34.
[49]Author's interview with SLRLS officers.

4. *Ceylon Bank Employees' Union*

One of the more widely respected unions among trade unionists is the Ceylon Bank Employees' Union, formed in 1943 as the Ceylon Bank Clerks' Union. In 1957, long-brewing rank-and-file dissatisfaction with an "outsider" leadership culminated in the overthrow of the "outsiders" and capture of the leading union offices by persons who were themselves union members and bank employees.[50] Originally limited to clerical employees, the union was expanded in 1956 to include bank employees below the clerical grades. The change in membership was accompanied by a change of name to the Ceylon Bank Employees' Union.[51] Although now including peons, messengers, and other "minor" employees, the union remains very strong among the clerical employees in banks and appears to retain a predominately white-collar orientation and character.[52] The CBEU contained about 5,000 members in 1967.

For a decade after the 1957 leadership change, the CBEU was engaged in a hard and frequently bitter struggle to obtain specific job-related demands of its members. An eleven-day strike ending early in 1959 won concessions on salaries, allowances, and holidays. A strike in April, 1961, was called off after it was denounced by the Prime Minister, but the grievances remained and the following December erupted into one of the longest and most bitterly contested strikes in the history of Ceylonese trade unionism. While the bank strike was in progress, port workers and petroleum workers struck and a widely effective one-day general strike was called to protest government use of troops to maintain port operations. In late January, the discovery and collapse of an attempted *coup d'etat* by a small group of police and military officers led to a political crisis and the termination of the port strike. The bank strike continued, however, although in its first days the dispute was referred to compulsory arbitration by the government and its subsequent continuation became illegal. In February, all striking bank employees were notified of their dismissal from their jobs. General meetings of the membership twice voted unanimously to continue the strike. In March, after ninety days, the union conceded defeat and called off the strike without winning any of its objectives.[53]

The exhausting strike of 1961–1962 did not alleviate the discontent of

[50]The overthrow of the "outsiders" was discussed in Chapter III.

[51]See "The Short History of the Ceylon Bank Employees Union," *Bank Worker*, February–March, 1961, pp. 4–5. *Bank Worker* is the official journal of the CBEU.

[52]The union not only includes a large proportion of clerks, but also some administrative-grade officers in the state-owned People's Bank and Bank of Ceylon. See "Report of Commission on Promotions in Banks, 1966" (mimeographed; Colombo, September 20, 1966), p. 2.

[53]On the background and course of the 1961–1962 strikes, see *Bank Worker*, June–July, 1962, pp. 1–5, and March, 1963, pp. 3–4.

bank employees, and in a few years the same issues were joined by union grievances regarding the right of members to retain membership in the union on promotion to lower supervisory grades and suspected discrimination against union members in promotions. In 1965 a strike was called in support of a clerk who refused to resign from the union on promotion. A strike at the National and Grindlay's Bank commencing in May, 1966, grew into a union-wide strike in July, which was suspended after the Minister of Labour announced that a commission would investigate bank promotion practices and the retention of union membership by promoted bank employees. The report of the commission, issued later in the year, generally supported the position of the union. Finally, in 1967, a bitter two-month strike won for the union a collective agreement with the Commercial Banks' Association, the Bank of Ceylon, and the People's Bank which included virtually all the longstanding CBEU demands on salaries, allowances, and pensions and was considered a major triumph for the union.[54] After a decade of arduous struggle, the CBEU had established a reputation as a cohesive and aggressively led trade union.

Despite the dominant influence of a politically conscious and articulate section of society, the urban white-collar workers, the union has not been conspicuously identified with partisan politics. The energy and attention of the union have been primarily directed toward occupational concerns and the winning of immediate job-related demands. The union's top leaders readily concede their personal partisan attachments, but are unanimously agreed that the CBEU as an organization should shun partisanship in the interest of unity and solidarity. Members and officers include suporters of various parties, although the LSSP is said to enjoy the widest support, followed by the Communist Party and the LSSP(R). Most members are considered to be in sympathy with the political "Left."[55]

Union behavior regarding the 1959 political strike, as described by its leaders, indicates in part the style of the union's political involvement. The 1959 strike was organized by the LSSP, but opposed by the Communist Party, the MEP, and the SLFP. The CBEU leaders, who are considered by observers outside the union to be predominantly pro-LSSP, claim to have favored joining the strike not because of its partisan sponsorship but because they viewed the proposed amendment to the Public Security Act as a threat to the labor movement. Opposition to the union's participation existed among Communist Party supporters within the membership, but prior to the strike the leaders spent about two weeks discussing the question and attempting to persuade the membership to

---

[54]The CBEU journal commented editorially that the banks had been forced to concede "in full every major demand of the Union." *Bank Worker*, May, 1967, p. 13.

[55]Based on the author's interviews with CBEU officers between June and September, 1967. Among the top officers, two professed to be LSSP supporters, one was a member of the LSSP(R), and one described himself as "pro-coalition."

back the strike. Eventually, it is claimed, a wide area of agreement in favor of the strike was achieved, and once the union was committed to the strike virtually every CBEU member took part.[56]

The CBEU has not been hesitant to take positions on political issues or denounce actions of the party in power which were considered detrimental to trade unionism and has been an active participant in the labor movement's struggles for unity. The union vigorously attacked both the SLFP and National Governments for "anti-trade union activities" and prolonging states of emergency.[57] Following its participation in the 1959 political strike, the CBEU helped form the Continuing Committee of Trade Union Organisations and was active in the successor Joint Committee of Trade Union Organisations until the 1964 JCTUO split. Despite the leanings of many of its leaders toward the LSSP and the coalition, the CBEU did not join the post-1965 JCTUO reconstituted as a pro-coalition grouping. Since 1966, the CBEU has been a member of the United Committee of Ceylon Trade Unions, which is politically aligned with neither the Government nor the opposition coalition.

The CBEU thus presents a picture of a prominent and aggressive union which has played a major role in the labor movement but has not aligned or identified itself with a political party. Over the years, the union has primarily represented employees of private banking institutions who are less immediately and obviously affected by political decisions than are public servants and consequently may feel themselves less directly concerned with political developments. Furthermore, the union contains a strong and dominant segment of white-collar, lower-middle-class clerks with secondary school educations. While seemingly inconsistent with the union's militancy in industrial relations and stress on solidarity with the working class, many of the clerks aspire to occupational advancement and social mobility.[58] Their interest, therefore, tends to focus on their job and industry, and while they may possess vocal political attitudes they may be more fundamentally concerned with occupational questions. The union's members in the private banks are educated in the English language and a significant proportion are Tamils, Burghers, and Christians. The political activism and radicalism generally attributed to the articulate, politically conscious, frequently frustrated and insecure lower-middle class may be attenuated by the increasingly uncertain privilege of education in English and the disillusionment with politics of the ethnic and religious minorities.

[56] As related to the author by CBEU officers W. E. V. de Mel and Oscar P. Pereira, July 5, 1967.

[57] E.g., *Bank Worker*, June–July, 1962; March, 1963; June, 1963; and June, 1965; and Ceylon Bank Employees' Union, *Annual Report* (leaflet; Colombo, May 26, 1967), p. 3.

[58] On the bank clerks' concern with opportunities for promotion, see "Report of Commission on Promotions in Banks, 1966."

The CBEU's preoccupation with specific occupational demands and the difficulty of the struggle for these demands over the past decade probably tended to absorb the union's energy and distract it from playing a vigorously partisan role. While partisan sentiments within the CBEU leadership presumably are weighted most heavily in the direction of the coalition, the lack of consensus may have made expedient the course of remaining detached from the coalition camp while simultaneously opposed to the Government.[59] Perhaps because of the need for solidarity to win the union's job-related demands, the leadership has not been willing to attempt to force the union into a partisan alignment and pay the price in disunity which marked partisanship is likely to involve. The CBEU officers have professed a strong belief in an autonomous labor movement free of partisan control as a more effective instrument for realizing workers' aspirations.[60] Although it is clearly not always the case, leaders drawn from the occupational group which the union represents, even though possessing firm partisan loyalties, may tend to be more deeply concerned with the union and the immediate employment grievances of the membership than with the party and the eventual benefits of its program.[61]

[59]One perceptive politician remarked in an interview by the author that the CBEU leaders "are LSSP, but think like the LSSP(R)."

[60]In interviews by the author. Virtually all leaders of trade unions, even those most firmly bound to a party, profess belief in trade union autonomy. In contrast with many other organizations, however, the actions of the CBEU do not reveal conspicuous partisan motivations.

[61]This was, of course, Lenin's contention when he asserted that the working-class movement itself was capable only of developing "trade unionism" and insisted on the need for party leadership and control. V. I. Lenin, *What Is To Be Done?* (Moscow : Foreign Languages Publishing House, n.d.), pp. 159–160 and *passim*. However, many individual trade unionists in Ceylon, who were themselves workers in industries represented by the union, are ardent partisans and dedicated party activists.

VIII

THE POLITICAL IMPACT OF STRIKES AND DISORDER

A major political significance of trade unions stems from their capacity to exert pressure by strikes in strategic industries and to precipitate civil disorder, which may intimidate or discredit the governing politicians and produce other major political consequences. The strike has been viewed as a political weapon since before independence, when colonial rule prevented a fully effective political process. In 1936, within a few months of the founding of the Lanka Sama Samaja Party, a strike of motor transport workers was staged by the party to protest a legislative enactment dealing with motor vehicle licensing.[1] As the colonial administration or British-owned firms were the principal employers of wage labor, strikes might simultaneously involve demands for improved wages and working conditions and attempts to weaken or undermine colonial rule.[2] Strikes have continued to be used as conscious political instruments since independence, and strikes and occasional outbursts of disorder resulting from trade union action have had important political consequences, both intended and unintended.

1. Types of Political Strikes

Some strikes have no discernible political ramifications, while others are expressly political and have slight industrial impact. There are, in addition, a considerable number of strikes which contain elements of both industrial and political conflict, either in intent or consequences or both. Most politically significant strikes can be classified into three categories:

---

[1] *The C.F.T.U. and the Working Class Movement* (Colombo: Ceylon Federation of Trade Unions, 1966), p. 10. Strikes in the early 1940's were attributed by Samasamajists to the inadequacies of the colonial legislature as a channel for realizing objectives. "The Real Situation in Ceylon," *Fourth International*, III (October, 1942), 301–302 (reprinted from *Samasamajist*, June 10, 1942).

[2] The general strike of 1947 is thought by many to have hastened the grant of independence, which came in February, 1948. Keuneman, for example, claimed that despite its failure to win immediate demands, the strike "nevertheless played a decisive part in the struggle for independence." Pieter Keuneman, *Twenty Years of the Ceylon Communist Party* (Colombo: Communist Party, [1963]), p. 9.

(1) overtly political strikes, called solely and explicitly for political reasons; (2) general strikes and strikes which combine political with industrial demands and objectives; and (3) strikes which are primarily the result of industrial disputes but which involve the prestige or interests of the political Government because they occur in industries operated by the state or essential to the normal life of the community.[3]

Political Protest Strikes

Exclusively political strikes are brief, generally lasting one day, and are intended as a symbolic act of protest and a means of dramatizing an issue, rather than as a serious effort to topple the Government. The political strike is called in protest over a specific immediate grievance or event, and takes the form of a general strike of all workers in all industries who are willing to participate. Invariably, a mass rally and, unless prevented by the police, a street procession accompany the strike. The objective sought is to display the strength and determination of the participants to the Government and the public and to generate popular concern with the issue. A one-day political strike in 1959, for example, was described as intended "to register a working class protest in an emphatic manner against a reactionary and anti-democratic piece of legislation."[4]

The hartal is closely related to, and can be considered along with, the exclusively political strike. A hartal, technically, is not limited to a strike by organized workers, but involves the closing of all shops, businesses, and schools and the suspension of normal activities by all members of the community. Like the political strike, the hartal is an act of protest, and includes the flying of black flags as a sign of mourning. Hartals are called by organizations other than trade unions, generally political parties. Several hartals, for example, were called by the Federal Party to protest official-language policy between 1956 and 1965. The distinction between a political strike and hartal is not always carefully maintained, and any politically motivated strike and demonstration may popularly be referred to as a hartal.

Relatively few exclusively political strikes have been staged.[5] The only one which produced profound repercussions was a hartal organized by the

---

[3]In his well-known study, K. G. J. C. Knowles has categorized "consciously" political strikes as (1) revolutionary general strikes, (2) strikes having political objectives and intended to force action on the government, and (3) strikes having industrial objectives, but timed according to political considerations. He has also cited "unconsciously" political strikes as those called for industrial reasons but requiring government action or those which because of their impact are liable to lead to government action. K. G. J. C. Knowles, *Strikes—A Study in Industrial Conflict* (Oxford: Basil Blackwell, 1952), p. 292.

[4]Leslie Goonewardene, *A Short History of the Lanka Sama Samaja Party* (Colombo: Lanka Sama Samaja Party, 1960), p. 61.

[5]Excluded from consideration here are a few hartals which did not involve significant participation by trade unions and organized workers.

Marxist parties and the Federal Party in 1953, attacking a Cabinet decision to increase the price of subsidized rice. The forerunner of the Ceylon Workers' Congress, the Ceylon Indian Congress, called a one-day hartal in 1946 to protest legislative approval of constitutional proposals. A general strike led by the LSSP in March, 1959, was called to protest against a proposed amendment to the Public Security Act under consideration in Parliament. Trade unions associated with the SLFP, LSSP, and Communist Party called a half-day general strike and demonstration protesting the defeat in Parliament of the SLFP-LSSP coalition Government late in 1964, and ordered a one-day strike and demonstration, which erupted into rioting and disorder, as a protest against official language regulations introduced in Parliament in January, 1966. As a result of the political divisions in the labor movement, political strikes frequently receive only partial support and their impact is consequently weakened. The 1959 LSSP-led strike, for example, was considered to have achieved slight success because of the opposition of the Communist- and MEP-controlled unions.[6] The force of the January, 1966, strike was considerably reduced by the refusal of the Ceylon Mercantile Union, Ceylon Workers' Congress, Democratic Workers' Congress, and a number of other important unions to participate.

No revolutionary general strike seriously expected to overthrow the Government has ever been staged, and the political and trade union leaders of Ceylon do not look upon the unlimited revolutionary general strike as a practical weapon in present or foreseeable circumstances.[7] The hartal of 1953, later described by a CTUF publication as "undoubtedly the highest expression of revolutionary action by the working class and people of this country,"[8] had by far the most serious political consequences of any explicitly political strike. The resignation of the Prime Minister, Dudley Senanayake, two months later is generally attributed to the hartal, and ramifications of the hartal were thought to have contributed to the defeat of the United National Party in the 1956 election. The hartal, however, was planned for only a single day and was called off by its sponsors the following morning.[9] The 1966 political strike was described by a leading Cabinet minister as "a strike which, if successful would have meant the downfall of the Government. . . . In other words, the purpose of the strike was to bring to a standstill the whole Government machinery deliberately and designedly."[10] The strike fell far short of this result,

[6]Goonewardene, A Short History of the Lanka Sama Samaja Party, pp. 60–61.

[7]Reported in interviews by the author in 1965 and 1967.

[8]The History of 25 Years of Proud Service to the Working Class by the Ceylon Trade Union Federation (Colombo : Ceylon Trade Union Federation, 1965), p. 17.

[9]Goonewardene, A Short History of the Lanka Sama Samaja Party, p. 45.

[10]Ceylon, House of Representatives, Parliamentary Debates (Hansard), vol. 65, col. 613 (March 11, 1966).

however. It has consistently been referred to subsequently by the participating trade unionists as a "token" strike. The impact of the work stoppage
seems to have been much less than that of the demonstration, which
produced considerable momentary disorder in Colombo.

General Strikes and Strikes Including Political Demands

Political objectives are frequently combined with or are implicit in other
objectives, particularly in general strikes or strikes by government employees. General strikes almost invariably include explicit or implicit
political demands and generate important political ramifications. Although
the principal immediate objective of a general strike may be related to
wage or trade union issues, the strike nonetheless is likely to challenge a
major policy or position of the Government. As LSSP leader N. M. Perera
observed, "Every general strike must be a political strike. The moment
you have a general strike, you knock against the Government and the
Government machinery comes into play. Even a trade strike must be a
political strike in the end."[11]

The general strikes of 1946 and 1947, which were spearheaded by public
employees, developed into direct clashes between the Government and
the strikers. The strike in October, 1946, began in the government-
operated railroads and spread to other public employees, mostly laborers.
Port workers, municipal employees, and workers in a number of private
firms also came out on strike a short time later. The striking public servants
demanded the right to form trade unions, which was then denied them,
and wage increases. The strike ended after a little more than a week with
the promise of some concessions.[12]

The issue of trade union rights for public servants flared up again in
the general strike of May-June, 1947. The 1947 strike commenced among
Colombo municipal employees and spread to several private-sector
industries. Along with wage demands were included demands for constitutional reform, the nationalization of the tea and rubber industries,
and several other demands of a political nature.[13] At the end of May,
the strikers were joined by a large number of public servants, principally
clerical employees. The public servants' strike followed the dismissal of
several public servants for convening a mass rally demanding trade union
rights for public servants, which was addressed by politicians in violation
of public service regulations. The strikers demanded the reinstatement of
the dismissed public servants and the grant of the right to form trade
unions. The strike met with the determined opposition of the Government

[11]*Ibid.*, vol. 15, col. 2496 (September 1, 1953).

[12]*Administration Report of the Commissioner of Labour for 1946* (Colombo: Government Press, 1947), p. 14; Goonewardene, *A Short History of the Lanka Sama Samaja Party*, pp. 28–30.

[13]*Memorandum by the Chief Secretary on Trade Unionism among Public Servants in Ceylon*, Sessional Paper VI—1947 (Colombo: Government Press, 1947), p. 8.

and collapsed on June 19 without winning any of its objectives. Many public servants were dismissed or disciplined for participating in the strike.[14] The following year, however, the Trade Unions Ordinance was amended to allow the formation of unions by public servants.

A one-day general strike was called in January, 1962, by the unions aligned with the Marxist parties in support of striking port workers. The objective of the general strike was to force the withdrawal from the port of military personnel who were maintaining harbor operations during the port workers' strike. The port strike, which involved 17,000 workers and was then in its third week, closely followed a transport workers' strike and coincided with strikes by bank clerks and employees of a petroleum distribution company. Immediately preceding the general strike, the Prime Minister had firmly declared that the port workers' demand for a monthly wage could not be granted and that troops would not be withdrawn from the port until the strike ended.[15] Leaders of the general strike asserted that its objective was not to undermine the Government, but to defend trade unionism by opposing the use of troops to replace strikers.[16] The strike was, however, intended to force a reversal of a major policy decision on the Government. Prime Minister Sirimavo Bandaranaike charged that there was "no doubt what so ever that the strike of the 5th January had political objectives."[17] The Government refused to alter its position and the port strike was abandoned after fifty-one days as a sign of solidarity with the Government when a plot by military and police officers to overthrow the Government was uncovered at the end of January.[18] Although leaders of the 1962 general strike denied it had political aims, a trade union journal subsequently claimed it "demonstrated to the present anti-working class Government in a most convincing manner the fighting spirit of the workers."[19]

In addition to general strikes, other strikes sometimes are called on a combination of demands, some of which have clear political implications. After a large number of public servants and employees of public corporations were penalized for participation in the January, 1966, political strike called by the SLFP-Marxist coalition, a demand that the punishments be revoked became a standard item in lists of demands formulated by the pro-coalition unions. The National Government regarded the political strike as a direct political challenge on an issue with little relevance

---

[14]*Administration Report of the Commissioner of Labour for 1947* (Colombo : Government Press, 1948), pp. 26–27; *First and Second Interim Reports of the Strike Committee*, Sessional Paper XIV — 1947 (Colombo Government Press, 1947).

[15]*Ceylon Observer*, December 29, 1961, p. 8.

[16]*Ibid.*, December 29, 1961, p. 1, and January 4, 1962, p. 7.

[17]*Ibid.*, January 8, 1962, p. 3.

[18]The developments surrounding the attempted *coup d'état* are described in Robert N. Kearney, "The New Political Crises of Ceylon," *Asian Survey*, II (June, 1962), 19–27.

[19]*Bank Worker*, March, 1963, p. 2.

to trade unionism and took an uncompromising stand on the punishments imposed on strikers, who had defied public service regulations by participating in a political strike. During 1968, several public servants' organizations, led by the Government Clerical Service Union, joined in a "consultative committee," which drafted two demands, calling for a salary increase for all public service grades and the withdrawal of punishments against those who participated in the January, 1966, strike.[20]

A strike on the two demands was launched in late November, 1968, by the unions associated in the consultative committee, coinciding with a strike for pay increases by a front of postal workers' unions. Within a few days, the strikers were joined by the three pro-coalition federations of public servants' unions, the PSWTUF, GWTUF, and Sri Lanka Nidahas Rajaya Seva Vurthiya Samithi Sammelanaya, which claimed a combined membership of 200,000 public servants. On the eve of the federations' entry into the strike, a large number of government departments were declared essential services under the Public Security Act, subjecting strikers to loss of employment and possible criminal prosecution. The postal workers pulled out of the strike after four days, but the contest was continued by the remaining unions although about 11,000 strikers in the departments designated as essential services were declared to have vacated their posts. Leaders of the three coalition parties met twice with the Prime Minister on behalf of the strikers. Eventually, strikers were told that those who lost their jobs for disregarding the essential services order would be re-employed and a salaries commission would look into wage demands, and the strike was ended after twenty-five days without achieving either of its original objectives.[21] The contest led the GCSU to conclude that public servants agitating for demands were to "be faced with the might of the Government and all its oppressive machinery."[22]

Political Implications of Industrial Disputes

Strikes often are called as a result of industrial disputes and have no discernible political objectives, but nonetheless develop political overtones because they come to involve the prestige or challenge policies of the Government. This is often the case with strikes in government-operated industries. The dispute producing the strike may be an uncomplicated question of wages or working conditions, but because the political Government takes a stand on the issue the strike assumes a political dimension. At the time of the 1963 Ceylon Transport Board strike, an unofficial LSSP publication commented editorially that "in the context of a wage-freeze every wage demand acquires a political flavour."[23]

[20]*Red Tape,* July, 1968, pp. 1-3.
[21]*Ceylon Daily News,* December 1, 2, 6, and 22, 1968.
[22]*Red Tape,* June, 1969, p. 8.
[23]"Editorial Notes," *Young Socialist* (Colombo), No. 9 (1963), p. 182.

The 1958 strike of public servants, called primarily on a wage issue, led to the declaration of a state of emergency and the assignment of troops to patrol the streets. The emergency and troop call-up produced a threat of a general strike by the major public and private sector labor organizations to protest the Government's action.[24] Strikes in the major public corporations between 1961 and 1964, precipitated by disciplinary questions and wage demands, were regarded by the SLFP Government as challenges to its authority and in some cases as politically motivated. A transport strike late in 1961 prompted the Minister of Labour to assert, "We cannot hold the public to ransom nor can we try to cripple the day-to-day working of the Government because some trade unionists, inspired by their political gurus, want to embarrass the Government at whatever cost."[25] The Government's response probably heightened the political significance of the strikes. It is unlikely, however, that strikes in major state-operated industries essential to the normal life of the community, led by trade unions associated with opposition political parties, can be insulated from political implications.

Collective barganing on issues of wages and conditions of employment is often suggested as an alternative to political involvement by trade unions. Collective bargaining rests on the ability of the union to use strikes or other forms of coercion to force the employer to concede demands. So long as collective bargaining is directed against fairly numerous private employers, the implicit threat of coercion does not seem directed against the community or the government, and therefore appears to be non-political. However, in Ceylon, and in many other developing countries, the government increasingly is becoming the major employer of industrial labor. Trade unions representing public employees can scarcely engage in collective bargaining without threatening or applying coercive pressure against the government. Conflicts between trade unions and the government need not necessarily become partisan contests, but the collision between trade unions and the machinery of government is likely to be seen by the political party in power as a threat to its policies or prestige, and by the opposition parties as an opportunity to discredit or harass the governing party. Trade unions representing public employees are very likely to view control of the government by one party as favorable and another as hostile to their aims. Thus the result of the government's increasing economic role and the growing bargaining power of trade unions may be to thrust trade unions more firmly into the political arena.

[24]Public Service Workers' Trade Union Federation, *Fifth Congress Report- From 1965 to 1967* (Colombo: Public Service Workers' Trade Union Federation, 1967), pp. 9–10; Goonewardene, *A Short History of the Lanka Sama Samaja Party*, p. 59.

[25]*Ceylon Observer*, December 12, 1961, p. 1.

2. *The Political Impact of Strikes*

The political consequences of strikes, whether in pursuit of political objectives or not, have become so great that strikes and labor strife are viewed as among the most serious threats facing the political party in power. A Communist leader underlined the potential consequences of united action by trade unions when, after the one-day general strike on January 5, 1962, he warned the Government:

> I ask my hon. Friends opposite, please do not fail to take note of the lessons of the January 5th strike. About a million workers took part in that strike. Do you think all your army, all your police force and all your pioneer corps can deal with such a situation if it continues for more than one day?[26]

The SLFP decision in 1964 to form a coalition Government with the LSSP was motivated, at least in part, by the need to contain mounting trade union militancy. When asked if the coalition was formed to stem growing labor strife, Prime Minister Sirimavo Bandaranaike responded, "We have brought into the Government a party which plays a dominant role among the urban working class.... Without the working class lending their [sic] full support I just cannot see how enterprises like the CTB [Ceylon Transport Board] or the Port Cargo Corporation can operate effectively."[27]

The political impact of a strike may be quite different from its economic impact. Some strikes have considerably more political significance than others, irrespective of their duration or the number of strikers involved. Generally, strikes which are apparent and disruptive in Colombo, or which dislocate the island's railroad or bus transport or block the port, through which vital imports of food and other essentials flow, have a great and immediate political impact. Transportation, especially buses, the popular mass transportation in Ceylon, is a particularly important target for general strikes because of its high visibility and its tendency to magnify the effectiveness of the strike by preventing many non-strikers from reaching work. It is said that on the day of a general strike many workers first determine whether or not the buses are running, as a guide to whether the strike is a success or failure, before deciding whether or not they will attempt to appear for work.

A strike of a single day which halts public transportation through much of the island and closes workshops, port facilities, and government offices in Colombo will almost certainly have important political ramifications, although its economic consequences may be slight. Strikes on the estates, on the other hand, are much less visible and disruptive to the normal life

[26]House, *Debates*, vol. 46, col. 931 (January 25, 1962).
[27]*Ceylon News*, September 24, 1964, p. 6.

of the community and consequently have minimal immediate political reverberations, although their economic consequences for the nation may be much more severe. An estate strike called by the Democratic Workers' Congress in 1966, for example, was claimed to have cost the country nearly Rs. 240 million in desperately needed foreign exchange and, hence, to have been extremely costly to the economy.[28] The strike continued for forty-five days, however, with slight political consequences. Strikes with the least political significance are those against private employers not prominently identified with the political party in power and not involving a particularly sensitive industry. The CBEU's long and bitter strikes against foreign-owned commercial banks, for example, produced only minor political reverberations, although they were among the most sharply contested strikes in the history of Ceylonese trade unionism.

Strikes led by politicians opposed to the party in power are much more likely to develop political significance than strikes called by unions sympathetic with, or at least not hostile toward, the existing political Government. Thus, an LSSP leader, Bernard Soysa, complained that during strikes by LSSP-controlled trade unions in 1957–1958:

> the Government party and Hon. Ministers ... [went] through the country stating, "This diabolical Lanka Sama Samaja Party is trying to overthrow the Government by means of these strikes." That, however, has not been said when the Government Party-organized trade unions launched strikes.... When ... [a union sponsored by the governing party] also launched a strike in certain sectors, when an Hon. Minister led the strike, then, apparently, the Government was not in danger.[29]

The National Government in power after 1965 repeatedly warned that the opposition parties were attempting to organize strikes to weaken or discredit the Government, but treated with tolerant forbearance a grueling forty-two day strike in the sensitive Colombo harbor called in 1968 by the Ceylon Mercantile Union, which, although not aligned with the Government, was harshly critical of the SLFP-Marxist opposition.

The National Government, opposed by parties with strong labor support, displayed serious concern with the potential political impact of strikes from its inception. In a brief message on becoming Prime Minister in March, 1965, Dudley Senanayake appealed to "the employees in both the public and private sectors not to be misled by those who may seek to nullify the people's verdict by undemocratic means."[30] The January 8, 1966, political strike represented the first major challenge

---

[28]*Ceylon Daily News*, August 28, 1967, p. 1.
[29]House, *Debates*, vol. 34, cols. 736–737 (February 12, 1959).
[30]*Ceylon Today*, XIV (March–April, 1965), 3.

to the National Government by the pro-coalition trade unions, and severe action was taken against strikers in the public service and public corporations. Prior to the strike, the Treasury circulated a warning that, since the strike was called on a political issue, disciplinary action would be taken against any public servant or employee of a public corporation who participated in the strike.[31] Striking public servants were fined a week's pay and a sizable number of strike leaders, including the officers of most participating unions, were suspended from duty pending dismissal proceedings.[32] In some public corporations, wholesale dismissals occurred, allegedly in order to provide employment for political supporters of the parties in power. More than 3,000 employees of the Ceylon Transport Board were said to have been dismissed, although about three-quarters of them were later re-hired with a loss of seniority.[33] Several heads of major public servants' unions who had been released for full-time trade union work and consequently had not absented themselves from duty were charged with circulating leaflets urging other public servants to strike on a political issue, in violation of public service regulations.[34]

The Government's strong reaction to the strike seems to have intimidated the pro-coalition unions and considerably reduced their militancy and daring, at least temporarily. Many private employers reportedly were encouraged by the Government stand to toughen their attitude toward trade unions. Although strikes on industrial issues were launched by the CMU and DWC, neither of which supported the coalition or joined in the 1966 political strike, it was not until the end of 1968 that pro-coalition unions mounted a major strike.

3. Trade Unions and Civil Disorder

In some cases, it is not the economic losses or disruption of normal activities produced by work stoppages but the eruption of civil disorder which produces the major political impact of trade union action. In virtually all circumstances, the incumbent holders of governmental power wish to maintain order and view an outbreak of disorder as a threat to their authority and power.[35] Trade unions are not solely, or even primarily,

[31]*Ceylon Daily News*, January 8, 1966, p. 1.

[32]Government Clerical Service Union, *45th Annual Report and Statement of Accounts, 1965–1966* (Colombo: Government Clerical Service Union, 1966), pp. 35–36. An opposition leader claimed nearly 40,000 public employees were fined for participating in the strike. House, *Debates*, vol. 65, col. 589. (March 11, 1966).

[33]Based on the author's interviews with trade union officers and leaders of Government and opposition political parties during 1967.

[34]See *Nation* (Colombo), June 22, 1967, p. 12. Charges were brought under rule 261 of the public service regulations, which prohibits public servants from "disseminating political publications." *The Ceylon Government Manual of Procedure* (4th ed.; Colombo: Government Press, 1957, with correction slips through no. 26, dated April 19, 1967), p. 44.

[35]It is conceivable that some individuals or groups holding governmental power might

responsible for serious disorders. The communal riots of 1958, which were unrelated to trade unions or labor issues, constituted the most violent and sanguinary outbreak of disorder in modern times.[36] Ceylonese trade unions apparently seldom seek to create disorder, and union-promoted violence or disorder has not become a major facet of politics or collective bargaining.[37] Nonetheless, the capacity of trade unions to create disorder— whether in pursuit of political or economic objectives—contributes to the coercive effect and heightens the political significance of trade union action.

Political and general strikes commonly involve processions and rallies in addition to work stoppages. Not infrequently, demonstrations lead to some disturbances, often involving a few stone-throwing and window-smashing incidents. Sometimes clashes occur between demonstrators and police or troops, and in a few instances demonstrators have been fired upon by police. Serious outbursts of violence involving deaths and extensive destruction have been surprisingly few in Ceylon, relative to other countries in the region. Incidents connected with the 1947 general strike, the 1965 May Day rallies, and the 1966 political strike resulted in one fatality each. The most serious eruption of violence and destruction occurred in connection with the 1953 hartal.

The 1953 Hartal

The hartal on August 12, 1953, was called to protest a decision by the UNP Government to abolish a consumer subsidy on rice, which produced a rise in the price of rice from Rs. 0.25 to Rs. 0.70 a measure. The hartal not only closed business places and government offices but produced widespread riots and disorders and extensive damage to transportation and communications facilities throughout the southwest corner of the

---

accept or even encourage disorder and destruction directed toward certain groups—perhaps foreign business or other interests—against whom the governmental authorities themselves fear to move. However, such cases are, in all likelihood, highly exceptional and do not appear relevant to contemporary Ceylon. The holders of governmental power normally are able or expect to achieve their objectives by use of the machinery of the state, and would view unauthorized violence as tending to discredit their rule and bring into question their capacity to hold and exercise power.

[36]One commentator, however, claimed that labor strife helped to create a climate of disorder and an appearance of governmental paralysis preceding the riots. Tarzie Vittachi, *Emergency '58: The Story of the Ceylon Race Riots* (London : Andre Deutsch, 1958), pp. 29–32, 104.

[37]In a stimulating study, James L. Payne has argued that labor organizations in Peru have utilized their capacity to threaten or create violence to coerce the political executive and win demands they could not obtain through applying economic pressure on employers, due to their weak economic bargaining position. James L. Payne, *Labor and Politics in Peru* (New Haven and London : Yale University Press, 1965). The situation in Ceylon is dissimilar in several ways, primarily because, in the absence of a tradition of military overthrows, the Government is less insecure. Also, many labor organizations have had relative success in collective bargaining, and the nature of the political and economic systems may make it more difficult for the Government to impose settlements in many instances. Despite a lesser magnitude and role, however, the coercive power of potential disorder is apparent in union relations with the Government in Ceylon as well.

island. Railroad tracks were blocked by trees and boulders, telephone lines were cut, and vehicles and buildings were set afire. A state of emergency was declared and at least ten persons died in clashes between police and rioters.[38] Property damage was estimated at Rs. 3,500,000 (nearly $750,000).[39] Damage to railroad facilities alone amounted to approximately Rs. 450,000 (nearly $100,000), and normal service was not resumed for a week.[40] The spectre of the hartal has probably haunted many subsequent Governments. In 1966, in an announcement of a reduction in the ration of subsidized rice—the issue which touched off the 1953 hartal—Prime Minister Dudley Senanayake warned against challenging the decision by creating "civil commotion."[41]

The Disorders of 1965 and 1966

Within a year of the 1965 election, two outbreaks of disorder, both involving trade unions, occurred in Colombo. The first confrontation between the newly formed National Government and the SLFP-Marxist coalition occurred on May Day, a month after the election. The May Day incidents resulted in the death of one participant in a procession moving toward the scene of the coalition-sponsored rally and some destruction of property. The disturbances, although not of great magnitude, were the subject of a report made on orders of the Government by a senior public servant. The report said of the May Day observances:

> The evidence indicates that all parties made a special effort to display their strength on this occasion. . . . Colombo was to be the rallying point of large numbers of persons from many areas of the Island. . . . The only conclusion that could be drawn was that May Day, 1965, became an occasion for a matching of political strengths in Colombo. . . . The National Government feeder processions and main procession were an expression of triumph and jubilation at its [the Government parties'] victory at the General Election. The characteristic feature of the coalition organisation seemed to be aimed at demonstrating their feelings of frustration, envy, and disappointment at their failure at the General Elections.[42]

M. G. Mendis, general secretary of the CFTU and a Communist Party leader, described the occasion in these words:

---

[38] The sponsors of the hartal claim that twelve lives were lost as a result of firing by police.

[39] Administration Report of the Government Agent, Western Province, for 1953, in *Administration Reports of the Government Agents and Assistant Government Agents for 1953* (Colombo: Government Press, 1954), pp. 4–5.

[40] *Administration Report of the General Manager, Ceylon Government Railway, for 1953* (Colombo: Government Press, 1954), p. 20.

[41] *Ceylon Today*, XV (December, 1966), 2.

[42] Ceylon, House of Representatives, *Report on the Incidents in Colombo on 1st May, 1965,*

May Day 1965 provided the opportunity not only to celebrate the traditional Workers' holiday but also to stage the first mass demonstration against the newly formed Hath Howla [i.e., seven-part coalition, a term of derision applied to the National Government by its opponents]. Our Federation joined with all the other leading trade union centres and progressive political parties to organise what was undoubtedly the biggest May Day rally ever seen in Ceylon. This mammoth May Day rally and procession proved to be such a challenge to the reactionary forces that they made a feeble effort to disrupt it by staging a provocation in which one worker who took part in the procession was killed, the first such incident to mar May Day which had been peacefully celebrated by workers in Ceylon for the last 33 years.[43]

The second and more serious disturbance accompanied the political strike and demonstration called by the opposition parties on January 8, 1966. Since formation of the National Government, which included the Federal Party and Tamil Congress representing the Ceylon Tamil minority, the opposition had charged that the Government was planning to alter the official-language policy to undermine the position of Sinhalese as the only official language. When announcement was made that regulations providing for the use of the Tamil language for certain public purposes would be presented to Parliament on January 8, a huge protest rally was held on January 5, at which plans were announced for a general strike and demonstration on the day the language regulations were to be debated. Demonstrators were to mass at various points and converge on the Parliament building. The Government issued orders that demonstrations were not to be allowed in the vicinity of the Parliament building, and army and naval personnel were called out to assist police in maintaining order.[44]

Because of the opposition of the CMU, CTUF, and other labor organizations, the strike appears to have been less widely supported than several previous general strikes, but at least 20,000 public servants were conceded to have participated,[45] along with employees of many private enterprises. Black flags appeared throughout the city and huge crowds

---

Parliamentary Series No. 6 of the Sixth Parliament (First Session, 1965–66), (Colombo: Government Press, 1966), p. 10.

[43]M. G. Mendis, *Ceylon Federation of Trade Unions : Report of the General Secretary to the 17th Sessions* (Colombo : Ceylon Federation of Trade Unions, 1966), p. 5.

[44]*Report of the Special Committee Appointed to Inquire into and Report on the Police Arrangements on the 8th January, 1966, in Connection with the Motion in the House of Representatives on the Regulations under the Tamil Language (Special Provisions) Act,* Sessional Paper V — 1966 (Colombo : Government Press, 1966), pp. 2–6, 14–15.

[45]House, *Debates,* vol. 64, col. 1066 (January 26, 1966). Opposition leaders claim that at least twice that number of public servants participated in the strike.

began assembling for the demonstration early in the morning, eventually totalling more than 15,000. By mid-day, a group of demonstrators had collected across from the Parliament building, were driven away by police, and reassembled in front of the Prime Minister's residence a short distance away. Later, a procession estimated to include 8,000-10,000 demonstrators, led by Buddhist bhikkhus, began to march toward the Parliament building. The procession was finally broken up and the demonstrators dispersed by police and military personnel using batons, tear gas, and rifles.[46] Rioting broke out and extensive damage was done to vehicles and buildings for several blocks adjacent to the major clash between police and demonstrators. In the firing and rioting, one man, a bhikkhu, was killed and at least ninety-one persons were injured.[47] A committee investigating police arrangements for the strike and demonstration summarized the later stages of the disturbances as follows:

(16) Between 1.30 and 1.45 p.m. Police resorted to firing tear gas and baton-charging to disperse the crowd at Kollupitiya. This was followed by stone-throwing and damage to property. ...

(17) At 2.15 p.m. information was received that persons dispersed by Police at Kollupitiya were on the railway tracks between Kollupitiya and Slave Island and were attacking passing trains;

(18) At 2.20 p.m. ... [a police officer] reported that the same persons who had been dispersed were attacking houses and shops along Galle Road and that trouble would spread immediately to other parts of the city;

(19) At 2.45 p.m. the C.I.D. reported that drivers and conductors of the C.T.B. [Ceylon Transport Board] were deserting their buses and refusing to take the vehicles out unless armed escorts were provided as the buses were attacked and some of them had been injured;

(20) Between 2.00 p.m. and 3.30 p.m. Police Headquarters had received numerous reports from all parts of the city that the crowds that were dispersed at Kollupitiya were resorting to stone-throwing and violence;

(21) Between 1.45 p.m. and 3.00 p.m. ... [a police party] had resorted to firing on four occasions at Kollupitiya junction, Kollupitiya railway station and along Galle Road towards Bambalapitiya;

(22) Finally, the death of a Buddhist priest as a result of gun shot injuries was known ... [to police officials] sometime after 2.00 p.m.[48]

[46]Report of the Special Committee ... on the 8th January, 1966 ..., pp. 25-28.
[47]Ceylon Daily News, January 9, 1966, p. 1.
[48]Report of the Special Committee ... on the 8th January, 1966 ..., p. 29.

With the outbreak of rioting, a state of emergency was declared and the Prime Minister, reflecting the almost inevitable concern of governmental authorities faced with spreading disorder, told the House of Representatives,

> This Government is responsible for the safety of the subjects, for the preservation of law and order. ... And if it is necessary to shoot to perserve law and order we will shoot. Am I just to stand by when people are being attacked, when stones are being thrown at trains, when bus drivers are pulled out and hammered for driving their buses?[49]

While the capacity to strike, and to precipitate disorder, has given labor organizations a highly significant element of political power, resort to "direct action" in serious political confrontations runs the twin risks of failing to be effective and creating an adverse public reaction against the unions and their associated parties. The entire labor movement is seldom united on action with political ramifications, and strikes often lack sufficient backing by organized labor and the public to generate effective coercive pressure. Furthermore, trade unions represent only a small fraction of the society, and their efforts to use coercion frequently appear to the public to be contrary to the wider interests of the community. When Prime Minister Senanayake was denounced by the opposition parties for his determined stand against the 1968 public servants' strike, he threatened to call an election on the issue, claiming his actions were supported by public opinion.[50] A Government confronted with strikes or disorder faces the danger of appearing either irresolute or repressive, but may also appear in the role of defender of the basic interests of the community as a whole.

[49]House, *Debates*, vol. 64, col. 165 (January 8, 1966).
[50]*Ibid.*, vol. 83, cols. 390–391, 396 (December 7, 1968).

IX

UNITY AND DISUNITY IN THE LABOR MOVEMENT

Deep cleavages of political origin have divided the labor movement since the youthful Marxists first challenged A. E. Goonesinha for the leadership of organized labor in the 1930's. Following the decline of Goonesinha, a split in the Marxist ranks between the Samasamajists and Communists created a new rift which produced bitter trade union rivalry for more than twenty years. The schism in the LSSP in 1950 leading to the formation of the party now called the Mahajana Eksath Peramuna added a third, though less significant, division in the labor movement. The unions associated with the Marxist parties acted in concert on a few occasions, the most notable being the 1953 hartal. More commonly, differing political positions prevented co-operation and considerably reduced the political strength of the trade union movement. While labor disunity was universally deplored, the adherents of each party blamed the others for the existing divisions. The Communist-sponsored Ceylon Trade Union Federation thus claimed in 1950:

> The unity of [the] entire trade union movement is an ideal that we have strived at [sic] from the start. In fact, the CTUF developed as an organisation embracing trade unions of all political complexions. It was the starting of rival trade unions by the Trotskyite leaders in 1945 and [19]46 that split the movement.[1]

After 1960, a strong trend toward coalescence appeared in the labor movement, probably reinforced by the growth of trade unionism in the period since 1956, but primarily produced by political circumstances. Briefly, an unparalleled degree of labor unity was achieved and then lost. The growth and rapid collapse of the unity dramatically illustrates the Ceylonese labor movement's vulnerability to the shifting currents and changing circumstances of politics.

[1]Ceylon Trade Union Federation, *Ten Years of the Ceylon Trade Union Federation, 1940–1950* (Colombo : Ceylon Trade Union Federation, [1950]), p. 17.

1.   *The JCTUO and the Twenty-One Demands*

The trend toward labor unity is generally traced to the 1958 strike by the Public Service Workers' Trade Union Federation and the CTUF. After a declaration of a state of emergency and the deployment of troops in the streets of Colombo, a group of prominent labor organizations with diverse political leanings threatened a general strike and succeeded in forcing the withdrawal of the troops. The following year the LSSP took the initiative in organizing a one-day general strike to protest an amendment of the Public Security Act, which was regarded as detrimental to trade unionism. Political considerations caused the two other Marxist parties and their labor following to refuse to participate, but several politically uncommitted unions which had been involved in the 1958 strike threat supported the political strike. The participating organizations subsequently formed a Continuing Committee (soon changed to Coordinating Committee) of Trade Union Organisations.[2] The Coordinating Committee included the Ceylon Federation of Labour, Government Workers' Trade Union Federation, Ceylon Mercantile Union, Ceylon Bank Employees' Union, Ceylon Workers' Congress, and Democratic Workers' Congress and essentially represented an alliance of the pro-LSSP organizations and a few major unaligned unions.

In 1960, following the second electoral alliance of the LSSP, SLFP, and Communist Party, the Communists contended .

> A basis has now been laid to unify the trade union movement which has hitherto been split into different detachments on the basis of political loyalties. Unity between the C.T.U.F. and the C.F.L. can and should be the basis for bringing in the S.L.F.P. trade unions, the C.W.C. and the independent unions in order to create a single trade union movement with a common directing centre.[3]

A major obstacle to Marxist collaboration resulted from differing attitudes toward the SLFP. Although the LSSP and Communist Party both initially supported the SLFP Government formed in 1960, the Samasamajists soon became critical of the Government. The small MEP had been bitterly hostile toward the SLFP since its leader had been forced out of the S. W. R. D. Bandaranaike Cabinet in 1959. Growing labor militancy commencing late in 1961 produced a series of clashes between

[2]Colvin R. de Silva, "The Co-ordinating Committee of Trade Union Organisations," *Bank Worker*, March, 1963, p. 7.
[3]*Draft Thesis for the 6th National Congress of the Ceylon Communist Party* (Colombo : Communist Party, 1960), pp. 57–58. Relations between the LSSP and Communist Party, and both parties' relations with the SLFP, are discussed further in Robert N. Kearney, "The Communist Parties of Ceylon : Rivalry and Alliance," in Robert A. Scalapino (ed.), *The Communist Revolution in Asia* (2nd ed., rev.; Englewood Cliffs, N.J. : Prentice-Hall, Inc., 1969), pp. 391–416.

the Marxist trade unions and the Government, which contributed to a widening rift between the Marxists and the SLFP. A turning point in the trend toward labor unity was the general strike of January 5, 1962. The strike was supported by the unions aligned with all three Marxist parties and the other unions associated with the Coordinating Committee, and was claimed to have represented an unprecedented level of labor unity, involving about one million workers. Following the general strike, the LSSP and Communist Party became increasingly estranged from the SLFP Government. A Communist statement for the following May Day denounced the SLFP's "hostile attitude to the trade unions,"[4] while the Samasamajists' May Day resolutions condemned "the strike breaking efforts of the stooges of the Government."[5] The rift between the Marxists and the SLFP led to the most serious attempt at Left unity in more than two decades. A common May Day rally was held by the three Marxist parties in 1963, and later in the year the LSSP, MEP, and Communist Party banded together to form a United Left Front based on a common program.[6]

The coalescence of the Marxist parties made possible an unprecedented unity of the labor movement. The LSSP and unaligned labor organizations associated in the Coordinating Committee were joined by the MEP and Communist federations, and the Coordinating Committee was transformed into the Joint Committee of Trade Union Organisations. The fourteen organizations associated in the JCTUO represented more than three-quarters of all organized employees in Ceylon and included all the significant labor federations, except that of the SLFP, and the most influential uncommitted unions. For the first time, a labor body was created which brought together organizations with conflicting partisan sentiments, although unions sponsored by the SLFP, UNP, and Federal Party remained outside the grouping.

A JCTUO conference in September, 1963, drafted a list of twenty-one demands to be presented to employers and the government. The demands incorporated a wide assortment of grievances and aspirations concerning wages, hours, and working conditions in both the public and private sectors and legislation on social and labor questions.[7] The pinnacle of labor unity was reached on March 21, 1964, when the twenty-one demands were endorsed by a gigantic JCTUO-sponsored mass rally. The demands

[4]*Forward* (Colombo), April 27, 1962, p. 2. For the Communist viewpoint on the deterioration of relations with the SLFP and the trend toward Left unity, see Pieter Keuneman, "Towards Unity of the Working Class," *World Marxist Review*, VI (December, 1963), 10–14.

[5]Lanka Sama Samaja Party, "May Day 1962 Resolutions" (mimeographed; Colombo, 1962), p. 3.

[6]*United Left Front Agreement* (leaflet; Colombo, August 12, 1963).

[7]Among other places, the famous "twenty-one demands" are listed in Government Clerical Service Union, *43rd Annual Report and Statement of Accounts, 1963–1964* (Colombo : Government Clerical Service Union, 1964), pp. 7–9.

became the symbol of growing labor solidarity, militancy, and exhilaration.

The Fight over the Twenty-One Demands

The enthusiasm engendered by the JCTUO and the twenty-one demands was quickly extinguished by political developments, however. In early 1964, Mrs. Bandaranaike began negotiations with the United Left Front parties on a coalition Government. When the talks stalled, primarily as a result of conditions imposed by MEP leader Philip Gunawardena, the LSSP abruptly agreed to enter the Government without its United Left Front allies.[8] Plans for the presentation of the demands were thrown into confusion by the formation of the SLFP-LSSP coalition Government in June, three months after the demands had received their enthusiastic public endorsement. Although on becoming Minister of Finance, LSSP leader and CFL president N. M. Perera indicated his desire to implement at least a part of the demands,[9] the LSSP leadership asked that agitation for the demands be suspended as a result of the changed political situation. The Samasamajist appeal for restraint was bitterly assailed by the ex-Samasamajists who had left the party to form the LSSP(R) and by the "left" Communists and many other trade unionists.[10]

The fight over the twenty-one demands opened a three-way split in the JCTUO. After heated debate, the issue came to a head in October, 1964. The pro-LSSP CFL, GWTUF, and Public Services League acquiesced in the LSSP request and opposed consideration of the demands.[11] The GCSU central executive committee on a closely divided vote decided to defy the LSSP appeal and continue to press for immediate presentation of the demands, then a short time later reversed its decision and acceded to the party's request.[12] The "regular" Communist trade unionists, after first advocating immediate presentation, proposed that the demands be forwarded to the Government with a "political preamble" stating that, "while seeking a satisfactory settlement between the Government and the working class in the matter of the 21 demands," the JCTUO was opposed to attacks being made against the Government by "vested interests." The political preamble was accepted by neither the LSSP nor the unaligned unions, and in November only the pro-Communist CFTU, PSWTUF,

---

[8]On the formation of the coalition, see Robert N. Kearney, "The Marxists and Coalition Government in Ceylon," *Asian Survey*, V. (February, 1965), 120–124.

[9]N. M. Perera, *Budget Speech, 1964-65* (Colombo: Government Press, 1964), p. 75.

[10]An LSSP(R) spokesman, liberally employing quotations from Trotsky, warned of the dangers of trade union degeneration under state patronage which could result from LSSP participation in the coalition Government. Wilfred Pereira, "The Strategy of Betrayal," *Young Socialist* (Colombo), No. 12 (1964), pp. 67–68.

[11]*CMU Bulletin*, August–September, 1964, p. 1.

[12]Government Clerical Service Union, *44th Annual Report (Part I), 1964-65* (Colombo: Government Clerical Service Union, 1965), pp. 8–10. On the GCSU, see Chapter VI.

and SLJGS presented the demands with the qualifying preamble.[13] On December 16, the remaining JCTUO members, consisting of the federations of the "left" Communists and the MEP, along with the CMU,CWC, and DWC, signed the demands and forwarded them to the Government.[14] Two days later, the coalition Government fell on the loss of a vote of confidence in Parliament, precipitating the 1965 election. The conflict surrounding the coalition and the twenty-one demands had demolished the JCTUO and shattered the brief unity of the labor movement.

The LSSP efforts to forestall action on the widely heralded demands undermined the party's credibility as a champion of labor and at least momentarily sapped the strength and solidarity of the LSSP's trade unions. The Samasamajists, and to some extent the "regular" Communists as well, were accused of creating the United Left Front and formulating the twenty-one demands as a lever to obtain entrance into a coalition with the SLFP, and when a favorable political opportunity appeared the demands were unceremoniously abandoned.[15] LSSP members, however, argued that the labor movement and working class would have benefited greatly—even beyond the gains represented by the twenty-one demands—by Samasamajist participation in the Government, and that the rank-and-file union members were generally content to give the coalition Government a reasonable opportunity to fulfil its pledges. However, the ex-Samasamajists of the LSSR(R) and "left" Communists exploited the issue of the twenty-one demands in order to harass and embarrass the LSSP.[16]

2. *Post-1965 Polarization*

The aftermath of the 1965 election found the labor movement sharply divided on partisan lines. While the enthusiasm and optimism for labor unity evaporated with the battle over the twenty-one demands the preceding year, the labor movement did not return to the multi-polar

[13] *The C.F.T.U. and the Working Class Movement* (Colombo: Ceylon Federation of Trade Unions, 1966), p. 36.

[14] *Ceylon Workers' Congress Report, 1964–1965* (Colombo: Ceylon Workers' Congress, 1965), pp. 35–36; *The History of 25 Years of Proud Service to the Working Class by the Ceylon Trade Union Federation* (Colombo: Ceylon Trade Union Federation, 1965), pp. 40–42. PSWTUF general secretary Wilfred Perera was also associated with the organizations presenting the demands, but he had been repudiated by the federation's central executive committee, which on November 26 voted to accept the Communist-sponsored political preamble, and he soon left the federation.

[15] *CMU Bulletin*, August–September, 1964, p. 1; author's interviews with Bala Tampoe, June 28, 1965, and N. Sanmugathasan, July 1, 1967.

[16] Based on the author's interviews with a number of Samasamajists during 1965 and 1967. N. M. Perera reportedly later claimed that if the coalition Government had survived another two months most of the demands would have been met. *Times Weekender*, September 11, 1967, p. 1.

Chart 2

COMPARISON OF MEMBERSHIP IN THE PRE-1965 JOINT COMMITTEE OF
TRADE UNION ORGANIZATIONS AND POST-1965 LABOR GROUPINGS

Pre-1965 JCTUO Membership	Post-1965 Labor Groupings
	1. *Joint Committee of Trade Union Organisations*
Ceylon Federation of Labour	Ceylon Federation of Labour
Government Workers' Trade Union Federation	Government Workers' Trade Union Federation
Government Clerical Service Union	Government Clerical Service Union
Public Services League	Public Services League
Ceylon Federation of Trade Unions	Ceylon Federation of Trade Unions
Public Service Workers' Trade Union Federation	Public Service Workers' Trade Union Federation
Sri Lanka Jathika Guru Sangamaya	Sri Lanka Jathika Guru Sangamaya
	Sri Lanka Nidahas Vurthiya Samithi Sammelanaya
	Sri Lanka Nidahas Rajaya Seva Vurthiya Samithi Sammelanaya
	Samastha Lanka Rajaye Lipikaru Sangamaya
	Lanka Petroleum Employees' Union
	2. *United Committee of Ceylon Trade Unions*
Ceylon Mercantile Union	Ceylon Mercantile Union
Ceylon Bank Employees' Union	Ceylon Bank Employees' Union
Democratic Workers' Congress	Democratic Workers' Congress
	Ceylon Estate Staffs' Union
	3. *Ceylon National Trade Union Confederation*
Ceylon Workers' Congress	Ceylon Workers' Congress
Central Council of Ceylon Trade Unions	Central Council of Ceylon Trade Unions
	National Employees' Union
	Lanka Jathika Estate Workers' Union
	Ilankai Thollilalar Kazham
	Kankesan Cement United Workers' Union
	Thuraimuga Navai Iyackunar Kazham
Ceylon Trade Union Federation	
Government Technical Officers' Trade Union Federation	

fragmentation which had existed before the formation of the JCTUO. Reflecting the political party polarization produced by the election, the trade union movement tended to split into pro-Government and pro-coalition groups, but several major labor organizations banded together outside either camp, producing a tri-polar division of the labor movement. The members of the now defunct JCTUO scattered among the new groupings according to political considerations. A comparison of the membership of the original JCTUO and the labor groupings formed after 1965 appears in Chart 2. The emerging cleavages in the labor movement were symbolized by the rival May Day demonstrations staged a month after the election. The SLFP, LSSP, and "regular" Communist Party and their associated trade unions held a joint rally. Another rally was staged by the MEP, UNP, and Federal Party unions. The CMU, after attempting unsuccessfully to organize a common rally of all unions which had been affiliated with the JCTUO, organized a rally separate from that of either political group.[17]

At the end of 1965, the name of the JCTUO was resurrected for a labor grouping clearly aligned with the SLFP-Marxist coalition. The eleven member organizations of the reconstituted JCTUO included only the seven members of the original committee associated with the LSSP and "regular" Communist Party, which were joined by the SLFP's unions and somewhat later by the Samastha Lanka Rajaye Lipikaru Sangamaya. Although the new JCTUO represented a formidable association of labor organizations, the absence of the CWC, DWC, CMU, and other unions deprived the reconstituted committee of the strength and broad inclusiveness enjoyed by the earlier group. The new JCTUO sponsored the January, 1966, political strike on the language issue and drafted a list of fifteen demands which were adopted at the coalition-JCTUO May Day rally in 1966.[18]

The post-1965 JCTUO provided the labor equivalent for the political coalition of the SLFP, LSSP, and Communist Party, and attempted a similar meshing of activities. The public servants' federations aligned with each of the three coalition parties, for example, formed united fronts in a number of government departments to campaign jointly for the three demands of the JCTUO in 1966–1967.[19] The JCTUO unions co-operated in strikes in 1967–1968 and, with JCTUO backing, the public servants' organizations joined in a major strike in late 1968. Apparently, however, some difficulty had been experienced in securing support of the coalition unions behind a GCSU campaign for a salary increase in 1968, which was an issue in the public service strike later in the year. Talks by leaders of the pro-coalition public servants' unions failed to reach agreement at

[17]*CMU Bulletin*, May, 1965, p. 1.

[18]As an indication of the intimate ties between the new JCTUO and the coalition, the CFTU reported that the JCTUO's fifteen demands were endorsed by the "1966 SLFP-LSSP-CP May Day rally." *The C.F.T.U. and the Working Class Movement*, p. 42. The first of the demands asked cancellation of punishments imposed on public servants and public corporation employees for participating in the political strike. The demands appear in M. G. Mendis, *Ceylon Federation of Trade Unions : Report of the General Secretary to the 17th Sessions* (Colombo : Ceylon Federation of Trade Unions, 1966), pp. 22–24.

[19]Public Service Workers' Trade Union Federation, *Fifth Congress Report—From 1965 to 1967* (Colombo : Public Service Workers' Trade Union Federation, 1967), p. 23.

one point and a conference called by the GCSU in July was attended by the GWTUF and Government Technical Officers' Trade Union Federation, but the SLFP's federation of public servants' unions, the PSWTUF, and the SLRLS were absent.[20]

Less significant but more frequent have been minor problems of maintaining co-operation and harmony at the lower levels, after many years of open competition among some of the JCTUO unions. Due usually to personal or factional squabbles in the branches, a few workers occasionally have sought to leave a union associated with one coalition party and join the union of another. As leaders have not wished to complicate relations with coalition and JCTUO allies for trivial reasons, they have been faced with a few delicate situations, often urging the rebels to remain independent for a time before joining their union to avoid the appearance of rivalry. In the port, where rivalry has been endemic for decades, some tensions between Samasamajist and Communist unions have continued.[21]

During 1966, the unions aligned with the parties composing the National Government were brought together in a loose association called the Ceylon National Trade Union Confederation. One of the professed aims of the confederation was to "establish a powerful and effective confederation composed of free and democratic trade unions, independent of political parties. ..."[22] The confederation, dominated by the huge CWC, with which the MEP's labor federation and five relatively small unions sponsored by the UNP and Federal Party were associated, had little coherence and apparently almost immediately subsided into inactivity.[23] It did, however, provide an instrument for convening pro-Government May Day rallies and facilitating some co-ordination of actions by the pro-Government unions. The existence of the confederation also served to underscore the fact that the Government parties, too, enjoyed the support of a segment of the labor movement and consequently dulled coalition attacks on the Government as anti-labor and anti-working class.

In April, 1966, the third grouping of trade unions was formed. The United Committee of Ceylon Trade Unions was created by the CMU, CBEU, DWC, and Ceylon Estate Staffs' Union. The four constituent unions represented a heterogeneous group of employees. Three were composed primarily of clerical and office workers and one of estate laborers. Two were associated with the estates and two with urban commercial

---

[20]*Red Tape*, July, 1968, pp. 1–2.

[21]Author's interviews with Pieter Keuneman, August 3, 1967, and D. G. William, August 24, 1967.

[22]"Constitution of the Ceylon National Trade Union Confederation" (mimeographed; Colombo, n.d.), p. 1.

[23]An unsympathetic observer, Bala Tampoe, claimed that the confederation's "main activity consists in arranging classes for 'workers' education.'" Ceylon Mercantile Union, "Ninth Annual Delegates Conference, 16th and 17th April 1967: General Secretary's Report" (mimeographed; Colombo, April 14, 1967), p. 27.

and financial enterprises. The UCCTU represented an effort of major labor organizations to coalesce in a group which was aligned with neither the coalition nor the National Government. The four unions all had traditions of activism in politics and the labor movement and generally radical political leanings. None, however, was willing to be associated with the coalition. The CMU had drawn away from the LSSP at the time of the party split in 1964, when CMU general secretary Bala Tampoe had played a leading part in establishing the Lanka Sama Samaja Party (Revolutionary). The leadership of both the CESU and DWC had supported the coalition during the 1965 election. As organizations composed primarily of Tamils, both unions were repelled by the post-election emphasis on communal issues and championing of Sinhalese Buddhist claims by the coalition parties.[24] The CBEU leaders explained that their union desired a united labor movement without partisan cleavages and favored the reconstruction of the old, broadly inclusive JCTUO, but, with the 1965 election, the CWC and the MEP's federation moved into alliance with the UNP and other JCTUO organizations firmly aligned themselves with the coalition, leaving only the unions which subsequently formed the UCCTU.[25]

The UCCTU displayed no partisan linkage, although LSSP(R) influence was apparent not only in the leading role played by Tampoe but also in the selection of another LSSP(R) leader, Prins Rajasooriya, as the UCCTU's general secretary. While the labor group's basic political posture of association with neither the coalition nor the National Government coincided with that of the LSSP(R), the UCCTU did not seek or obtain complete agreement on partisan questions. Shortly after the committee was formed, Rajasooriya described the bond uniting the four unions as "our common desire to act together in the interests of the workers of Ceylon without distinction of race, nationality, religion, language, or political adherence."[26]

The UCCTU was willing to find some common ground with the coalitionists, particularly on issues which seemed to involve the defense of trade unionism, but on other issues was strongly opposed to the coalition. Typical of the UCCTU position was the group's 1966 May Day resolution, which sharply condemned the coalition-led political strike in January but denounced with equal severity the disciplinary action taken against government employees participating in the strike.[27] The UCCTU

[24]Author's interviews with A. Aziz, July 26, 1967, and August 1, 1967; Bala Tampoe, June 25, 1967; and Prins Rajasooriya, June 27, 1967.
[25]Author's interviews with CBEU officers, July 5, 1967.
[26]"Letter of the UCCTU to the Prime Minister," *Young Socialist* (Colombo), No. 16 (August, 1966), p. 11.
[27]"1966 May Day Resolutions: The United Committee of Ceylon Trade Unions," *Young Socialist* (Colombo), No. 16 (August, 1966), pp. 9–10.

leaders were not, however, in complete accord in their attitudes toward the coalition. Tampoe became a scathing critic of the coalition, whereas Aziz favored avoidance of open attacks on the coalition in the interest of maintaining communication with the coalition parties.[28] In August, 1967, the DWC announced it was withdrawing from the UCCTU in order to be "free to play an independent role in the cause of the Trade Union movement...."[29]

The bitter recriminations exchanged between Tampoe and the coalition, reflecting the ideological issues on which Tampoe broke with the LSSP, spilled over into the labor movement. Not long after the 1965 election, the LSSP declared that "in the Trade Unions we must strive for united action, although this task is harder because of the treacherous role played in politics by such trade union leaders as [CWC president S.] Thondaman and Bala Tampoe."[30] Tampoe in 1967 taunted the JCTUO unions for their lack of militancy and complained that they "continue to avoid any association with unions that do not subscribe to the politics of the Opposition Coalition, even on matters like the January 8th victimisation."[31]

A labor dispute in 1968 brought the CMU into direct collision with the LSSP and the Samasamajist trade unions. The dispute erupted with a CMU demand for the dismissal of twenty-three temporary clerks employed by the Port (Corgo) Corporation in Trincomalee whom the union alleged lacked the qualifications for their posts. The CMU called a strike of its members in the Trincomalee and Colombo ports, later backed by a union-wide strike of CMU members. The clerks were eventually dismissed, but the strike continued on the issue of disciplinary action taken against CMU members in connection with the dispute. The LSSP's United Port Workers' Union, to which a number of the dismissed clerks belonged, vigorously condemned the strike and urged workers to remain on the job. In an acrimonious exchange of charges, the UPWU was backed by the LSSP and the CMU by the LSSP(R). The CMU accused the LSSP of strike-breaking and providing blacklegs for the Port (Cargo) Corporation, while the LSSP charged the CMU with victimizing the twenty-three clerks and seeking the aggrandizement of the union.[32] In a statement issued on behalf of the LSSP(R) politbureau, Tampoe denounced the LSSP leadership for betrayal of the working class and claimed: "The general public and the working class in particular are now aware of the LSSP's strike-breaking role in relation to the current general strike of the

[28] Author's interview with A. Aziz, July 26, 1967.
[29] Letter from the DWC general secretary to the UCCTU, quoted in Ceylon Mercantile Union, *Tenth Delegates' Conference, 17th & 18th March 1969 : General Secretary's Report & Conference Resolution* (Colombo : Ceylon Mercantile Union, 1969), p. 40.
[30] *Samasamajist*, July, 1965, p. 4.
[31] CMU, "Ninth Annual Delegates' Conference," p. 27.
[32] *Ceylon Daily News*, April 22, 1968, p. 1.

Ceylon Mercantile Union, particularly in the port of Colombo."[33] The strike finally ended when a compromise settlement proposed by the corporation was accepted by the CMU.[34]

The UCCTU organizations found themselves neither restrained by Government desires to avoid labor militancy nor inhibited by the Government's curbs on the pro-coalition unions in the public service and public corporations following the 1966 political strike. Consequently, they were among the most aggressive and launched the most significant strikes of any labor organizations in the years immediately following the 1965 election. Although the ideological gulf between the UCCTU and the Government was wide, the unions seemed satisfied to concentrate on industrial demands which did not appear as politically motivated challenges to the Government. The leaders of the National Government, on the other hand, were aware of the potential labor strength already arrayed against them by the coalition parties and probably looked with favor on the non-aligned political position assumed by the important section of the labor movement grouped in the UCCTU. The CMU and CBEU, because of their location in strategic and highly visible sectors in Colombo, are considered to be of great importance in general strikes. Their refusal to join in the 1966 political strike undoubtedly did much to blunt the impact of the strike and their disinterest significantly reduced the coercive effect of subsequent strike threats by the pro-coalition unions. The UCCTU, however, sharply and repeatedly criticized the Government for resort to emergency powers in labor disputes.[35]

Outside the triangular alignment of the labor movement and largely isolated in both labor affairs and politics was the "left" Communists' CTUF. The leader of the party and federation, N. Sanmugathasan, had made a number of overtures to the coalition but was rebuffed.[36] The CTUF complained that it had sought labor unity for the mutual protection of the trade unions after the UNP came to power, "But inside the trade union movement, there are sections, like the revisionists [i.e., pro-Moscow Communists] and the Samasamajists, who behave like the Brahmins of Hindu society who claimed that they alone knew the language in which to talk to God. These sections claim that they alone know how to fight the UNP."[37]

The creation of the original JCTUO, followed by the shattering of labor unity and the opening of new rifts in the labor movement, illuminates

[33]*Ibid.*, April 27, 1968, pp. 1, 5.

[34]*Ibid.*, April 30, 1968, p. 1.

[35]E.g., *May Day 1967 : The United Committee of Ceylon Trade Unions, Resolutions* (leaflet; Colombo, 1967), pp. 2–4; *Ceylon Observer*, July 9, 1967, p. 1.

[36]Author's interview with N. Sanmugathasan, July 1, 1967; *Kamkaruvā*, July 10, 1965, pp. 1, 8; *Red Flag* (Colombo), May 1, 1967, p. 8.

[37]*The History of 25 Years of Proud Service* ..., p. 55.

the extent to which the labor movement has been influenced by the political strategies and requirements of the parties involved in trade unionism. Even the uncommitted unions were caught in the partisan clashes and tended to gravitate toward one of the new groupings created on the basis of political considerations. The triangular shape of the labor movement since 1965, only slightly blurred by the isolation of the CTUF, clarified and accentuated the lines of partisan division in the labor movement and signified a growing polarization parallel to the trend toward polarization of political parties.

While the abrupt collapse of the JCTUO and demise of the twenty-one demands underscored the vulenerability of trade unionism to partisan political developments, the episode does not necessarily suggest a weak and pliant labor movement. Vigorous opposition to the abandonment of the demands was widely expressed and union leaders were repeatedly required to debate the questions involved and explain and justify their actions. The LSSP experienced considerable difficulty in securing compliance with its request by unions closely aligned with the party, and a substantial part of the labor movement rejected the party's plea. The fight over the twenty-one demands, hence, suggests not only the impact of politics on trade unionism but also the limitations of party control over the labor movement.

X

CONCLUSION: AGGRESSIVE TRADE UNIONISM, SOCIETY, AND POLITICS

The labor movement represents and speaks for the hopes and aspirations of the working class, with no doubt some distortions and imperfections. The basic objective of trade unionism is to alter the distribution of resources to the advantage of the workers and to protect workers from some of the harsh and unfavorable features of their situation. In Ceylon, as in other states where unions are allowed to function with relatively few restraints and with some degree of autonomy, they serve as the bargaining instrument of the workers and seek a more egalitarian distribution of the product of the economic system and a more full, effective, and emotionally satisfying participation in the life of the society. Not only have Ceylonese unions sought material gains and more favorable conditions of life for their members, but they have asserted a virtually unfettered right to act in defense of organizational or members' interests. In a forceful statement justifying aggressive and unrestrained trade unionism, the Ceylon Mercantile Union exclaimed that:

> we [are] implacably opposed to any and every move towards State suppression or restriction of the democratic freedoms of workers to join, and to take collective action through trade unions of their choice, as and when they deem it necessary to take such action in their [own] interests. To deny workers this freedom would be to pave the way to naked capitalist dictatorship. Any attempt to do so will naturally mean a direct confrontation with the trade union movement.[1]

There is virtually unanimous agreement among spokesmen for the labor movement that unions must champion the demands and protect the interests of workers in a broader area than the immediate job-related questions of wages, hours, and conditions of work. S. Thondaman, who is scarcely one of the more radical of Ceylonese labor leaders, recently contended:

[1]Ceylon Mercantile Union, *Democratic Freedoms and Industrial Relations* (leaflet; Colombo, March 27, 1967), p. 3.

The functions of trade unions are no longer conceived in limited terms of safeguarding and promoting the economic interests of workers through collective bargaining. Though collective bargaining is still basic to the trade unions they have also to function as organizations expressing the views of the working class on the larger problems of economic and social life.[2]

In concluding this study of trade unions and politics in Ceylon, this chapter seeks to evaluate some of the social and political implications of the aggressive trade unionism which has emerged in Ceylon and to assess the position and significance of the labor movement in the Ceylonese political process.

1.   Aggressive Trade Unionism and Economic Development

Among the most serious challenges faced by labor movements in Ceylon and other economically underdeveloped countries is the allegation that strong and militant trade unionism retards swift economic growth, which is perhaps the most widely accepted societal goal in many of these countries. It has been argued that income gains by workers divert resources into consumption, thereby preventing capital accumulation and risking a rising price level. Therefore, it is claimed, the proper role of trade unions in the developing countries is to forego immediate demands and urge restraint, discipline, restricted consumption, and increased productivity on the labor force.[3] When Prime Minister Dudley Senanayake was asked his opinion of the proper role of trade unions in the Ceylonese economy, he replied that "they should address themselves to the task of maximizing production...."[4] Particularly subject to criticism are work stoppages called in pursuit of labor demands. The Minister of Finance in 1965 argued that "strikes are a luxury that an under-developed country like Ceylon can ill-afford in the present context of economic development."[5] Earlier, Mrs. Bandarnaike as Prime Minister had denounced strikes then in progress as detrimental to the economy and called on "organized labour and its leaders to do some re-thinking as regards their responsibility towards society."[6]

However, there are grounds on which to argue that a vigorous and

[2]S. Thondaman, "Trade Unions and Economic Development and Trade," *Asian Labour* (New Delhi), XVI (February–March, 1968), p. 7.

[3]The almost classic statement of this argument was made by the former Indian Minister of Planning and one-time socialist and labor leader, Asoka Mehta, "The Mediating Role of the Trade Union in Under-Developed Countries," *Economic Development and Cultural Change*, VI (October, 1957), 16–23. Also, Mehta's "The Role of the Trade Union in Under-developed Countries," in M. K. Haldar and Robin Ghosh (eds.), *Problems of Economic Growth* (Delhi : Prabhakar Padhye, for the Congress for Cultural Freedom, 1960), pp. 87–106.

[4]*Ceylon Observer*, September 3, 1967, p. 1.

[5]*Ceylon Today*, XIV (August, 1965), 18.

[6]*Ibid.*, XIII (February, 1964), 7.

relatively unrestrained labor movement will not retard economic development, but can make positive—perhaps essential—contributions to the
process.[7] The wage demands of unions are frequently efforts to recover
losses in real wages due to inflation, and hence represent an inevitable
effort on the part of workers to prevent a loss of real income and a declining
living standard. Seldom in the developing countries have unions been
powerful enough to produce a major impact on the wage structure of the
economy as a whole, capable of creating inflation and seriously altering
the level of consumption. In Ceylon, despite the high level of organization
and the militancy of public servants, public service pay remained stationary
for more than a decade until late 1967, when a special allowance was
granted to offset in part the effects of a currency devaluation. In a few
instances, workers have succeeded in obtaining wage gains far out of
proportion to those won in other sectors due to especially advantageous
circumstances. Workers in the Colombo port are a notable example. Such
instances, however, appear to be exceptional, although industrial workers
have fared much better in obtaining wage demands than agricultural
workers. Between 1957 and 1967, the index of real wages of all workers in
trades covered by wages boards, using 1952 as a base, had increased only
from 104.7 to 106.4, while the index for industrial workers climbed from
101.5 to 121.0. In contrast, the index of real wages of agricultural workers
slumped slightly, from 105.6 to 104.9.[8]

Often overlooked is the fact that strikes are a product of disagreement
between workers and employers, and the responsibility for strikes cannot
any more justifiably be placed on unions than on management. The Ceylon
Mercantile Union has asserted :

> The workers of our country cannot be expected to give maximum and
> uninterrupted output of work without adequate payment. Rates
> of remuneration have remained fixed for several years, in spite of the
> continual rise in the cost of living, even in sectors where employers are
> making large profits. Trade unions like ours, that are not prepared
> submit to this situation, naturally tend to come into conflict with the
> employers, sooner or later.[9]

Furthermore, many of the demands and a large proportion of the labor
disputes in Ceylon center around non-wage issues such as discipline,

[7]Arguments refuting Mehta's thesis, upon which much of the following discussion is based,
have been ably presented by Van Dusen Kennedy, *Unions, Employers and Government : Essays
on Indian Labour Questions* (Bombay : Manaktalas, 1966), pp. 207–218; and Paul Fisher,
"Unions in the Less-developed Countries : A Reappraisal of Their Economic Role," in
Everett M. Kassalow (ed.), *National Labor Movements in the Postwar World* (Evenston, Ill. :
Northwestern University Press, 1963), pp. 102–115.

[8]Central Bank of Ceylon, *Annual Report of the Monetary Board to the Minister of Finance for
the Year 1967* (Colombo : Central Bank of Ceylon, 1968), p. 140.

[9]CMU, *Democratic Freedoms and Industrial Relations*, p. 4.

working conditions, job security, and protest against abusive and degrading treatment, issues with slight potential impact on labor costs and inflation.

The vital social and political functions trade unions may perform in countries attempting swift economic growth are perhaps of even greater significance than the economic consequences of trade unionism. Industriazation and the accompanying rapid and disturbing social transformations are bound to produce labor protest and unrest. Unions play a valuable role by participating in and contributing to the management and ordering of industrial conflict. Aggressive trade unionism, as champion and defender of the worker, also provides an essential channel for the expression of protest and release of tensions which might otherwise explode in highly disruptive and destructive actions. The vigorous trade union which is able to articulate workers' grievances without inhibition and occasionally win some gains can provide workers with a sense of hope and stem the growth of alienation, futility, and despair, and thus forestall social and political upheavals that could choke off all prospect of economic progress.

Trade unions which are not suppressed or reduced to instruments of the state constitute one of the few existing types of relatively autonomous voluntary associations in the developing countries. They thus represent a check on authoritarian or arbitrary action by either the government or private groups. In Ceylon, the trade unions have almost universally defended the franchise, elective institutions, and government by popular consent, and generally have acted in defense of public liberties against governmental encroachments. Moreover, unions for the most part are supporters of modernization and change, and in comparison with other social structures are relatively successful in integrating the particularistic communal, caste, and religious groupings of the society.

Where the labor movement has already grown strong and willful, as in Ceylon, there is little prospect that trade unions will allow themselves to be emasculated or converted into pliant tools of the government in the claimed interest of economic development or any other social goal. A conference of Asian trade unionists in 1968 put the labor viewpoint with clarity and force :

> Trade unions exist to serve the interests of the working people and the community. This is their fundamental purpose which they cannot surrender without ceasing to be bonafide trade unions. Where governmental development policies run counter to the interests of the working people, trade unions simply cannot fully contribute to the success of such policies.[10]

[10]"Statement Adopted by the First Asian Trade Union Economic Conference," *Asian Labour* (New Delhi), XVI (February–March, 1968), p. 58.

2.   Trade Unions and Politics : Concluding Comments

Ceylonese trade unions have become deeply enmeshed in politics in part because so many objectives of unions and their members require or are believed to require political action. As organizations concerned with the collective interests of workers in a society where many workers' needs and aspirations require action on a scale and in areas only the state can undertake, unions are inevitably drawn towards politics. The role of the state in determining wages, working conditions, and other matters of immediate concern to workers, as well as the growing importance of public employment, further involves unions in political issues and decisions. Furthermore, it might be noted that partisanship pervades the social and economic structures of the country. The press, business and professional associations, educational institutions, the Buddhist sangha and other religious bodies, and to an increasing extent the bureaucracy all reveal strong partisan tendencies or cleavages. It should, hence, not be surprising that the labor movement displays the deep imprint of partisan politics.[11]

Most trade unions and trade unionists in Ceylon are hostile to the existing social order, which is associated with the economic, political, and social subordination and deprivation of the workers. Relief from the problems of workers is commonly sought through radical political action. The strength of Marxism in the labor movement is with little question related to its appeal as an inherently revolutionary doctrine legitimizing and providing guidelines for a fundamental reconstruction of society. Radical political sentiments are common not only among the Marxist trade unionists but also among other labor leaders, such as the late Dr. W. D. de Silva, the organizer of the SLFP unions, who was generally regarded as well to the left of the party leadership, and A. Aziz, president of the Democratic Workers' Congress and long a political associate of the Marxists. Distrust of private ownership and control of industry is widespread in the labor movement, leading to numerous demands for the expropriation of economic enterprises and their operation by the government. Thus, the Government Clerical Service Union declared, "The Union considers that only a change in the economic structure on a socialist basis can find an effective solution to the pressing problems of the working people of this country."[12] The Ceylon Bank Employees' Union argued, "Exploitation for profit, corruption and malpractice has been the conspicuously dismal record of the private sector in this country."[13]

[11]On the pervasiveness of partisan attitudes and outlooks in the developing countries, see Lucian W. Pye, *Aspects of Political Development* (Boston : Little, Brown and Co., 1966), pp. 27–29.

[12]Government Clerical Service Union, *43rd Annual Report and Statement of Accounts, 1963–1964* (Colombo : Government Clerical Service Union, 1964), p. 55.

[13]Ceylon Bank Employees' Union, *Annual Report* (leaflet; Colombo, May 26, 1967), p. 3.

Trade Unions and Political Parties

Trade unions function in Ceylonese politics both as vehicles for the articulation of workers' demands in the political system and as auxiliaries for political parties in the competitive mobilization of political support. Association with a political party has appeared to many trade unionists as the most feasible means for achieving union objectives in the political arena, and, for an important segment of the labor movement, it is doubtful that any alternative has been considered. The relationship between unions and parties is based on expectations of reciprocal benefits. Many groups of workers need outside leadership possessing the organizational, legal, and negotiating skills and the confidence and sophistication required for effective union leadership. The party also serves as the link between the union and the agencies of government, the general public, and the rest of the labor movement. The central role of the state in labor-management relations as arbitrator or employer has enhanced the advantages of labor leadership by politicians by heightening the value of access to the administrative and political decision-makers.

With universal suffrage and mass political awareness, trade unions have been seized upon by politicians as one of the few types of coherent, organized groups through which potential supporters can be mobilized in a highly competitive political situation. Awareness of the possible political impact of strikes, whether explicitly directed toward political objectives or not, and the usefulness of trade unions in mobilizing rallies and demonstrations has increased the concern of parties with trade unionism.

Labor organizations' relations with political parties have been considered in this study under the three-fold classification of party-sponsored, party-oriented, and uncommitted trade unions. The party-sponsored unions typically lack or in the past have lacked the requisites for an effective organization and are bound to the sponsoring party by dependence on the initiative, energy, and skills provided through party auspices. These unions frequently are organizations of unskilled laborers possessing neither the knowledge and training to manage organizational affairs nor the prestige and influence to achieve organizational objectives. The party-oriented unions, in contrast, are generally self-sufficient organizations linked to parties through the voluntary acceptance of party guidance by the leadership and possibly by a significant portion of the membership. The uncommitted unions, although interacting and occasionally allying themselves with parties, have maintained a separate political identity and have avoided the relatively durable links with a party and predictable response to partisan issues which characterize the party-oriented unions.

The character of a trade union's involvement in politics is essentially determined by four interrelated factors—the circumstances of the union's founding, its organizational capacity, its leadership, and the social and occupational composition of its members. As has been mentioned repeatedly, many labor organizations were formed by party activists under direct party auspices. The leadership thus established and the habits of association with a party, as well as the success of the party in building a "political base" in the union through indoctrination and identification of the party with the aspirations of the members, may create partisan ties that continue in existence even though the need for direct party support declines. Furthermore, many of the party-sponsored unions continue to lack organizational capability from their internal resources and to require the talents and energy provided by the party. An end to party sponsorship presumably would cause a serious decline in the effectiveness of the union, if not its total collapse. For such organizations, there is little practical alternative to close linkage with a party.

The preferences and loyalties of the leadership constitute the most obvious factor in determining the political posture assumed by a union. In the party-sponsored unions, the leaders are frequently outsiders who are also party activists and work in the union largely in furtherance of party objectives. The leaders of party-oriented unions are nearly always activists or close sympathizers of the party, whether outsiders or insiders, and their personal partisan sentiments are frequently able to determine the partisan orientation of the union.

While leaders of the party-oriented and uncommitted unions ordinarily have considerable latitude in determining the political behavior of the union, a sophisticated, articulate, and politically conscious rank-and-file membership imposes some constraints on the leadership. Party-oriented and uncommitted unions frequently are composed of politically conscious clerks and other comparatively sophisticated and educated urban employees. In some cases, the partisan sympathies of the leadership may be shared by significant elements of the rank and file. However, the membership may also contain supporters of other parties, and the leaders may be required to avoid too close or obvious an alignment with the party for fear of weakening the internal cohesion of the union and perhaps producing challenges to their control. Even among unions with a less articulate and sophisticated membership, political developments obviously affecting a basic interest of the members may require leaders to shift political positions to avoid rank-and-file desertions. Unions composed of public servants and employees of public corporations seem particularly prone to partisan alignment. The immediate relevance of political and administrative actions and decisions for their employment conditions has presumably stimulated political consciousness and partisanship among the public employees and their organizations.

There are indications, as yet feeble, of a re-evaluation of the party-union relationship from both sides. Some disillusionment with the efficacy of trade unions as political instruments seems to be developing. On the other side, a few of the stronger unions seem in practice to be shifting their major efforts and attention from politics to collective bargaining with employers on specific occupational questions. Nonetheless, no fundamental change in the basic partisan character of the labor movement appears to have commenced at this time. Despite some disenchantment with the utility of labor activities, additional parties have been entering the trade union field to meet the competition of those parties already active in the labor movement, and no party has significantly reduced its trade union efforts. Also, while some unions may in practice be tending toward a less intense concern with partisanship, others are becoming more deeply enmeshed in politics and more highly partisan.

Gains and Losses of Partisan Alignment

The heavy partisan commitment of Ceylonese trade unions has involved both gains and losses to the labor movement. While some unions might serve their members' occupational interests with more fidelity or vigor if they were free of partisan ties, many others would not exist or would be reduced to impotence without party support and assistance. There is little doubt that the Ceylonese labor movement has grown in size and strength in large measure because of the sponsorship, support, and encouragement given it by political parties. Two major charges, however, are repeatedly made against the partisanship of trade unionism. The disunity and rivalry resulting from partisan competition for influence with organized labor is claimed to weaken the labor movement and disrupt industrial relations, and, in addition, the domination and control by political parties is said to compromise the autonomy of the labor movement in the pursuit of the economic or political objectives of the union members. Both accusations were implied in a recent statement by the chairman of the Employers' Federation of Ceylon, who contended,

> There will be no hope for collective bargaining in this country as long as the workers are split into separate camps which tout various political ideologies.
>
> [The workers] have allowed themselves to be led into situations which cannot, by any stretch of the imagination, be said to be of interest to them either as workers or trade unionists. ...
>
> What is the function of a trade union? The essential character of a trade union is that its ultimate responsibility is to the workers who are its members, and its destiny cannot therefore be directed by any outside agency.... [14]

[14]Employers' Federation of Ceylon, "Thirty Eighth Annual General Meeting, Chairman's Address" (mimeographed; Colombo, 1967), p. 3.

Disunity has been the major price the labor movement has paid for the support of political parties. In an immediate sense, the disunity and rivalry resulting from partisan competition has reduced the strength of labor in both politics and industrial relations and has been detrimental to orderly collective bargaining. A part—although not the major part, as is frequently assumed—of the fragmentation of trade unionism results from competition among parties. Energies and resources are dissipated in rivalry and conflict designed less to meet serious needs of workers than to triumph over rival unions. Yet, over a period of several decades the competition has stimulated the growth and contributed to the strength of the labor movement as a whole by popularizing trade unionism and multiplying the efforts and resources devoted to union activities. Also, by creating the risk of organizational disintegration through rank-and-file desertions to competing unions, rivalry has tended to limit the subordination of unions to party considerations and irresponsible control by the leaders. Furthermore, the conflict between rival unions has generated discussion and debate on labor and political issues and required leaders to justify, defend, and explain their actions. Hence, rivalry has created circumstances which stimulate the growth of an alert and informed union membership and encourage increasing leadership responsiveness and accountability to the membership. In short, although rivalry has involved some costs, it has contributed to the growth and autonomy of the labor movement and encouraged meaningful rank-and-file participation in union affairs.[15]

The highly competitive struggle among political parties has led to increasing party interest and activity in the labor movement. As additional parties have sought to augment their capacity to mobilize political support by involvement in labor organizing, parties have been forced to pay increasing attention to the aspirations of workers and to advocate policies and proposals intended to appeal to workers. Partisan links provide the union with a channel to the agencies of government, communications media, and the general public which the union could not establish for itself. Many workers' grievances are given a hearing in the press, Parliament, and the bureaucracy as a result of the party connections of unions.

Demands made by politicians in the name of trade unionism and labor may be formulated for the purpose of embarrassing rival parties or the Government, but may still result in the grant of some concessions to workers. Even though the parties with which most unions are associated do not win governmental power, some labor demands may be realized. The strikes and agitation for the right of public servants to organize in

[15]Similar observations regarding the consequences of partisan rivalry for trade unionism in India have been made by Kennedy, *Unions, Employers and Government,* p. 197.

1946 and 1947, although led by the Marxist opposition, were followed by the 1948 amendment to the Trade Unions Ordinance, drafted by a UNP Government, which secured for public servants the right to form trade unions. After clashes with unions and an intransigent stand against strikes and labor demands, the SLFP Government was willing to make concessions in the harbor strike of 1963-64, and when the SLFP joined with the LSSP in the coalition Government six months later, it accepted a program containing many provisions for workers. Although the concerns of urban labor have been given low priority by the post-1965 Government, the UNP by 1965 had adopted a number of proposals which earlier had been advocated by trade unionists and pro-labor politicians, including profit sharing and workers' participation in management. Hence, while the preponderant part of the labor movement has been allied to parties out of power, workers' interests have not been ignored and their aspirations seem to have been communicated effectively in the political system.

Unions in Ceylon, and in other developing countries, are often charged with being servile instruments of political parties and, as a result, with inadequately performing their function of championing and defending the occupational interests of their members. Individual labor organizations can certainly be cited for uncritically following party directives in disregard of, or even in opposition to, the apparent interests of the membership. The Ceylonese labor movement as a whole, however, must be credited with a considerable degree of autonomy. The unions which are closely linked to and dependent on parties comprise only a portion of the labor movement. A number of powerful unions are not linked with parties and are dominated by neither the government nor any other organization. The unions associated with the United Committee of Ceylon Trade Unions, for example, constitute a significant combination of autonomous labor strength. Among the unions firmly oriented toward a party, organizational needs seem to be given high priority and the necessity to hold the loyalty of the membership effectively limits the leaders' ability to act or fail to act on significant matters unless they enjoy fairly broad rank-and-file support. Even the unions dependent on party sponsorship and support are not always pliant instruments of their associated parties. Although the rank-and-file members are often passive and inarticulate, the high degree of rivalry existing in the labor movement has prevented leaders from neglecting the moods and desires of the membership for fear of desertions to rival organizations.

Parties and party activists leading trade unions have urged militancy and counseled restraint according to political circumstances and calculations of partisan advantage, but do not appear to have been markedly successful in ordering union action which did not reflect relatively widespread rank-and-file sentiment, as was illustrated by the difficulties of the coalition parties in mobilizing effective trade union action after 1965. Similarly, the partisan leadership of unions has at times had little choice but to provide direction for spontaneous rank-and-file grievances, even if not consistent with the political strategies of the parties. The LSSP and Communist Party, thus, found themselves drawn into conflict with the SLFP Government in 1961–1963 by pressure from their unions for action on wages and other occupational questions.

It cannot be denied that the behavior of many unions is strongly influenced by the partisan interests of the parties with which the unions are associated. However, the subjugation of trade unionism to politics is found less in a total domination of parties over unions than in the vulenerability of the labor movement to political developments, which may produce solidarity and enthusiasm at one moment and disunity and confusion at another. The Communist schism in 1963, the Samasamajist split in 1964, the conflict following the collapse of the original JCTUO and abandonment of the twenty-one demands, and the political strike of January, 1966, each sent shocks through the entire labor movement. The party schisms, the fight over the twenty-one demands, and the controversy surrounding the 1966 political strike not only contributed to conflict between labor organizations but injured some strong and capable trade unions by causing resignations, internal dissension, and factional conflict.

Partisan commitment of trade unions unquestionably does lead to union action which does not help the members, either in the occupational or political field. The January, 1966, political strike is one of the more conspicuous examples of politically inspired action by trade unions that seems to have been detrimental to the interests of the unions and their members. The direct political challenge to the Government stimulated the distrust and hostility of the Government and led to stern measures which hurt and inhibited a number of the participating unions. If these unions had avoided an overt challenge to the Government on a controversial issue of slight relevance to trade unionism, they might not only have conserved their strength for battles on occupational issues, but have been in a better position to oppose the Government on political issues of more concern to the labor movement and on which they stood more chance of success. Furthermore, many unions were divided internally because of the communal implications of the strike. By committing the unions to action without general rank-and-file agreement, or at least acquiescence, the leaders of several unions seriously weakened the cohesion of their organizations, leading to some loss of members and considerable confusion and disillusionment.

It can be argued, as some pro-coalition trade unionists have done, that the National Government was irredeemably opposed to the unions' and workers' goals, and that therefore achievement of labor objectives necessitated as a first step the undermining of the Government. The strike, however, did not in any demonstrable way shorten the life of the Government, and, indeed, was subsequently described by the participants as only a token protest. While the unions participating in the strike were recovering from the shocks of internal dissension and disciplinary action against their leaders in the public service and public corporations, unions which were willing to avoid head-on collisions with the Government on political issues were able to win some gains. The CMU, for example, although politically unsympathetic toward the Government, scored some important victories in this period, even in the public corporations. With the possible exception of one or two unions such as the Samastha Lanka Rajaye Lipikaru Sangamaya, which had a particularly deep interest in the language issue, it is difficult to conclude other than that participation in the strike was a partisan action which damaged and weakened the labor movement without any prospect of significant gains for either the unions or their members.

Trade Unions and the Political Process

In addition to their primary political function of representing workers' collective interests in politics, trade unions perform other highly significant functions in the political process of Ceylon. Unions are among the few associational groups with mass memberships in the society, and the union functions along with the political party as one of the few organizations mediating between the masses of the citizenry and the authoritative agencies of the state. Unions are particularly significant as voluntary associations because they incorporate members with few or no other links with the political system and the society beyond their immediate family and workplace. In a society with a hierarchical, ascriptive social ethos and tradition, unions provide one of the few relatively open channels for purposeful participation in the larger social and political realms by persons not born into the small elite and privileged social strata. Many workers have been introduced to the political process through unions, which undoubtedly constitute one of the most important agents of political socialization for workers. To the unsophisticated and scarcely literate worker, the union may provide a more satisfactory vehicle for expressing political sentiments and participating in the political process than the political party, which remains largely the preserve of the educated and the articulate.

Through their close association with political parties, unions also play a role of some importance in facilitating the operation of Ceylon's strikingly competitive, pluralistic political system. Unions help in the critical process of mobilizing political support, which is both difficult and vital in the Ceylonese political system. The predominately village society, rigid class structure, particularistic social cleavages, and limitations of mass communication media make broad political communication difficult. However, the style of politics and the predominant political values which have emerged require that issues be debated and consent be organized on a mass popular scale. Trade unions have assisted parties in performing this function by taking political discussion to sections of society not otherwise easily reached and by channeling dissatisfactions and hopes into actionable issues, explaining and defining partisan alternatives, developing partisan loyalties, and generally serving as a link between parties and the public. While large sections of the society are not reached by unions, they can be of considerable importance in performing this function with the industrial and estate workers and they represent one of the few auxiliaries available to parties. The much criticized partisanship of the labor movement, indeed, may have assisted in the development of the competitive political process based on mass participation in meaningful elections which is one of the most impressive achievements of contemporary Ceylon.

BIBLIOGRAPHY

Ceylon Government Publications

Administration Report of the Commissioner and Chairman, Colombo Port Commission, for 1960. Colombo : Government Press, 1961.

Administration Report of the Commissioner of Labour for the years 1944–1966/ 1967. Colombo : Government Press, 1945–1969.

Administration Report of the Controller of Labour for the years 1935–1943. Colombo : Government Press, 1936–1944.

Administration Report of the General Manager, Ceylon Government Railway, for 1953. Colombo : Government Press, 1954.

Administration Reports of the Government Agents and Assistant Government Agents for 1953. Colombo : Government Press, 1954.

Central Bank of Ceylon. *Annual Report of the Monetary Board to the Minister of Finance* for the years 1967 and 1968. Colombo : Central Bank of Ceylon, 1968–1969.

———. Department of Economic Research. *Survey of Ceylon's Consumer Finances, 1963.* Colombo : Central Bank of Ceylon, 1964.

The Ceylon Government Manual of Procedure. 4th ed. Colombo : Government Press, 1957 (with correction slips through no. 26, dated April 19, 1967).

Ceylon Investment Guide : The General Economic Environment. Colombo : Industrial Development Board, Ministry of Industries and Fisheries, 1968.

Ceylon Investment Guide : The Light Engineering Industry. Colombo : Industrial Development Board, Ministry of Industries and Fisheries, 1968.

Department of Broadcasting and Information. *Economic Changes Since 1956.* Information Brochure No. 5. Colombo : Government Press, [1964].

———. *Labour Policy Since 1956.* Information Brochure No. 3. Colombo : Government Press, [1964].

Department of Census and Statistics. *Census of Ceylon, 1953.* Vols. III–IV. Colombo : Government Press, 1960.

———. *Census of Commerce, 1961.* Colombo : Government Press, 1964.

———. *Census of Population, Ceylon, 1963.* Vol. I, Part II : "The Gainfully Employed Population, Tables Based on a 10% Sample." Colombo : Government Press, 1967.

———. *Ceylon Year Book* for the years 1948–1967. Colombo : Government Press, 1949–1967.

———. *Statistical Abstract of Ceylon, 1965.* Colombo : Government Press, 1966.

———. *Statistical Pocket Book of Ceylon, 1966.* Colombo : Government Press, 1966.

Department of Information. *Ceylon Today* (Colombo, monthly).

Department of Labour. "Collective Bargaining in Ceylon." (Mimeographed.) Colombo, January, 1960.

First and Second Interim Reports of the Strike Committee. Sessional Paper XIV— 1947. Colombo : Government Press, 1947.

House of Representatives. *Parliamentary Debates (Hansard).* Vols. 1–83.

———. *Report on the Incidents in Colombo on 1st May, 1965.* Parliamentary Series No. 6 of the Sixth Parliament (First Session, 1965–66). Colombo : Government Press, 1966.

Memorandum by the Chief Secretary on Trade Unionism among Public Servants in Ceylon. Sessional Paper VI—1947. Colombo : Government Press, 1947.

Ministry of Commerce and Industries. *Handbook on Labour Law and Legislation for Industrialists.* Colombo : Government Press, [1963].

Ministry of Labour, Employment, and Housing. *May Day, 1967.* Colombo : Government Press, 1967.

Perera, N. M. *Budget Speech, 1964–65.* Colombo : Government Press, 1964.

Report of the Commission of Inquiry on the Working of the Commercial Sector of the Port of Colombo. Sessional Paper II—1957. Colombo : Government Press, 1957.

Report of the Commission on Profit Sharing. Sessional Paper XXVII—1967. Colombo : Government Press, 1967.

Report of the Committee of Inquiry into the Law and Practice of the Trade Unions Ordinance. Sessional Paper XXVIII—1967. Colombo : Government Press, 1967.

Report of the National Wage Policy Commission. Sessional Paper VIII—1961. Colombo : Government Press, 1961.

Report of Reconnaissance Mission to Ceylon in Connection with State Industrial Corporations, February 16–March 16, 1966. By G. W. Naylor. Colombo : Ministry of Planning and Economic Affairs, October, 1966.

Report of the Special Committee Appointed to Inquiry into and Report on the Police Arrangements on the 8th January, 1966, in Connection with the Motion in the House of Representatives on the Regulations under the Tamil Language (Special Provisions) Act. Sessional Paper V—1966. Colombo : Government Press, 1966.

Report on the Sixth Parliamentary General Election of Ceylon. Sessional Paper XX—1966. Colombo : Government Press, 1966.

Trade Union Publications

Aziz, A. "Presidential Address of Mr. A. Aziz at the Annual Sessions of the Democratic Workers' Congress Held at the Colombo Town Hall on 16th and 17th October 1965." (Mimeographed.) Colombo, 1965.

———. *Presidential Address of Mr. A. Aziz at the Annual Sessions of the Democratic Workers' Congress Held at Yatiyantota on the 17th of August, 1963.* Colombo : Democratic Workers' Congress, 1963.

————. "Presidential Address of Mr. A. Aziz at the Annual Sessions of the Democratic Workers' Congress Held at Yatiyantota on 27th and 28th August 1967." (Mimeographed.) Colombo, 1967.

Bank Worker (Colombo, monthly).

Ceylon Bank Employees' Union. *Annual Report.* (Leaflet.) Colombo, May 26, 1967.

Ceylon Federation of Labour News (Colombo, irregular).

Ceylon Mercantile Union. "Annual Delegates' Conference, 1st November, 1964: General Secretary's Report." (Mimeographed.) Colombo, November 1, 1964.

————. "Answer to the Questionnaire of Industrial Disputes Commission." (Mimeographed.) Colombo, n.d.

————. *The Constitution.* Colombo: Ceylon Mercantile Union, n.d.

————. *Democratic Freedoms and Industrial Relations.* (Leaflet.) Colombo, March 27, 1967.

————. "Draft Resolutions for the 9th Annual Delegates Conference of the Ceylon Mercantile Union." (Mimeograph~d.) Colombo, April 2, 1967.

————. "Ninth Annual Delegates Conference, 16th and 17th April 1967: General Secretary's Report." (Mimeographed.) Colombo, April 14, 1967.

————. "The Struggle for a Collective Agreement with the Employers' Federation of Ceylon—1966." (Mimeographed.) Colombo, n.d.

————. *Tenth Delegates' Conference, 17th & 18th March 1969 : General Secretary's Report & Conference Resolution.* Colombo: Ceylon Mercantile Union, 1969.

Ceylon Workers' Congress. "Constitution of the Ceylon Workers' Congress." (Mimeographed.) Colombo, September 1, 1965.

————. *Ceylon Workers' Congress Report, 1964–1965.* Colombo: Ceylon Workers' Congress, 1965.

————. "Report of the Seventeenth Annual Sessions of the Ceylon Workers' Congress Held at 'Sarvodhaya Sadukkam,' Nuwara Eliya, on 28th September, 1958." (Mimeographed.) Colombo, 1958.

Ceylon Trade Union Federation. *Ten Years of the Ceylon Trade Union Federation, 1940–1950.* Colombo: Ceylon Trade Union Federation, [1950].

The C.F.T.U. and the Working Class Movement. Colombo: Ceylon Federation of Trade Unions, 1966.

CMU Bulletin (Colombo, monthly).

"Constitution of the Ceylon National Trade Union Confederation." (Mimeographed.) Colombo, n.d.

Democratic Workers' Congress. *Democratic Workers' Congress Administrative Report, 1963/64.* Colombo: Democratic Workers' Congress, 1964.

————. "Resolutions of the Democratic Workers' Congress Passed at the Annual Sessions Held on the 28th of August 1967 at Yatiyantota." (Mimeographed.) Colombo, August 31, 1967.

De Silva, Colvin R. "The Co-ordinating Committee of Trade Union

Organisations," *Bank Worker*, March, 1963, p. 7.

Government Clerical Service Union. *Annual Report* for the years 1962/
1963–1968/1969. Colombo: Government Clerical Service Union,
1963–1969.

———. *47th Annual Conference of Delegates*. (Leaflet.) Colombo, May 5,
1967.

———. *Onslaught Against Trade Unions?* (Leaflet.) Colombo, July 23, 1965.

*The History of 25 Years of Proud Service to the Working Class by the Ceylon
Trade Union Federation*. Colombo: Ceylon Trade Union Federation, 1965.

Kamkaruvā (Colombo, weekly).

May Day 1967 : The United Committee of Ceylon Trade Unions, Resolutions.
(Leaflet.) Colombo, 1967.

Mendis, M. G. *Ceylon Federation of Trade Unions : Report of the General
Secretary to the 17th Sessions*. Colombo: Ceylon Federation of Trade
Unions, 1966.

Perera, Wilfred. "Presidential Address of Mr. Wilfred Perera at the
U.P.T.O. Conference of Delegates Held on 28th and 29th June, 1967."
(Mimeographed.) Colombo, 1967.

Public Service Workers' Trade Union Federation. *Fifth Congress Report—
From 1965 to 1967*. Colombo: Public Service Workers' Trade Union
Federation, 1967.

Red Tape (Colombo, monthly).

Samastha Laṅkā Rajayē Lipikaru Sangamaya 1966/67 Varshika Vārthāva
[Samastha Lanka Rajaye Lipikaru Sangamaya 1966/67 Annual
Report]. Colombo: Samastha Lanka Rajaye Lipikaru Sangamaya,
[1967].

Sanmugathasan, N. *17th Congress Session of the CTUF (Colombo, November
1965) : Report by General Secretary*. Colombo: Ceylon Trade Union
Federation, 1965.

Sri Lanka Jathika Guru Sangamaya. *1965–66 Varshaya Sambandayen
Idiripath Karaṇalada Pradhana Lēkam Mahathāgē Avurudu Vārthāva* [Annual
Report of the General Secretary Presented for the Year 1965–66].
Colombo: Sri Lanka Jathika Guru Sangamaya, 1966.

———. "Srī Laṅkā Jāthika Guru Saṅgamayē Pasvāni Avurudu Maha
Sabhāva Vetha Idiripath Kerena Lēkam Mahatāgē Vārthāvayi
[General Secretary's Report Presented at the Sri Lanka Jathika Guru
Sangamaya's Fifth Annual Conference]." (Mimeographed.) Colombo,
August 23, 1967.

Thondaman, S. *Presidential Address, Ceylon Workers' Congress, Twenty-First
Sessions*. Colombo: Ceylon Workers' Congress, 1965.

Vinayagmoorthy, K. "Paranthan Chemicals Employees Sangam," in
Sri Lanka Nidahas Vurthiya Samithi Sammelanaya, *1962 Mäyi Dina*
[1962 May Day]. Colombo: Sri Lanka Nidhas Vurthiya Samithi
Sammelanaya, 1962, pp. 139–140.

Political Party Publications

"The C.P. in the Struggle for Teachers' Rights," *Forward* (Colombo), July 2, 1965, p. 8.

Draft Thesis for the 6th National Congress of the Ceylon Communist Party. Colombo : Communist Party, 1960.

Forward (Colombo, weekly).

Goonewardene, Leslie. *A Short History of the Lanka Sama Samaja Party.* Colombo : Lanka Sama Samaja Party, 1960.

Jayakody, Lakshman. "Śrī Laṅkā Nidahas Pakshaya saha Kamkaru Samithi Vyāpāraya [Sri Lanka Freedom Party and the Labor Union Movement]," in *Śrī Laṅkā Nidahas Pakshaya Dasavāni Sāṅvathsarika Kalāpaya, 1961* [Sri Lanka Freedom Party Tenth Anniversary Volume, 1961]. Colombo : Sri Lanka Freedom Party, 1961, pp. 115–116.

Jayawardena, Harold."Kamkaru Handa[Voice of Labor]," in *Śrī Laṅkā Nidahas Pakshayē Saṅvathsara Kalāpaya, 1964* [Sri Lanka Freedom Party's Anniversary Volume, 1964]. Colombo : Sri Lanka Freedom Party, 1964, pp. 81–86.

Keuneman, Pieter. *Twenty Years of the Ceylon Communist Party.* Colombo : Communist Party, [1963].

———. *Under the Banner of Unity : Report of Pieter Keuneman, General Secretary, on Behalf of the Central Committee.* Colombo : Communist Party, 1964.

Lanka Sama Samaja Party. "May Day 1962 Resolutions." (Mimeographed.) Colombo, 1962.

———. *Programme of Action, Adopted at the Unity Conference, June 4th, 1950.* (Leaflet.) Colombo : Lanka Sama Samaja Party, 1950.

———. *Visipas Vasarak : Laṅkā Sama Samāja Pakshayē Rajatha Jayanthiya Nimiththen Nikuth Kerena Saṅgrahayayi* [Twenty-Five Years : Publication Issued for the Lanka Sama Samaja Party's Silver Jubilee]. Colombo : Lanka Sama Samaja Party, 1960.

Mendis, M. G. "The Communist Party and the Workers," *Forward* (Colombo). July 2, 1965, pp. 4–5, 7.

On Questions of the International Communist Movement : Statement of the Central Committee of the Ceylon Communist Party. Colombo : Communist Party, September 26, 1963.

"Open Letter to the Members of the Lanka Sama Samaja Party from the Lanka Sama Samaja Party (Revolutionary)." (Mimeographed.) Colombo, August 9, 1969.

Perera, Basil. *Pieter Keuneman : A Profile.* Colombo : Communist Party, 1967.

Perera, N. M. *To the Voters of Colombo Central.* (Leaflet.) Colombo, January 4, 1960.

"The Real Situation in Ceylon," *Fourth International,* III (October, 1942), 301–302. Reprinted from *Samasamajist,* June 10, 1942.

Red Flag (Colombo, weekly).

Reply to the Central Committee of the Ceylon Communist Party. Colombo : Worker Publication, n.d.

Samasamajist (Colombo, irregular).

Sanmugathasan, N. *How Can the Working Class Achieve Power?* Colombo : Worker Publication, [1963].

———. *The Lessons of the October Revolution.* Colombo : Worker Publication, 1964.

———. "Outsiders in the Trade Unions," *Red Flag* (Colombo), July 14, 1967, p. 8.

Siyarata (Colombo, weekly). Until 1962, published under the title *U.N.P. Journal.*

Śrī Laṅkā Nidahas Pakshayē Pasalosväni Sāṅvathsarika Kalāpaya [Sri Lanka Freedom Party's Fifteenth Anniversary Volume]. Colombo : Sri Lanka Freedom Party, 1967.

Śrī Laṅkā Nidahas Pakshayē Vyavasthā [Sri Lanka Freedom Party's Constitution]. Colombo : Sri Lanka Freedom Party, 1958.

Statement of Ten Central Committee Members of the Ceylon Communist Party. Peking : Foreign Languages Press, 1964.

25 Years of the Ceylon Communist Party. Colombo : People's Publishing House, 1968.

United Left Front Agreement. (Leaflet.) Colombo, August 12, 1963.

United National Party 18th Annual Sessions, 23rd & 24th February, 1969. Colombo : United National Party, 1969.

United National Party. *Progress Through Stability : United National Party Manifesto.* Colombo : United National Party, 1958.

———. *What We Believe.* Colombo : United National Party, 1963.

Employers' Association Publications

Ceylon Estates Employers' Federation. *Annual General Meeting* for the Years 1960–1963. Colombo : Ceylon Estates Employers' Federation, n.d.

———. "Annual General Meeting, 19th August, 1964." (Typescript.)

———. *Rules.* Colombo : Ceylon Estates Employers' Federation, 1948.

———. *XXth Annual Report and Accounts, 1963–1964.* Colombo : Ceylon Estates Employers' Federation, n.d.

Employers' Federation of Ceylon. *Annual Report and Accounts* for the years 1963/1964–1966/1967. Colombo : Employers' Federation of Ceylon, n.d.

———. "Chairman's Address to Members, 35th Annual General Meeting, 11th September, 1964." (Mimeographed.) Colombo, n.d.

———. "Chairman's Address to Members, 36th Annual General Meeting, 30th September, 1965." (Mimeographed.) Colombo, n.d.

———. "Chairman's Address to Members, 37th Annual General Meeting, 22nd September, 1966." (Mimeographed.) Colombo, n.d.

———. "The Chairman's Speech, Annual General Meeting, 20th August, 1963." (Mimeographed.) Colombo, n.d.

———. "Reply to Questionnaire Issued by the Industrial Disputes Commission (Ceylon)." (Mimeographed.) Colombo, January 7, 1967.

———. *Rules (Revised 1964).* Colombo : Employers' Federation of Ceylon, n.d.

———. "Thirty Eighth Annual General Meeting, Chairman's Address." (Mimeographed.) Colombo, 1967.

Books, Monographs, and Reports

Almond, Gabriel A., and G. Bingham Powell, Jr. *Comparative Politics : A Developmental Approach.* Boston : Little, Brown and Co., 1966.

Bandarage, D. S. (ed.). *Hand Book of Personnel Management (Ceylon).* Colombo : Institute of Personnel Management, [1964?].

Bandaranaike, S. W. R. D. (ed.). *The Handbook of the Ceylon National Congress, 1919–1928.* Colombo : H. W. Cave & Co., 1928.

Ceylon Daily News. *Parliament of Ceylon, 1947.* Colombo : Associated Newspapers of Ceylon, Ltd., n.d.

———. *Parliament of Ceylon, 1956.* Colombo : Associated Newspapers of Ceylon, Ltd., n.d.

———. *Parliaments of Ceylon, 1960.* Colombo : Associated Newspapers of Ceylon, Ltd., [1962].

Davies, Ioan. *African Trade Unions.* Harmondsworth, England : Penguin Books, Ltd., 1966.

De Silva, W. P. N. *Industrial Law and Relations in Ceylon.* Colombo : K. V. G. de Silva & Sons, 1964.

Duverger, Maurice. *Political Parties.* London : Methuen & Co., Ltd., 1954.

Eisenstadt, S. N. *Modernization : Protest and Change.* Englewood Cliffs, N.J. : Prentice-Hall, Inc., 1966.

Farmer, B. H. *Pioneer Peasant Colonization in Ceylon.* London : Oxford University Press, 1957.

Galenson, Walter (ed.). *Labor and Economic Development.* New York : John Wiley & Sons, 1959.

———, and Seymour M. Lipset (eds.). *Labor and Trade Unionism : An Interdisciplinary Reader.* New York : John Wiley & Sons, Inc., 1960.

Ghosh, Subratesh. *Trade Unionism in the Underdeveloped Countries.* Calcutta : Bookland Private, Ltd., 1960.

Great Britain. Colonial Office. *Ceylon : Report of the Special Commission on the Constitution.* Cmd. 3131. London : His Majesty's Stationery Office, 1928.

Hammond, Thomas T. *Lenin on Trade Unions and Revolution, 1893–1917.* New York : Columbia University Press, 1957.

Huntington, Samuel P. *Political Order in Changing Societies.* New Haven and London : Yale University Press, 1968.

International Labour Office. *Report to the Government of Ceylon on Labour-Management Relations and Personnel Management at the Gal Oya Development Board.* ILO/TAP/Ceylon/R.24. Geneva : International Labour Organisation, 1963.

Jayawardena, Kumari. *Labour, Politics and Religion in Ceylon : The Rise of the Labour Movement, 1893–1933.* Durham, N.C. : Duke University Press, in press.

Karnik, V. B. *Indian Trade Unions : A Survey.* 2nd ed., rev. Bombay : Manaktalas, 1966.

――――. *Strikes in India*. Bombay: Manaktalas, 1967.

Kearney, Robert N. *Communalism and Language in the Politics of Ceylon*. Durham, N.C. : Duke University Press, 1967.

Kennedy, Van Dusen. *Unions, Employers and Government : Essays on Indian Labour Questions*. Bombay: Manaktalas, 1966.

Knowles, K. G. J. C. *Strikes—A Study in Industrial Conflict*. Oxford : Basil Blackwell, 1952.

Lenin, V. I. *"Left-Wing" Communism, an Infantile Disorder*. Moscow: Foreign Languages Publishing House, n.d.

――――. *What Is to Be Done?* Moscow: Foreign Languages Publishing House, n.d.

Lerski, George J. *Origins of Trotskyism in Ceylon : A Documentary History of the Lanka Sama Samaja Party, 1935–1942*. Stanford, Calif. : Hoover Institution on War, Revolution and Peace, 1968.

Lozovsky, A. *Marx and the Trade Unions*. New York : International Publishers, 1942.

Michels, Robert. *Political Parties*. New York : Dover Publications, Inc., 1959.

Millen, Bruce H. *The Political Role of Labor in Developing Countries*. Washington, D.C. : Bookings Institution, 1963.

Moore, Wilbert E. *The Impact of Industry*. Englewood Cliffs, N.J. : Prentice-Hall, Inc., 1965.

――――, and Arnold S. Feldman (eds.). *Labor Commitment and Social Change in Developing Areas*. New York : Social Science Research Council, 1960.

Myers, Charles A. *Labor Problems in the Industrialization of India*. Cambridge, Mass. : Harvard University Press, 1958.

Obeyesekere, Gananath. *Land Tenure in Village Ceylon*. Cambridge, England : Cambridge University Press, 1967.

Oliver, Henry M., Jr. *Economic Opinion and Policy in Ceylon*. Durham, N.C. : Duke University Press, 1957.

Orde Browne, G. St. J. *Labour Conditions in Ceylon, Mauritius, and Malaya*. Cmd. 6423. London : His Majesty's Stationery Office, 1943.

Payne, James L. *Labor and Politics in Peru*. New Haven and London : Yale University Press, 1965.

Pieris, Ralph. *Sinhalese Social Organization : The Kandyan Period*. Colombo : Ceylon University Press Board, 1956.

Pye, Lucian W. *Aspects of Political Development*. Boston : Little, Brown and Co., 1966.

Raman, N. Pattabhi. *Political Involvement of India's Trade Unions*. New York : Asia Publishing House, 1967.

Reports on the Visit of a Joint Team of Experts on Labour-Management Relations to Pakistan and Ceylon, September-November 1959. ILO Labour-Management Series No. 10. Geneva : International Labour Office, 1961.

Riggs, Fred W. *Administration in Developing Countries : The Theory of Prismatic Society*. Boston : Houghton Mifflin Company, 1964.

Ross, Arthur M., and Paul T. Hartman. *Changing Patterns of Industrial Conflict*. New York : John Wiley & Sons, Inc., 1960.

Ryan, Bryce. *Caste in Modern Ceylon.* New Brunswick, N.J.: Rutgers University Press, 1953.

―――. *Sinhalese Village.* Coral Gables, Fla.: University of Miami Press, 1958.

Snodgrass, Donald R. *Ceylon: An Export Economy in Transition.* Homewood, Ill.: Richard D. Irwin, Inc., 1966.

Sufrin, Sidney C. *Unions in Emerging Societies.* Syracuse, N.Y.: Syracuse University Press, 1964.

United States. Department of State. Bureau of Intelligence and Research. *World Strength of the Communist Party Organizations, 1968.* Washington, D.C.: Government Printing Office, 1968.

Vittachi, Tarzie. *Emergency '58: The Story of the Ceylon Race Riots.* London: Andre Deutsch, 1958.

Weerawardana, I. D. S. *Ceylon General Election, 1956.* Colombo: M. D. Gunasena & Co., Ltd., 1960.

Wriggins, W. Howard. *Ceylon: Dilemmas of a New Nation.* Princeton, N.J.: Princeton University Press, 1960.

Articles and Papers

Almond, Gabriel A. "A Comparative Study of Interest Groups and the Political Process," in Harry Eckstein and David E. Apter (eds.), *Comparative Politics: A Reader.* New York: Free Press of Glencoe, 1963, pp. 397–408.

Beer, Samuel H. "Group Representation in Britain and the United States," *Annals of the American Academy of Political and Social Science,* CCCXIX (September, 1958), 130–140.

Corea, Gamani. "Ceylon," in Cranley Onslow (ed.), *Asian Economic Development.* New York: Frederick A. Praeger, 1965, pp. 29–65.

De Mel, Wimalasiri. "Trade Unions Cannot Escape Politics," *Nation* (Colombo), July 6, 1967, pp. 6–7.

"Editorial Notes," *Young Socialist* (Colombo), No. 9 (1963), pp. 179–184.

Fernando, B. R., and P. U. Ratnatunga. "Discipline, Absenteeism and Lateness," in D. S. Bandarage (ed.), *Hand Book of Personnel Management (Ceylon).* Colombo: Institute of Personnel Management, [1964?], pp. 120–129.

Fisher, Paul. "Unions in the Less-developed Countries: A Reappraisal of Their Economic Role," in Everett M. Kassalow (ed.), *National Labor Movements in the Postwar World.* Evenston, Ill.: Northwestern University Press, 1963, pp. 102–115.

Goonesinha, A. E. "My Life and Labour," serialized in *Ceylon Observer,* commencing July 4, 1965.

Green, T. L. "The Cultural Determination of Personality in Ceylon," *School and Society,* LV (March 15, 1952), 164–166.

Jayaraman, R. "Caste and Kinship in a Ceylon Tea Estate," *Economic Weekly* (Bombay), XVI (February 22, 1964), 393–397.

Jayawardena, Kumari. "Pioneer Rebels among the Colombo Working

Class," *Young Socialist* (Colombo), No. 18 (November, 1968), 80–87.

Kassalow, Everett M. "Trade Unionism and the Development Process in the New Nations: A Comparative View," in Solomon Barkin, *et al* (eds.), *International Labor.* New York: Harper & Row, 1967, pp. 62–80.

———. "Unions in the New and Developing Countries," in Everett M. Kassalow (ed.), *National Labor Movements in the Postwar World.* Evenston, Ill.: Northwestern University Press, 1963, pp. 225–253.

Kearney, Robert N. "Ceylon: The Contemporary Bureaucracy," in Ralph Braibanti and associates, *Asian Bureaucratic Systems Emergent from the British Imperial Tradition.* Durham, N.C.: Duke University Press, 1966, pp. 485–549.

———. 'Ceylon: Political Stresses and Cohesion," *Asian Survey,* VIII (February, 1968), 105–109.

———. "The Communist Parties of Ceylon: Rivalry and Alliance," in Robert A. Scalapino (ed.), *The Communist Revolution in Asia.* 2nd ed., rev. Englewood Cliffs, N.J.: Prentice-Hall, Inc., 1969, pp. 391–416.

———. "The Marxists and Coalition Government in Ceylon," *Asian Survey,* V (February, 1965), 120–124.

———. "Militant Public Service Trade Unionism in a New State: The Case of Ceylon," *Journal of Asian Studies,* XXV (May, 1966), 397–412.

———. "New Directions in the Politics of Ceylon," *Asian Survey,* VII (February, 1967), 111–116.

———. "The New Political Crises of Ceylon," *Asian Survey,* II (June, 1962), 19–27.

———. "The Partisan Involvement of Trade Unions in Ceylon," *Asian Survey,* VIII (July, 1968), 576–588.

Keuneman, Pieter. "Towards Unity of the Working Class," *World Marxist Review,* VI (December, 1963), 10–14.

Knowles, William H. "Industrial Conflict and Unions," in Wilbert E. Moore and Arnold S. Feldman (eds.), *Labor Commitment and Social Change in Developing Areas.* New York: Social Science Research Council, 1960, pp. 291–312.

Kuruppu, N. S. G. "A History of the Working Class Movement in Ceylon," *Young Socialist* (Colombo), No. 1 (July-September, 1961), pp. 12–16; No. 3 (October–December, 1961), pp. 152–156; and No. 4 (January–March, 1962), pp. 201–205.

"Labour Conditions in Ceylon," *International Labour Review,* Part I: LX (December, 1949), 572–616; Part II: LXI (January, 1950), 1–20.

LaPalombara, Joseph. "The Utility and Limitations of Interest Group Theory in Non-American Field Situations," in Harry Eckstein and David E. Apter (eds.), *Comparative Politics: A Reader.* New York: Free Press of Glencoe, 1963, pp. 421–430.

"Letter of the UCCTU to the Prime Minister," *Young Socialist* (Colombo), No. 16 (August, 1966), pp. 11–12.

Lipset, Seymour M. "The Political Process in Trade Unions: A Theoretical Statement," in Walter Galenson and Seymour M. Lipset (eds.), *Labor and Trade Unionism : An Interdisciplinary Reader.* New York : John Wiley & Sons, Inc., 1960, pp. 216–242.

Mehta, Asoka. "The Mediating Role of the Trade Union in Under-Developed Countries," *Economic Development and Cultural Change,* VI (October, 1957), 16–23.

————. "The Role of the Trade Union in Underdeveloped Countries," in M. K. Haldar and Robin Ghosh (eds.), *Problems of Economic Growth.* Delhi : Prabhakar Padhye, for the Congress for Cultural Freedom, 1960, pp. 87–106.

"1966 May Day Resolutions : The United Committee of Ceylon Trade Unions," *Young Socialist* (Colombo), No. 16 (August, 1966), pp. 9–10.

Oliver, Henry M., Jr. "The Economy of Ceylon," in Calvin B. Hoover (ed.), *Economic Systems of the Commonwealth.* Durham, N.C. : Duke University Press, 1962, pp. 202–237.

Ornati, Oscar A. "Problems of Indian Trade Unionism," *Annals of the American Academy of Political and Social Science,* CCCX (March, 1957), 151–161.

Pereira, Wilfred. "The Strategy of Betrayal," *Young Socialist* (Colombo), No. 12 (1964), pp. 61–68.

Pieris, Ralph. "Speech and Society : A Sociological Approach to Language," *American Sociological Review,* XVI (August, 1951), 490–505.

Ranawake, Eric. "The Right to Strike," *Enterprise* (Journal of the Ceylon Chamber of Commerce), II (March, 1968), 29–33.

Rasaratnam, C. T. "Trade Unionism in Ceylon," *Ceylon Labour Gazette,* XVIII (August, 1967), 589–598.

Ross, Arthur M. "The Natural History of the Strike," in Arthur Kornhauser, Robert Dubin, and Arthur M. Ross (eds.), *Industrial Conflict.* New York : McGraw-Hill, 1954, pp. 23–36.

Ryan, Bryce, L. D. Jayasena, and D. C. R. Wickremesinghe. "Secularization Processes in a Ceylon Village," *Eastern Anthropologist,* XI (March-August, 1958), 155–161.

Sartori, Giovanni. "European Political Parties : The Case of Polarized Pluralism," in Joseph LaPalombara and Myron Weiner (eds.), *Political Parties and Political Development.* Princeton, N.J. : Princeton University Press, 1966, pp. 137–176.

Sarvaloganayagam, V. "Trade Unionism in Ceylon," *Ceylon Today,* VII (May, 1958), 28–31 ; and VII (June, 1958), 13–21.

"Statement Adopted by the First Asian Trade Union Economic Conference," *Asian Labour* (New Delhi), XVI (February–March, 1968), 51–59.

Straus, Murray A. "Childhood Experience and Emotional Security in the Context of Sinhalese Social Organization," *Social Forces,* XXXIII (December, 1954), 152–160.

————. "Westernization, Insecurity, and Sinhalese Social Structure," *International Journal of Social Psychiatry,* XII (Spring, 1966), 130–138.

————, and Jacqueline H. Straus. "Personal Insecurity and Sinhalese Social Structure : Rorschach Evidence for Primary School Children,"

Eastern Anthropologist, X (December, 1956–February, 1957), 97–111.

————, and Solomon Cytrynbaum, "Support and Power Structure in Sinhalese, Tamil, and Burgher Student Families," *International Journal of Comparative Sociology*, III (September, 1962), 138–153.

"A Survey of Employment, Unemployment and Underemployment in Ceylon," *International Labour Review*, LXXXVII (March, 1963), 247–257.

Tambiah, S. J. "Ceylon," in Richard D. Lambert and Bert F. Hoselitz (eds.), *The Role of Savings and Wealth in Southern Asia and the West*. Paris: UNESCO, 1963, pp. 44–125.

Tampoe, P. B. "Absenteeism," *Young Socialist* (Colombo), No. 10 (September, 1963), pp. 257–259.

Thondaman, S. "Trade Unions and Economic Development and Trade," *Asian Labour* (New Delhi), XVI (February–March, 1968), 7–8.

Vaikunthavasan, K. "Coalition Splinters within the GCSU," *Ceylon Daily News*, June 2, 1968, p. 11.

Weerawardana, I. D. S. "The General Elections in Ceylon, 1952," *Ceylon Historical Journal*, II (July–October, 1952), 111–178.

Wickrema, I. J. "A Great Leap Forward," *Ceylon Daily News*, April 2, 1966, p. 13.

Newspapers

Ceylon Daily Mirror (Colombo, daily).
Ceylon Daily News (Colombo, daily).
Ceylon News (Colombo, weekly).
Ceylon Observer (Colombo, daily).
Nation (Colombo, weekly).
Times of Ceylon (Colombo, daily).
Times Weekender (Colombo, weekly). Until 1966, published under the title *Sunday Times of Ceylon*.
Tribune (Colombo, weekly).

Other Materials

"Readership Survey, Ceylon, April–June 1964, Conducted for the Audit Bureau of Circulations Limited by the Market Research Department of Lever Brothers (Ceylon) Limited." (Mimeographed.) Colombo, September, 1964.

"Report of Commission on Promotions in Banks, 1966." (Mimeographed.) Colombo, September 20, 1966.

INDEX

* 9 7 8 0 5 2 0 3 3 1 7 4 7 *